Ten Sisters

A True Story

Ten Sisters

A True Story

Written By
Virginia Ruth Waggoner Rackley
Deloris Maxine Waggoner Hart
Rhita Jean Waggoner Brniak
Mary Margaret Waggoner Hickmott
Irma Joan Waggoner Swierk
Roberta Pauline Waggoner Ariel
Phyllis Ann Waggoner Ferguson
Vera Mae Waggoner Barber
Audrey Faye Lee Waggoner Cole Alford
Doris Evon Jean Waggoner Replogle Wenzel

Mayhaven Publishing

Published by
Mayhaven Publishing
803 Buckthorn Circle
P. O. Box 557
Mahomet, IL 61853
U. S. A.

Thanks for permission to use material from *Timeless Memories* compiled and edited by
Audrey Lee Waggoner Alford, 1995

Thanks for the use of information in *The Waggoner Family*, compiled by John Garland
Waggoner, Clem Martin Boling, Joshua Waggoner Tull, George A. Daughtery, and Mary
Daughtery, published in 1922 and revised in 1929.

Copyright © 1997 Mayhaven Publishing
Jacket Design by Aaron M. Porter
Printing & Binding: BookCrafters, Chelsea MI

First Edition 1997
10 9 8 7 6 5 4 3 2
Library of Congress Catalog Number: 96-77711
Hardcover ISBN 1-878044-49-4

Acknowledgements

We wish to thank all those who contributed documents and photos and bits and pieces of history so that we might put these chapters together. We thank Bonnie Brooks for first bringing the 1942 articles to us, to Elsie Thomas and Joyce Golden for additional information, and to Laura Emerson and Bill Lair whose own award-winning articles inspired us to tackle this project. We also thank Tonya Abbott, Neva Swartz, Georgia Howe, Aaron Porter and Michelle Scott for their very helpful assistance.

Contents

The last photo of the entire Waggoner family until 1975. From left to right: Back row: Glen (Dad) holding Doris Evon*; Ruth (Mom), Carl Alfred, and Jesse Dale (Dale); Third row: Rhita Jean (Bede), Deloris Maxine (Dodo), and Virginia Ruth (Jenny); Second row: Mary Margaret (Margy), Irma Joan, Roberta Pauline (Bertie), Phyllis Ann; First row: Vera Mae and Audrey Faye. Mattoon, Illinois. Summer 1940.
*Evon is the spelling on the original Birth Certificate, but in other court documents it is spelled Evonne or Yvonne—probably a clerical assumption.

Introduction

In 1942 the world was in chaos. World War II dominated the news. Everything else that was happening was almost incidental. So it is no wonder that the swift and permanent decisions made in one historic courtroom in one small midwestern town made little impact on the general public. The entire event seems to have been summarized in two local newspaper articles. But for the participants in that civil court case, the effects would linger a lifetime. While the two oldest brothers sailed the seas serving their country, ten sisters found themselves adrift in an unfamiliar world.

This book is about those sisters; what happened to them, how they survived. It is not a single story. It is many intertwining stories. Each sister has written her own chapter from her own singular perspective. Sometimes the events reported are similar. Sometimes they are diverse. On occasion they contradict. Many stories are filled with passion. A few are strangely dispassionate. But read in their entirety, these chapters provide an interesting tapestry of ten personalities, ten characters, and ten lives over a period of more than fifty years.

Most of the sisters are not writers. They have not even read each other's chapters. They have simply recorded what they remember, what influenced them, and what they think and feel about what happened before, during, and after the winter of 1942. While every effort has been made to retain the "voice" of each sister, this is not meant to be a literary work, but a sort of personal journal of shared experiences. In writing about their lives, each sister hopes to enlighten her children and answer some disturbing questions that have lingered over the years.

While this was a remarkably cooperative effort, the one item that could not be compromised was the dedication. Because each sister differed about who or what was the overriding influence in her life, as it pertained to this work, they chose not to compromise at all on this matter, but to allow each sister to dedicate her chapter to whomever or whatever she chose. Those dedications, alone, provide further insight into the effect the dissolution of this family had on each and every heart and mind of these ten sisters.

The heroines of this story are most certainly the older sisters, who never once gave up the dream of reuniting their family. Despite their limited resources, their many responsibilities, and their own disappointments, they have, at every opportunity, kept open the complex lines of communication.

This work is timely. While it deals with events that happened a half century ago, it reflects, unfortunately, far too many situations in today's world. How we handle families in this country is often appalling. Each time we see a child wrenched from his parent's arms—a parent with or without blood ties—who has nurtured and loved him; each time we see siblings standing in the shadows of some judicial storm that tears families asunder, we weep. As long as the courts play judicial games, allowing children to be used as chattel in legalistic wars and as salve for wounded egos, there will always be families like ours. Childhood is a brief and fragile thing. All children should be allowed to feel the security and stability of living with the people they know and trust, for all their fleeting young lives.

Vera Mae Barber, Anchorage, Alaska
Doris R. Wenzel, Mahomet, Illinois
July 1996

Ten Sisters

This photo at the Coles county courthouse on March 30, 1942, is believed to have been taken by a Kentucky newspaper photographer. Amanda Replogle (Mother to Doris) had talked about it, but Doris did not actually see the photo until 1985, when, while moving from Glen Ellyn, Illinois to Normal, Illinois, her son, Quintin, dropped a framed photo and the negative fell out from behind another picture. From left to right: Back row: Virginia (Jenny) holding Doris, Rhita (Bede), Deloris (Dodo) holding Audrey; Mary Margaret (Margy) is alone in middle row, and Pauline (Bertie), Irma, Phyllis and Vera in the front row. Interestingly, a negative of this photo was also found among our natural mother's belongings after her death in 1993. Despite the fact that her house was filled with photos of family members, she had never had her negative made into a photo.

Prologue

Several documents about this incident exist. The following news-paper articles and court orders outline *what* happened in the winter of 1942. *Why* it happened has not been as easy to document.

TEN CHILDREN ON MERCY OF WORLD

Ten children of a Mattoon family will be arraigned in the Coles county court at 10:00 o'clock Friday morning, March 27, to answer to a petition charging them with being dependents. The petition was filed by Clarence W. Shoot, the court's probation officer.

The ten defendants, children of Glen and Ruth Waggoner, ranging from sixteen years down to two years are Virginia, Delores, Rita, Roberta, Phyllis, Vera, Audra, Doris, Mary Margaret, and Irma.

It is charged that the father and the mother, who are living apart, have abandoned their children, thus permitting them to depend upon the public for their care and future welfare.

Charleston Courier
March 19, 1942

TEN SISTERS ARE TAKEN FROM PARENTS

Ten sisters, ranging from sixteen years down to two years, children of Glen Waggoner, forty, and Ruth Waggoner, thirty-eight, of Mattoon were found to be dependents, without proper parental care and almost homeless in the Coles county court today by Judge John T. Kincaid, who has had the case under advisement for some days. Judge Kincaid entered an order on his docket by which he removed the children from their parents and placed them in the charge of Mrs. Alice Caton, the court's west side probation officer and also named her as the guardian of the ten girls. The court also granted her the power to place them in homes by adoption.

It was stated today that homes have been found for six and possibly seven of the children. The grandparents are to assume the control, care and education of two; several to be committed to the Cunningham Home at Urbana, and two others were given to the care of Charleston couples, who will adopt them and give them their names.

Audra, four years old, has been awarded to Mr. and Mrs. Jess Cole of Charleston, and the youngest, Doris, aged two years, will enter the home of Mr. and Mrs. Dale Replogle.

The Waggoners are the parents of twelve children, two sons having enlisted in the United States Navy some months ago.

At the same time Judge Kincaid ordered the father to pay the sum of a $20 a month, and the mother to pay a $10 a month to assist in the care of the children, if needed. It is doubtful if the couple could carry out these orders.

Charleston Courier
March 30, 1942

Prologue

On this and the next two pages are the court papers dealing with the
preliminary hearing of March 19, 1942 in the Coles County Court,
Charleston, Illinois.

unwilling to care for, protect, education, control, and discipline said children.

Your petitioner further represents that it is for the best interes of said children and the People of the State of Illinois that said children be taken from said parents and placed upon the guardianship of some suitabl person to be appointed by this Honorable Court.

Your petitioner represents further that said parents of said children are unable to contribute to the support of said children.

Your petitioner further represents that Glen Waggoner is the fathe: of said children, and that Ruth Waggoner is the mother of said children, and that said parents are living separate and apart and have become estranged, and that there is little possibility of said parents ever living together again; and that said parents have neglected to care for said children and are unfit and improper guardians and are unable and unwilling to care for, educate, control, and discipline said children.

Your petitioner further represents that said VIRGINIA WAGGONER; DELORES WAGGONER; RITA WAGGONER; MARY MARGARET WAGGONER; *Irma* ~~RITA~~ WAGGONER; *Pauline* ~~ROBERTA~~ WAGGONER; PHILLIS WAGGONER; VERA WAGGONER; AUDREY WAGGONER; and DORIS WAGGONER should be taken from said Glen Waggoner and Ruth Waggoner and thereafter be and remain wards of this Honorable Court, to be awarded by this Court to the guardianship of some proper and suitable person or persons or committed to the care, education, and training of some suitable person or persons or any institution provided by the city, county, or state, or any association or institution that has been accredited according to law by the Department of Public Welfare of the State of Illinois, and for the appointment of a guardian with power to consent to the adoption of, and the giving of, said child or children out for adoption, if the Court should so see fit.

And that upon the hearing of this cause, this Honorable Court make such disposition of the custody of said children as will best serve the interests of said children and the People of the State of Illinois, in accordance with the Statute in such case made and provided.

-2-

14

Prologue

And that the Court appoint some suitable and proper person or persons guardian or guardians of the persons of said children, with power to conse. to adoption and to further give said children out for adoption, and make such other orders in this case as to Your Honor shall seem meet, according to equity and good conscience and according to the Statutes made and provided.

Clarence Shoot
Petitioner

STATE OF ILLINOIS)
) SS.
COUNTY OF COLES)

Clarence Shoot
~~ALICE CATON~~, being first duly sworn upon oath, deposes and says that she is the petitioner in the foregoing petition named; that she has read the same and knows the contents thereof; and that the same is true and correct to the best of her knowledge, information, and belief.

Clarence Shoot

Subscribed and sworn to before me, a
~~Notary Public~~ in and for the County and
State aforesaid, this *19* day of
March, A. D. 1942.

Elmer H. Elston
Clerk of County Court, Coles County

On the next three pages are the documents related to the March 27, 1942 hearing in the Coles County Court, Charleston, Illinois.

STATE OF ILLINOIS)
) SS.   IN THE COUNTY COURT THEREOF.
COUNTY OF COLES)

IN THE MATTER OF THE DEPENDENCY OF VIRGINIA   )
WAGGONER; DELORES WAGGONER; RITA WAGGONER;   )
MARY MARGARET WAGGONER; *Irma* WAGGONER; *Pauline*   )   NO._____
WAGGONER; PHILLIS WAGGONER; VERA WAGGONER; AUDRAY   )
WAGGONER; AND DORIS WAGGONER, ALL MINORS.   )

         Now on this _27th_ day of March, A. D. 1942, the above cause
coming on to be heard, the Court finds that the petition was duly sworn to
by a reputable person, a resident of said county, and that the Court has
jurisdiction of the parties and of the subject matter thereof; that the said
petition was filed on the _19th_ day of March, A. D. 1942, and that on the
_27th_ day of March, A. D. 1942, Glen Waggoner ~~and Ruth Waggoner~~, parents
of said VIRGINIA WAGGONER; DELORES WAGGONER, RITA WAGGONER; MARY MARGARET
WAGGONER; *Irma* ~~RITA~~ WAGGONER; *Pauline* ~~ROBERTA~~ WAGGONER; PHILLIS WAGGONER; VERA WAGGONER;
AUDRAY WAGGONER; and DORIS WAGGONER, all minor children, entered ~~their~~ *his*
appearance ~~and the appearance of each~~ in this cause in writing, and *has* ~~have~~
waived all and any service of process or summons in this cause, and ~~have~~ *has*
consented that this Court may proceed to the hearing of said cause and
enter any and all orders and decrees and take any other proceedings herein
at any time on and after the _27th_ day of March, A. D. 1942, with the
same force and effect as if ~~they and each of them~~ had been duly and regularly
served with process in this cause, as provided by law, and which consented
that this Court may take any action from time to time until said cause is
fully determined. *Summons issued March 19th 1942 and served on Ruth Waggoner, mother, Jones Thacker on March 20th 1942 return filed March 27th 1942*
         The Court further finds from the evidence that Glen Waggoner and
Ruth Waggoner, parents of said minor children heretofore named, were of full
age and under no legal disability.

         The Court further finds from the evidence that all of the
material allegations in said petition contained are true as therein stated;
that said VIRGINIA WAGGONER; DELORES WAGGONER; RITA WAGGONER; MARY MARGARET

            1   -1- 2   3   4

Prologue

WAGGONER; ~~ETTA~~ *Irma* WAGGONER; ~~ROBERTA~~ *Pauline* WAGGONER; PHILLIS WAGGONER; VERA WAGGONER; AUDREY WAGGONER; and DORIS WAGGONER are female children under the age of eighteen years and of the ages of sixteen years, fifteen years, thirteen years, twelve years, ten years, nine years, seven years, six years, four years, and two years, respectively, and are dependent child in this: That the said children do not have proper parental care and guardianship and are destitute, homeless, and abandoned, and are dependent upon the public for support; that said Glen Waggoner and Ruth Waggoner, parents of said children, are now living separate and apart and are estranged, with little possibility of ever living together again; and that said parents are not financially able to properly educate, control, and have the custody of said children; that said minor children above-named are dependent children within the meaning of the Act of the General Assembly of the State of Illinois entitled: "An Act Regulating the Treatment and Control of Dependent, Neglected, and Delinquent Children," approved April 21, 1899, and all Acts amendatory thereto.

The Court further finds from the evidence that it is for the best interests of said minor children above-named and of the People of the State of Illinois that said minor children be taken from their parents, Glen Waggoner and Ruth Waggoner, and that a guardian be appointed to have the care, custody, control, and education of said children above-named; and that said guardian be authorized to consent to the adoption of said children without notice to, or assent from, the parents, or either of them, of said children.

IT IS, THEREFORE, ORDERED, ADJUDGED, AND DECREED BY THE COURT that the said VIRGINIA WAGGONER; DELORES WAGGONER; RITA WAGGONER; MARY MARGARET WAGGONER; ~~ETTA~~ *Irma* WAGGONER; ~~ROBERTA~~ *Pauline* WAGGONER; PHILLIS WAGGONER; VERA WAGGONER; AUDREY WAGGONER; and DORIS WAGGONER be, and each of them is, hereby declared to be dependent and neglected children, said VIRGINIA WAGGONER; DELORES WAGGONER; RITA WAGGONER; MARY MARGARET WAGGONER; ~~ETTA~~ *Irma* WAGGONER; ~~ROBERTA~~ *Pauline* WAGGONER; PHILLIS WAGGONER; VERA WAGGONER; AUDREY WAGGONER; and DORIS WAGGONER being female children under the age of eighteen years and being of the ages of sixteen years, fifteen years, thirteen years, twelve years, ten years, nine years, seven years, six years, four years, and two years, respectively.

-2-

Ten Sisters

And that the Court appoint some suitable and proper person or persons guardian or guardians of the persons of said children, with power to conse to adoption and to further give said children out for adoption, and make such other orders in this case as to Your Honor shall seem meet, according to equity and good conscience and according to the Statutes made and provided.

Clarence Shoot
Petitioner

STATE OF ILLINOIS)
) SS.
COUNTY OF COLES)

Clarence Shoot
~~ALICE CATON~~, being first duly sworn upon oath, deposes and says that she is the petitioner in the foregoing petition named; that she has read the same and knows the contents thereof; and that the same is true and correct to the best of her knowledge, information, and belief.

Clarence Shoot

Subscribed and sworn to before me, a Notary Public in and for the county and State aforesaid, this 19 day of March, A. D. 1942.

Elmer H. Elston
Clerk of County Court, Coles County

These documents appear as they did when we received them from the Coles County Court archives.
Note the many corrections and changes.

On the following pages are Audrey and Doris' Adoption Decrees.

18

Prologue

Decree of Adoption

STATE OF ILLINOIS,
County of......**Coles**......}ss. In the..............**County**............Court.

....Jesse L. Cole and Lotta Belle Cole,
vs.
............Alice Caton............

PETITION TO ADOPT

............**AUDREY FAYE WAGGONER**

And Now, on this............**3rd**............day of............**June**............A. D. 19....**42**....
he same being one of the regular days of said............**County**............Court, come.... said
............**Jesse L. Cole and Lotta Belle Cole**............
petitioner.... herein, and it satisfactorily appearing to the Court that on the............**21st**............
lay of............**May**............A. D. 19....**42**...., said petitioner.... filed in the office of the Clerk
of this Court a petition in the words and figures following, to wit:

PETITION TO ADOPT CHILD

STATE OF ILLINOIS,
County of......**Coles**......}ss. In the..............**County**............Court.
To the Honorable Judge of said Court:

Your petitioner....   **Jesse L. Cole and Lotta Belle Cole**
............respectfully show.... unto your Honor that............**they are**....desire....
resident.... of the County of....**Coles**............and State of Illinois, and that....**they**....
to adopt a....**fe**....male child, who is a resident of the County of....**Coles**....first aforesaid, and who
was of the age of....**4**....years on the....**24th**....day of....**March**............A. D. 19....**42**....
and whose name is....**Audrey Faye Waggoner**............
Your petitioner.... further show.... unto your Honor that said above named child is now in the custody of....
............**these petitioners**............whose place of residence is
....**407 Thirteenth Street, Charleston, Illinois**............
Your petitioner.... further show.... unto your Honor that the............of said child....dead.
Your petitioner.... further show.... unto your Honor that the name of the father of said child is............
............**Glenn Waggoner**............and that his place of residence is
............**Riverton, Illinois**............

Your petitioner.... further show.... unto your Honor that the name of the mother of said child is............
............and that her place of residence is
............**Ruth Waggoner**............
............**Chicago, Illinois**............

Your petitioner.... further show.... unto your Honor that....   **Alice Caton**
is the legal guardian of said child, and that the place of residence of said guardian is............
............**1101 Broadway,**
Mattoon, Illinois............

Your petitioner.... further show.... unto your Honor that....**they**....desire.... that the name of said child shall be
............**Audrey Lee Cole**............
Your petitioner.... further show.... unto your Honor that....**petitioners sustain to each**
other the relationship of husband and wife.

Ten Sisters

Your petitioner**s** further show.... unto your Honor that ...**said child is a ward of the County Court of Coles County, Illinois, having been deserted by its natural parents, and said parents have been deprived of the custody of said child by the County Court of Coles County, Illinois, and such Court in the order appointing a guardian over the person of the child, has authorized such guardian to consent to the adoption of such child without notice to or assent by the parents, and that such guardian consents to such adoption, and it is to the best interests of said child that said adoption be made.**
Your petitioner**s**. therefore pray.... that said above named ...**Alice Caton**......

may be made defendant.... to this.................petition, and that a summons may issue for ~~her~~xxxxxxxxxxxx **her**,
returnable the ...**10th**.....day of......**June**.......A. D. 19..**42**, and that xxxxxx **she**
xxxxxxxxx may be required to answer this petition as is by the statute provided.'

And your petitioner**s** further pray.... that your Honor will, on the final hearing of this petition, order, adjudge and decree that the said ......**Audrey Faye Waggoner**......

shall, to all legal intents and purposes, be the child of your petitioner**s**., and that the name of said child shall thereafter be........**Audrey Lee Cole**......
And that your Honor will make such other and further orders in the premises as may be in accordance with law.

.......**Jesse L. Cole**......

.......**Lotta Belle Cole**......

STATE OF ILLINOIS, }
County of....**Coles**........ }ss.   .....**Jesse L. Cole and Lotta Belle Cole**......

being duly sworn, depose.... and say.... that **they are**....the petitioner**s**. in the foregoing petition by....**them**.....subscribed, and that the matters and things alleged in said petition are true as therein stated.

.......**Jesse L. Cole**......

.......**Lotta Belle Cole**......

Subscribed and sworn to before me this.......**20th**........day
of.......**May**........A. D. 19**42**.

.......**Bert E. Brainard,**......

.......**Notary Public**......

And it satisfactorily appearing to the Court that said defendant....**Alice Caton,** *guardian*

in said petition named, ha..**s**.... been duly notified of the filing of said petition and of the pendency of this proceeding ~~by service of summons upon xxxxx xxxxxxxxxxxxxxx more than three days prior to the~~ ~~day of xxxxxxxxxxxxxxxxxxxx A. D. 19xxxx the same being the return day in said summons mentioned; and that said defendant.~~

~~in said petition named xxx x x x been duly notified of the filing of said petition and of the pendency of this proceeding by publication of a notice thereof in x~~
~~the same being a newspaper of general circulation in this County of.~~
~~onxxxx.   xxdayxxx.   xxA.D.19xxx;~~

~~And it further satisfactorily appearing to the Court that within ten days after the publication of said notice as xxx sixty a copy of said notice was by the Clerk of this Court sent by mail to said defendant.~~

~~xxxxxxxxxx place x of residence~~   *guardian*
And said defendant, **Alice Caton,** having heretofore....entered....her....appearance herein in writing and having consented in writing to such adoption.
~~having filed xxx xxxxxx answer to said petition x~~

20

Prologue

And this cause now coming on to be heard by the Court upon evidence heard in open Court, the Court finds that the allegations of said petition are true as therein set forth;

And particularly does the Court find from the evidence that said petitioner s are of sufficient ability to bring up said child and to furnish to her suitable nurture and education, and that it is fit and proper and for the best interest of said child that the adoption prayed for in said petition should be made;

And the Court does further find from the evidence that the child was 4 years of age on the 24th day of March A. D. 19 42, and that the name of such child is Audrey Faye Waggoner

and that such child is a resident of this County and is in the custody of Jesse L. Cole and Lotta Belle Cole

And the Court further finds from the evidence that said defendant x Glenn Waggoner is the father of said child

And the Court further finds from the evidence that said defendant Ruth Waggoner is the mother of said child

And the Court further finds from the evidence that the legal guardian of said child is said defendant Alice Caton

And the Court further finds from the evidence that said petitioner s are husband and wife

And the Court further finds from the evidence that said child is a ward of the County Court of Coles County, Illinois, having been deserted by its natural parents, and said parents have been deprived of the custody of said child by the County Court of Coles County, Illinois, and such Court in the order appointing a guardian over the person of the child, has authorized such guardian to consent to the adoption of such child without notice to or assent by the parents, and that such guardian consents to such adoption, and that it is to the best interests of said child that said adoption be made.

It is Therefore Ordered, Adjudged and Decreed by the Court that from this day the said Audrey Faye Waggoner

shall, to all legal intents and purposes, be the child of said Jesse L. Cole and Lotta Belle Cole petitioner s herein.

And it is further ordered, adjudged and decreed by the Court that the name of said child shall be, and the same is, hereby changed and that her name shall from and after this day be Audrey Lee Cole

It is further ordered that said petitioner x pay the costs of this proceeding. be, and the same are hereby, remitted.

John I. Kincaid
Judge.

21

STATE OF ILLINOIS
DEPARTMENT OF PUBLIC HEALTH

CERTIFICATE OF ADOPTION

STATE OF ILLINOIS

County Court

Coles County

Case No. _13146_

TO THE DEPARTMENT OF PUBLIC HEALTH:

By a Decree of Adoption entered by the _County_ Court

of _____ County on the _____ day of _____, 19___,

it was adjudged that _Doris Yvonne Waggoner_ a (fe)male child, whose

natural mother is _Mrs. Ruth Waggoner_, and

whose natural father is _Mr. Glen Waggoner_, and who was

born at _Paradise Twp._, County of _Coles_
(City, Village, Township, or Road District)

State of _Illinois_, on the _11th_ day of _February_, 19_40_
is deemed to all legal intents and purposes the child of the following parents:

(All the following information should be as of the date of birth of this child)

FOSTER FATHER	FOSTER MOTHER
1. Full Name _Forest Dale Replogle_	7. Full Maiden Name _Sarah Amanda Tho_
2. Residence _Charleston Ill._ (City or Place and State or Country)	8. Residence _Mode Ill._ (City or Place and State or Country)
3. Color or Race _White_	9. Color or Race _White_
4. Birth Date _Oct 20 1906_ (Month) (Day) (Year)	10. Birth Date _Feb 13 1909_ (Month) (Day) (Year)
5. Birth Place _Charleston Ill._ (City or Place and State or Country)	11. Birth Place _Mode Ill._ (City or Place and State or Country)
6. Occupation _Owner & operator Skating Rink_	12. Occupation _House wife_

13. Number of Children of the Foster Mother (at time of this birth and including this child):

(a) Born alive and now living _none_, (b) Born alive and now dead _none_, (c) Stillborn _none_

It was further ordered that the name of the child should be:

Doris _Yvonne_ _Waggoner_
(First) _Doris_ (Middle) _Jean_ (Surname) _Replogle_

Signed _____

Dated _____, 19___.
[SEAL]

Clerk of the _____ Court

of _____, County, Illinois.

We, the foster

ATTORNEY OF RECORD:

Name _____

Street and No. _____

City and State _____

FOSTER PARENTS' MAILING ADDRESS:

Name _____

Street and No. _____

City and State _____

Although Doris' Decree of Adoption (not shown here) was signed. This Certificate is not. It may have been an unsigned copy made at a later date.

Virginia Ruth
(Jenny)

This chapter is dedicated to Mom and Dad

Ten Sisters

When I was really small we lived in Dorans, Illinois. There was me, Carl, Dodo, Bede, and Jess. Margy might have been a baby then, but I don't remember. I do remember Carl and I playing in the coal shed. He fell and cut himself and probably carried a piece of coal in his chin for ever after.

We lived near a railroad and every chance we got we were running on the rails. I don't know if this place used to be a train station or what, but we lived in it, and it had a big blackboard on the wall. I remember getting a splinter from that blackboard. We never went to the doctor for anything at that time, though.

I realize, now, it was a dangerous place to live. One time Bede was on the track and the train almost got her. Mom made it just in time. I tell you I know the Lord was with us, then, because we never had any kind of tragic accident or anything.

Jess never did go to the tracks much. He was always helping Mom. If she had a baby, which she always did, he was helping her with the house and the little ones. Mom said she always depended on Jess because he loved to rock. She could put a baby in his arms and let him rock for hours.

But the highlight of living in that little station by the tracks was the hoboes that used to come to the door for food. Mom always accommodated them. No matter what, she would give them something to eat.

When I was about six or so we moved from Dorans to Paradise Township, Illinois. Mom was pregnant again. I guess with Irma. This time the house set back off the road a little ways and we had a big yard. Our house only had two rooms. Dad and Mom's brother, Uncle Nolan, eventually built another room onto the back. It was supposed to be a bedroom, and there was room enough for a bed and a couch, but all of us girls slept in the same bed and Jess and Carl slept on the couch. In the winter time we used to wake up and be covered with snow. It came through the cracks. There was no siding or insulation—just boards. Mom and Dad slept in the living room. We never had dressers, end tables—nothing. Our house was so small. Looking back I wonder how we all survived in that house for so many years.

I don't know when Grandpa Waggoner died, but Grandma Waggoner lived at the top of the hill southwest of our little house.

Us kids used to have a ball on the hill. We were always sliding down it. We would come down in old tires, or in wintertime with snow on the ground we'd slide down on our hindends. We spent half the winter sliding down it.

In the summer and fall we had plenty to eat. We had corn in the field and vegetables in the garden. And whatever we had we ate it. We ate lots of berries and grapes before they were ripe. And we'd sit in the tree and eat lots of Mulberries. It's a wonder we lived without getting sick. We picked gooseberries, blackberries, and anything else we could eat—and anything Dad could find to sell. Us girls got the bulk of picking when the boys got old enough to go off to CCC Camp. But before they went our brothers helped. I remember one time Jess got stung by a bumblebee and his lip swelled up so bad we laughed for a whole week and a half.

We had lots of blackberries in summer and Mom made cobblers and pies. And we had fruit from Grandma Waggoner's apple and peach orchards. We used to keep those orchards pretty well cleaned out if we could keep her from knowing we were there.

Dad grew beautiful watermelons. One time we went up and plugged each one of those darned melons and then turned them upside down so he wouldn't notice. Oh, he liked to killed us for that.

In the fall we gathered hickory nuts and walnuts and hulled those big walnuts with our feet. The walnut tree was handy—right in front of our house.

But winters could be tough. We never had much milk, only canned or goat's milk. Once in awhile, Gram gave us some warm cow's milk. Sometimes all we had was a biscuit with some canned milk and sugar spread on it. Mom used to make jelly, but it never lasted very long. One time at school somebody stole someone's lunch out of the boys' cloak room and everybody had to put their lunch out on the table. Carl had this great big bag, but he only had two little biscuits in the bottom. When he took them out and put them on the desk everyone made the expected comments and I giggled most of all, but he was so embarrassed. He just about died. And I couldn't stop giggling. I think he beat the shit out of me all the way home, but I still couldn't keep from laughing.

It was a funny thing about those biscuits. Us kids would trade those biscuits to one girl. I can't remember her name, but she always had chocolate cake or something like that. She would trade us that cake, and even bananas, for our biscuits because she never had anything like that at home. She loved them.

Carl, Dodo, and all of us used to stop and pick pears for something extra. Sometimes we filled our bags full of pears. After the Fuller boys started working at the Sally Ann Bakery in Mattoon, Dad would stop there and pick some bread up, and we finally got made-up bread pretty regular. We'd never had anything like that in our lives before unless somebody came to visit and brought some along. Day-old bread was good.

Once in awhile, Mom would go to town and she'd come by school and bring us kids lunch. We would get half a bologna sandwich, half a banana, and some kind of cookie. God! We thought we had the world by the tail with a downhill pull. Those were the greatest lunches we ever had in our lives.

Meat, though, was always scarce. We lived on fish in the summer and rabbit in the winter. Once in awhile they would butcher up the hill at Grandma Waggoner's and they would give us pork. Dad used to take us fishing with him. He'd cut the bottom out of a tub and set it down over the fish. We always went home with plenty.

He was a good shot, too. People would say he was the only guy in the county that could kill two rabbits with one shot. We would go home and anyone big enough to clean, cleaned. We never had any refrigerator—didn't need any. We had plenty of nails on the outside walls and that's where the rabbits hung.

Dad never bought a fishing or hunting license in his life. When I used to go with him he'd tell me to sit and watch for the Game Warden. When I saw him coming I'd run down yelling, "The Warden's coming! The Warden's coming," and Dad would hold off a bit.

We had a lot of fun. Us kids nailed big boards up in the tree in front of our house and we used to sit up there all the time. That's where us kids would play. We would go from board-to-board to each other's houses.

We didn't have many toys, but I remember a bike Dad got us. We would take turns, but I was an ornery cuss. I wouldn't get off the bicycle when my turn was over. Jess got in the tree and jumped down right on top of me. There went the bicycle, the spokes and everything was broken. I got my hindend paddled and so did Jess.

I remember the first radio we got. We took it apart trying to see where the voices came from. It was amazing to us that you could turn it on and there would be people talking, but we couldn't put it back together so that was the end of the radio.

When we got whipped, and we did quite a bit, we usually had to cut our own switches. If we didn't, Mom would pick asparagus. She would get us with that. I hated that asparagus. When she would tell us to get down out of the tree, soon as our legs were in sight we started getting it, but you didn't dare turn loose, or you'd fall out.

After school there was always plenty of work for the older kids. We used to wash about every day of the week. Lots of dirty diapers, of course, made out of whatever Mom could find. I faced a tub of diapers in the morning and a tub of diapers in the evening. The line was always full of diapers—white ones, purple ones, or seed-sack patterns. Dodo and I had to help Carl carry the water from the branch after Jess left for CCC Camp.

Carl aggravated us girls to death. We used to pick up little pieces of glass and pottery and wash them—and pretend they were our dishes. When they killed the pigs we got to play in the hog pen—I guess it was the only building available. We would go out there and set those little pieces of glass up and make it look like our house. We even put boards down where we could walk on them. Carl used to go out and hit the shed with rocks and, man, our 'dishes' would shatter into a hundred pieces. It would make us so darn mad. But you know, after Carl went off to CCC Camp, I was the one who used to throw rocks and hit the wall of the pig pen.

Us kids never had dolls or anything like that. I was thirteen-years-old before I had my first doll. But we used to dress up the posts out in front of the house. We called them Mrs. Iggley and Mrs. Jumley. Us girls used to get behind them and every time a car came down the road we'd yell, "Hello. I'm Mrs. Iggley. Hello. I'm Mrs. Jumley." I'm sure everyone knew what we were doing, but they never said anything.

Like I said, when we moved to Paradise there must have been five of us kids, and Bertie was born there. Irma was born there, too, but I can't remember a thing about that time. Bertie is the one I remember. She was born in the daytime and Dr. Richardson thought I was old enough to watch. As far as I know he delivered all the kids born in Paradise—if he got there on time. Dr. Richardson named Bertie—Roberta Pauline. She was so sweet and little—and fat!

I can still remember the first day of school. Mom told Jess and Carl to hold on to my hand because I was so little. We stopped at every bridge. We'd look over to see if the water was running.

One bridge was by the Freese's. We thought they were rich because they had a big house. I was excited and looking around when Jess says, "I smell shit!" It was me. He made me go all the way back home by myself. I slipped into the house unnoticed. We had an old rollaway bed. I crawled in between the mattress and stayed there. Every time Mom would come into the room she would say "What's that smell in here?" She finally chased the smell down and I got my butt busted for that. I might have had to wash out my own clothes, too, because even though I was little I was already helping Mom wash clothes.

The mailman used to ask Mom "How many kids you going to have, Mrs. Waggoner?" and she'd say, "I want to have a dirty dozen." That certainly did come to pass. I remember Jess used to say, "Now if they're girls you sisters can take care of them, and if they're boys me and Carl will take care of them." Every time the doctor came he always opened up the door to our bedroom, especially if he spent the night, and said, "It's another split-tail!" and we would all go "Oh no!" As far as I know, most of the kids were born at night and he used to get a big kick out of opening that door and telling us. He was a great doctor, and even before we went to Chicago we were seen by Dr. Richardson.

Mrs. Hyland was the one and only teacher I ever had. I went to the first through the eighth grade with her. I was so bad to write notes. If I was passing one on to somebody I'd get caught and was sent to the cloakroom and got my butt paddled—many times. She would come in there, make me pull down my underpants, and wallop me with the paddle, but it didn't really hurt. Carl got me in more trouble than anybody. He'd stick his ruler up under my desk and even though there was never anything funny about that, I would giggle. I was always a giggler when I was little.

It seemed like we had a long walk to school. To make it seem shorter we'd walk to the first telephone pole and run to the next, walk to one, run to the other, over and over toward school. If it was storming or real cold sometimes Mrs. Hyland would give us a ride to the dirt road. Of course, she never went *down* the dirt road, but it helped us to get a little bit closer. During the winter we spent half the day in that school warming ourselves by the big stove in the back of the room. Us kids wore socks over our shoes for extra warmth. We never had boots or anything like that. In the spring and fall we went to school barefooted most of the time.

We'd draw names at school for Christmas. We used to say, "Oh, I hope we don't get gloves," but that's what we usually got, and what we needed. At the time, though, we didn't think we needed them.We wanted something to play with.

Jess and Carl used to be the picks of the teacher. She used to give them a little picture, maybe 2x3 inches, and they would make a big poster of it by drawing all the characters in the picture. I would love to know what happened to those posters. They were beautiful.

Me, Dodo, and Bede used to sing a lot in school. You could hear us all over the countryside. Mrs. Hyland put on the best shows for the holidays—two or three a year. We'd have marches, and she made all our costumes out of crepe paper and stuff. It was wonderful. We used to have people from all over come and stand inside and outside—just everywhere. The school would only hold so many people.

I went to school eight years, but I had to quit just before Mom had another kid so I could help out by babysitting and doing housework for other families. Dad did farm work, low wages and long hours, but there was never enough money for all our needs.

There was never enough places to sit and eat. We used to fill our plates and cups and sit down by the wall or stand at the table. I know we ate a lot of gravy and bread. We had potatoes most of the time. And we had a big barrel that Dad used to put sugar in. I don't know why we always had so much sugar but we did. When he and

Mom would go somewhere they would mark the sugar barrel to keep us kids from getting into it, but we got into it, anyway, and made candy. We didn't know how to make candy, of course, but we did our best. We ate anything that was sweet. We loved sweets. Mom said we would have eat shit if we thought is was chocolate. Dad was a big chocoholic. Mom, though, never liked chocolate at all. I still love chocolate.

It seemed, when I was home, like Mom was always pregnant. I loved being around her, though, when I got older. She made quilts and blankets a lot out of pieces of material that people gave her. When she quilted back then she never had a frame or anything. And when she sewed, she sewed by hand. She'd buy yards of material and try to make something for everybody out of it. By the time she got to me, though, she usually ran out, so most of the time I got something made over that someone had give to us.

One time the 'Relief' gave clothes to Dad for us kids. There was one coat that I just loved, but Dodo got it. I used to tell Dad that he favored Dodo over me. The coat I got was so damn long that all the way to school everybody started pinning it up. By the time I got to school it was short enough for me, but it was pathetic.

Christmastime at our house was very low. We always hung our stockings up but Dad used to tell us, "no use hanging those socks up. I'm telling you kids, there is no Santa Claus, and we don't have any money, and you are not going to be able to have anything." But Mom always made some little something to put in our stocking, and most of the time Dad bought haystack candy (chocolate drops), and each of us would get one-half a piece at a time. We'd make them last as long as we could. It was so good.

Uncle Walter and Aunt Mary would always come on Christmas and bring a big box of candy and oranges and stuff, and us kids would go haywire. It was all delicious. And when they came they'd take a lot of pictures—most of what we have from that time.

Ten Sisters

When I got old enough I used to babysit a lot and work for other people. Later Mom and I cleaned houses together in Mattoon. We'd go from house to house and make 50-cents or a dollar for each one we cleaned depending on how long we were there. We pooled our money to buy things for the kids. Sometimes we'd spend the night at Grandma Coen's house because we had to work so early the next day, and we didn't have any way of getting around but to walk—and that's just what we did.

Our sister Vera used to stay at Grandma's most of the time, but before Vera was born I used to stay there a lot in the summer. As soon as school was out here would come Grandma and Grandpa Coen and Aunt Helen. Aunt Helen always wanted me to come in and stay with her. She liked me to comb her hair and I guess she'd let me comb it all day if I would. And when she got the two kids I used to stay there with her and Uncle Asa and play with those two kids. They had everything! I used to think they were the wealthiest people in the family, besides Uncle Don and Aunt Bessie who seemed like they always had a lot. Their kids were always nicely dressed.

Sometimes we'd go to Charleston to some relatives. We were at Uncle Arthur's and Aunt Irene's a lot. On Dad's side we went to Uncle Vine's and Aunt Freda's and also to Uncle Jess and Aunt Blanche's quite a lot. Other than that we were not invited too much of anyplace. I guess there were just too many of us kids.

Small as our house was several people came to see us. Uncle Nolan spent a lot of time at our house. Ruth Easton came to our house one time, too. She was related to Mom in some way. Jess and Carl threw a hose at her and she thought it was a snake. We thought she was going to have a heart attack! And I remember one time me and Dodo were supposed to cook the potatoes. We cut all of them up and put them in this big skillet. When the company came to the door we went to see who all had come, and when we got back in that kitchen there was a chicken sitting on the edge of the skillet. We never knew if it had crapped in the potatoes or not, but we scraped the top off and went ahead and cooked them up. Dodo and I did not eat any of those potatoes, believe me, when we didn't know what happened there.

When Dodo stayed with Grandma—now I don't know if Grandpa didn't like her or had something against her, anyway, she would bawl a lot. I would try to hold my hand over her mouth so she wouldn't bawl out loud because he might hear her. I knew if he heard her he was going to come in there and whip her hindend. And every time it happened. She'd bawl and he'd come in and whip her until she shut up, and then she'd bawl again. Deloris always was stubborn.

We always liked to go there, though. Grandma and Grandpa Coen, as far as I know, always lived on Moultrie Avenue in Mattoon, and they had a grocery store at the back of their lot. They had an outdoor john, too. Grandpa used to give us kids big pieces of Bologna to eat. It was wonderful and I'll never forget it.

One time when Mom and I were there I had an epileptic seizure—the one and only one I ever had. I had a high fever, so I probably got it from that. And it's strange, because when my youngest daughter Doris was little she got a high fever when she was cutting teeth and had a seizure, too—the only one she ever had. Anyway, I also remember me or Dodo sitting on Bede's back there one time when a big worm came out of Bede's mouth. She almost choked to death.

I want to tell you us kids never missed Sunday School. It got us out of the house. We looked forward to every Sunday. But when we'd cut across the field toward home we would always hear Mom and Dad fighting. It seemed to me they would start a fight when we were not home and, man, we'd run like hell to get there. Me and Jess were the only ones who ever tried to break the fights up. Carl and Dodo would run out of the house.

Ten Sisters

We had a hen house, but we didn't have many hens. Maybe a few chickens once in a while. So that's where we went to the toilet. We didn't have indoor plumbing or even an outhouse, and some of the kids never made it all the way to the chicken house. You would have to hip, hop, skip, and jump all the way without stepping in someone's pile.

Our cousins, Wanda and Catherine, used to be at our house a lot. They would come and stay most of the summer. In fact, we always had plenty of kids there all summer long. We built a boxing ring out in the yard. Lord have mercy! We boxed—everyone boxed. That's where we first seen Don Hart. Don and Carl used to take Dodo and I up to Arthur to the dances because we liked to dance with the Amish Dutch boys. Besides, Carl and Don didn't want to dance. All they ever did was play the jukebox. We had a lot of fun up there. Dodo and I had boyfriends, but Bede didn't have any. But we were always stuck on our cousins. I liked the Warfel boys. And with Carl and Jess both in the navy I used to write to a lot of service men—lots of them. I loved it! I still turn to look when a Navy man walks by, but that's probably because Carl and Jess were Navy men.

One morning I got up to help Dad. Mom was away working. After that I always got up early. Mom hitchhiked into Chicago to work, and she'd come home on the weekends. She always brought something for the kids. One day she brought this box of Kotex home. Lord! I thought she'd brought me a gift. Me and Dodo didn't know what they were. We took them out to the chicken house to read the instructions. We didn't know what to do with them and, of course, Carl had his nose out peeking through the cracks at us. It wasn't long until we learned what they were all about.

When Mom was in Chicago working I had to do the cooking, baking—whatever we ate—but I don't remember ever making coffee. Dad always ate breakfast before he left for work, so he must have made it. I know we had a coffee pot.

Virginia Ruth

We used to get a lot of company and when we did, Mom and Dad, no matter how hard they were fighting, quieted right up. That's why no one ever knew they fought. No one else ever seen them fight, but we saw them fight many times, and I tell you the truth, I never knew what they fought about. I know they would make up. Dad used to walk up behind Mom and put his arms around her and they would kiss and hug. They loved each other. I'm very sure they loved each other throughout their lives even though they separated—divorce and all. There was a lot of anger there, but I think when there's anger there has to be some kind of love. I think Mom and Dad loved each other regardless of what happened between them.

I remember when Mrs. Caton, from the State, started coming out to the house. One day I'd just mopped the kitchen and Irma and Bertie were laying on the cot in the living room. They had jelly all over their faces. Mrs. Caton asked me, "Where did they get those sores?" I wiped my finger across their faces and said, "them ain't sores. They're jelly and bread." Later, when we went to court, she would say the kids had sores all over their faces and Mom said, "Where are they. Where are the sores? Where are the sores on their mouths? They ain't got no sores now." And that was just a week before we went to court. I guess the Judge never believed us.

The kids and I knew there was something going on between Mom and Dad. I was fifteen years old and not any dummy. I knew something wasn't kosher. Dad said it was because Mom went off to work and left us, but believe me, when Mom worked we had little things that we never had before—like underwear. You know we didn't even own a comb in our house until Jim Burrwell gave one to Dodo. We used to use forks to comb our hair in the morning before going to school. Dad used to keep our hair short. He put a bowl over our head and cut around it and there we were.

Ten Sisters

In the summer we used to wash our clothes in the branch and our baths were taken in the branch with a bar of soap, but it done the job. In the winter we used to get a tub of hot water and Mom would start with the little ones first and up to the last ones. You know what the water was like before it got to me, but we still bathed in it. Water was scarce around our house. You couldn't go to the branch in winter like you could in the summer. We had a well, but it didn't furnish us with enough water.

We never starved at home and all the kids were usually healthy and healthy looking. We didn't have a lot of sickness. I went to the Doctor once when I was home. I couldn't walk and they had to carry me up the stairs to his office. I know this sounds strange, but he cut a little piece out of my groin and placed a piece of cotton in there. And today that cotton is probably still in there. I even have a little scar. I have no idea what was wrong. At the time I was a pretty good sized girl.

And one time when I was at the doctor with Mom she asked him why I never had my period. I was already fourteen years old. He told her "Hey, if she has no pain and is not complaining then don't worry about it. A lot of girls are very late in life." Mom said we never worried about it after that.

I remember when we all got the measles. Jess came home from service and he was sick. He went back and wrote to tell us he had the measles. Carl was in the CCC camp and he had the measles, too. All of us got the measles but not at the same time. I remember when I had them Bud Rickleman was out there and he had a beer. The Dr. asked him if "he could give some to the girl so that she will break out." I drank that beer, got drunk, and I guess I broke out. Dr. Richardson told Mom not to wash the floor until all the kids got through getting the measles. When we did Mom and I had to wash the floor—then Dad got the measles. He was so sick.

Phyllis had pneumonia one time and it seemed Mom rocked

36

her for two weeks. And Dodo had typhoid fever. That whole room had to be cleaned and no one could be in there but Dodo. Dad had typhoid, too, and he was very, very sick. So was Dodo.

Bertie got hit by a car once, and Jess got sick. He had something wrong with this stomach. It swelled all up. I understand, now, that it was Bright's disease. Mom took us all to school and then took Jess on to the hospital.

We had an old car. I don't remember where or when we got it. It was a Model T Ford. One morning Mom said, "I'm learning to drive that car." That evening she went to pick Dad up at work—and that was the first time she'd ever drove that dang car—and that's exactly when she learned to drive. She just stayed in the ruts.

Mom used to take us to a lot of dances. Me and Dodo won more jitterbug contests than you could shake a stick at. Mom never drank and neither did we. We had cokes or something like that if we had the money for it. Dodo and I used to win those jitterbug contests all the time.

In good weather we used to get on the bridge out in front of the house. If we seen a car coming we'd hide under the bridge and all the dirt would fall down between the cracks onto us when the cars went by. Another thing that was big for us was damming up the creek. Us kids used to dam it up 'till the water really ran through there. I tell you, I almost drowned there twice. Either Carl or Jess came in and got me. But when Carl and Jess left us girls used to dam it up, too. One day we were all out there naked as jaybirds. We used to take our clothes off—we sure didn't have bathing suits—when this car came down the road and the guy stopped. He came out there where we were and saw all our clothes on the bank and said, "I need a glass of water. Who's gonna come out and get me a glass of water?" Well all he could see was our heads shaking because nobody was going to go to the well to get him a drink. "Well," he said, "I'll give 10 cents to whoever will get me a glass of water."

Still nobody got out of the water. Then he got all the way up to a quarter, but nobody moved. I think cousins, Wanda and Catherine, were probably in the water with us. Anyway, he finally left. Later on he told Mom and Dad about it and they laughed. Dad said, "I tell them kids not to dam that water, but they do every time!"

Another thing that stands out about home is Mom, Uncle Nolan, and Aunt Vivian singing. Uncle Nolan played the guitar, and Mom played it a little bit, and they would sing, sing, sing. You could hear them all over. Even Dad sang *Red River Valley* because he loved that song so.

I always thought Uncle Nolan had a crush on Dad's sister, Aunt Vivian, until the day she died. She died very young from some kind of disease, but I don't know what it was. I always walked her home from school. She'd always tell me to wait for her. She had the most beautiful hair and she used to wave ours. I loved her so much and Mom was very close to her.

I remember when Uncle Pete and Aunt Virginia were going together. Us kids used to follow them all over, giggling.

And I remember when Carl went off to the Navy. I wanted to go into the service, too, but instead I went to work for a couple who worked outside the home. He was with the Hayes Truck Lines and she was with the Brown Shoe Factory. They had a little boy. I made three dollars a week and I took my first three dollars and bought myself a doll. Carl and Jess bought Dodo and Bede one and those were our first dolls. I was already fourteen years old and I loved that doll. I still love dolls. I can't stand to see a naked doll laying around anywhere. Today, I have a lot of dolls in my collection.

I remember the time Carl was in a tire we were rolling down the hill. Carl came right towards the back door and he came right on through—right through the the wall! We hurried up and patched the hole, and piled some wood in front of it to let the patch dry and keep people away from the wall, but when Dad came in that evening he decided to bring in another pile of wood. He threw it down with the rest and the whole wall caved in. O Lord! We had to explain that to him. We wasn't bad to tattle on each other. Rather than see one of us get a whipping we just kind of kept it back for ourselves.

Sister Margy wasn't the youngest, but she was the tiniest one at home. When we played house she was always our mom—that little, bitty, skinny thing. We played house a lot and put on programs at home. We used to strip the beds and hang the sheets up in the front room and put a light behind it and then we would get in there and perform. The rest of the kids set out in front and watched. When we heard Dad and Mom coming home we'd tear those sheets off them big nails in the wall. Of course Mom caught on, finally, but I don't remember if she ever done anything about it. She knew that was one of the only ways we had to entertain ourselves.

We had a goat. We loved that thing, but that dang goat! He'd get to chasing us and then we'd run into the house, and hell, he would come right through the screen door—didn't even pause. Mom liked to killed us. That screen was broken all the time. Somehow that goat disappeared and one day one of our neighbors brought some meat down to us. Mom said it was probably our goat and that was why he brought it.

Sometimes we would get a few cents on Sunday and after we got home from church we'd walk over to the store near the lake where Bea, Carl's wife, lives now. We'd spend our few pennies and walk back home. We loved to do that. Then we had Sunday dinner.

We didn't have many things brand new, but one time Carl and I got new readers from school, and we put them under the bridge 'cause we didn't want to take them home. We hated homework. It rained that night and boy! The next morning Carl and I got up and headed for that bridge first thing. The books were gone. Gone! The bridge had floated out.

Ten Sisters

Rain caused a lot of problems. I remember the time it rained so hard it looked like our house was sitting in the middle of a lake. Dad came up to the corner to meet us kids and walked us from the corner down to the house which was quite aways when you think about it. He didn't want us to cross the bridge alone. Dad was trying to get us across the bridge and he just about lost me. If he hadn't grabbed me when he did I would have been downstream—long gone. I guess that's why I'm so afraid of water today. I almost drowned so many times.

Uncle Nolan tried to teach all of us to swim. He'd throw us in the damn water and yell "Swim, you little devils! Swim!" I would not swim and so he'd give me to the last minute then come jump in and get me. He'd say, "Jenny, you're too damn stubborn to swim." I was stubborn. I loved to go into the water, but I didn't want to swim. Now Bede could swims like a fish. O God! She could swim good.

And there were other things we spent time doing. Dad and Mom used to kill rats. Us kids would crawl underneath the house and stir up the rats' nests and as they would come out, Mom and Dad would shoot them. If they missed the rats lit out for the branch and went downstream. We used to have cats and dogs coming there galore. At night you could hear a car door slam at the top of the hill and the next thing you knew a cat or a dog came running down towards our house. We'd tie them up in the front yard, but Dad used to kill them things. We never were cat or dog lovers. I can't ever remember petting and making over cats or dogs—ever. We made over the goat more than anything. We managed to entertain ourselves the best that we could.

Kids like us are bored to death if they have nothing to do. We never had puzzles, never had games. We played a lot of hopscotch, and we had the one bicycle and the one radio that never worked right. And Jess, and Carl, and us girls, and the neighbor-

hood kids played house a lot. The things that we did at home left no
scar on my life what-so-ever—only good memories.

Us kids were together a lot. Mom and Dad used to go away
—they even went to the World's Fair. And they used to go to dances
together, especially at the Smith's house. Where they started going
wrong I don't really know. I don't know how it all came about. I do
know Dad started going out. And the fights began to get more and
more regular. In a way I was happy to see the fighting ended. In fact,
the last time Jess was home he told Dad, "Don't you ever lay a hand
on Mom or when I come home, I'll kill you." I don't think Jess was
serious. He loved them both. Dad never did hit her another time after
that, but they didn't live together long after that, either.

The day we went to court all of us girls drove with Dad and
Mom in the car. Grandma and Grandpa Coen were already at the
courthouse and there were a lot of other people there. Us girls sang
You Are My Sunshine while everybody at the courthouse listened
and watched. I'm sure some people knew what was going on and a
lot probably didn't. At that point I figured Mom and Dad were
going to divorce, but Mom did not know that the kids had already
been placed in homes or had places picked out where they were
going. When we went in and they took us out of the room Mom
wanted to know where we were going. They told her "Just into the
other room. We will be back." But they never came back. They
marched us right out of that courthouse to the other side of the
square. We didn't know for sure what was going on. They took us
to a restaurant to eat. I remember that we had many forks, a special
fork for this and one for that, and a spoon for this and a spoon for
that. I told the guy "This is all new for us. We never had but a couple of forks and a couple of knives and a few spoons at home." So
this was a treat for us to get a big dinner like that. But half of us did
not even eat the food, especially us older kids who knew that something right was *not* happening here. We thought we were either

going to be taken away from Dad or from Mom. We didn't know which one, only that wrong was going on here. They took our picture on the courthouse steps. Each one of the kids have that picture today—but we didn't see the picture for over forty years. When Mom died in 1993 a newspaper took another picture on the courthouse steps. In that picture we were standing in the same sequence as the original one. The only regret is that Mom never got to know it or see it. She would have loved it.

That day in 1942 we left from the courthouse to many places—Dodo first—and then me.

I went to a Dr. Austinhager's house. He was married and they had two little boys, one a baby. I had to sleep in the room with those two kids and I had to be with them at night, changing diapers, feeding them. And I was responsible for washing dishes and cleaning house. His wife smoked and that was the first time I ever tasted cigarettes. The clothes I went there in was the same clothes I left there in. She never bought me one new thing. She had some clothes that someone had given her for me to wear. And she finally borrowed a bicycle for me to ride.

Dodo's place was different. She got a new bike and new clothes—new this and new that. But Dodo and I did get back together. I found out where she was by making a lot of phone calls and asking a lot of questions. Then at the skating rink I found out where Bede was. One night I was supposed to go the movies and the Doctor followed me. He told me the next morning "You didn't go to the movie. You went to the skating rink to see your sister."

He was right. I had heard that she was there, so I went to see. Mrs. Caton had told me there was a guy there that owned the skating rink that had her. And just as I walked into the skating rink Bede was standing at the top of the steps and she spotted me and we ran to meet each other and we hugged, and kissed, and cried. We were so happy to see each other. Well this guy said he wanted all of us.

He wanted me, and Dodo, Bede, and Margy, and as many as he could get. He also had kids of his own. He took us to Chicago in a trailer. We had never done anything like that before. But it didn't work out.

We never got to go back home. If we had anything personal, and that's doubtful, it was left behind. Dodo used to have quite a few little personal things, but I'm sure there were no belongings left even if we'd got to return. After we left that morning, that was the end of my ever living there. By the time I did get to go back, the house had already been moved and Dad lived in it. He'd moved it up to the corner where the house had once set. Several years ago it got moved back to where it set when we lived in it. All of us today have a part of that house. My brother-in-law Dick made something for each of us from it. He did that for us and we appreciate that very much. We went back there often just to see the tree. I have one of the posts that we used to dress up all the time, that Phyllis brought me from the house. I've still got the post and I'm hoping someday to dress that post up and place her somewhere in my yard with flowers around her.

Anyway, I just went down and told that woman that I was leaving and going to my Grandma's because we knew where grandma and Grandpa lived. Mrs. Caton, when she found out we all went to Grandma's, said she was going to have me and Dodo placed in a home in New York. I told her "You place me in there and I will run away. I'll not stay there." So we didn't go. Then she tried to put us in another home, saying we were pregnant. She sent us to Dr. Richardson. Grandma went with us. After he looked at each of us he said we were *not* pregnant, that we were all having our periods. Grandma was standing up so close to the door that when we opened it she fell. She was trying to hear what was going on in the room.

Then Bede went off to Cunningham Home in Urbana, Illinois, where Margy, Bertie, Irma, and Phyllis were. Before that,

Margy and Bertie had been in a home where this woman was nothing but a pig. How she ever managed to get the girls, I'll never know. The environment there was terrible, nothing like home.

I guess Grandma and Grandpa Coen needed the money so taking Vera to raise was one way of getting extra money as they were paid by the State to take care of her. The other people were also paid by the State to take care of the others that were minors. We were all minors. I remember the day they took Audrey. She kicked Mrs. Cole right in the stomach real hard, almost knocking the wind out of her. And Doris, of course, was too little to even know what was going on, but it was very sad when they walked out of that courtroom with those kids. Very, very sad. We were all crying and really didn't know what in the hell was going on—one of the saddest days of my life. We were glad Vera was going with someone we knew because nobody else was. We were all going to other homes. Vera was the sweetest little thing. When she was about a year or two old, Uncle Arthur had a child and that child was so big and fat that he sat in a chair and Vera stood alongside of him and he was way bigger than Vera. I'll never forget that.

Vera stayed with Grandma and Grandpa from then on. I think this was all set up. I guess Dad had planned it with them because Vera had, like me, stayed with them a lot. In fact, Vera's life didn't change much. Even when we were home they used to keep Vera. Mom used to bring her home on weekends and then Grandma and Grandpa would come and get her on Sundays. They always favored Vera very, very much. She was older than Audrey, but she was smaller and very cute. They favored me, too, until I got to be a brat. Even though they didn't pick me to live with them, I loved Grandma and Grandpa.

After I left the Doctor's me and Dodo went to work at an old folks' home. We worked there for a month. She worked cleaning rooms and I worked in the kitchen. And after we got our first paycheck, I don't remember how much, we went and bought us a new dress. Both dresses were black with white trim. We loved them! And we got us a pair of shoes and socks and we got us a train ticket to Chicago—to be with Mom. She met us at the station and took us to her apartment. We stayed with Mom part of the time, but we would be back and forth between her and Dad. He also lived in Chicago at that time and worked for R. R. Donnelly. He lived on the south side of the city with the Huffman family. We were back and forth, back and forth, between them.

Mom got all the kids out of the Cunningham Home when she married Paul Kopeck. Paul, being the most reasonable one, probably was the instigator of it. I don't think Mom would have ever got them out by herself. Bede was the first to come out of the home, but she came out because she was too old to stay. You could stay until you were sixteen—then you had to leave. Me and Carl went there on the train and got Bede and took her back to Chicago. Then after Mom got the kids, the authorities tried, again, to have them taken away. Well the kids did live here and there. Mom didn't have an apartment big enough for all of us, but when we went to court that day the judge said, "I want this woman left alone. This family loves each other no matter who they live with or what, so leave this family alone. I don't want this family brought back into this courtroom." So we all left, went out to eat, and then went our own ways.

I am fifteen years older than my sister Doris, and we didn't get to see her too often, but we always got to see Vera. She was at Grandma's, but we knew she was our sister and we loved her. Mom saw her a lot, too. I don't know if Dad did. Doris and Audrey lived with foster families.

In Chicago, Mom and I went to work at the same factory, a plastics factory. Dodo kept house as she was too young to work. We had a flat roof up on top of our apartment, and we used to go up there and dance—Mom, and me, and Dodo. We had a ball. We wore those overalls that had those little sailors and marines on them.

While Mom and I were working at the plastic factory I had an accident. I got my hair pulled out and had to go to a doctor. I had a big bald spot on the top of my head. I should have sued as they didn't have any guards on those machines I was working on, but we didn't know anything about suing in those days. I just leaned over a little and there went my hair. It went so fast it didn't even hurt. We worked there quite awhile. Mom and I saw a lot of our cousins, Marie and Marvin Woolems. They lived close by. Marie and Mom were very close.

I want to tell about when I went to New York. Jess had just married Betty Golden and I went there to be with Betty when she had her baby, Kenneth Dale. She lived in the Bronx. I stayed with her for quite some time. Carl and Jess were both stationed in New York—on the *U.S.S. Arkansas*. Jess only came there once while I was there, though. Then he was sent to the pacific coast. Carl stayed aboard the *Arkansas*. He invited me to come over where he and some friends, Gene Fudge and his sister Ella, were. Carl dated the sister. They were from Danville, Illinois. I was just eighteen years old. I guess it was puppy love. Gene and I were married a few weeks later. Carl and Ella stood up for us and we had a minister, but I don't recall his name or what denomination he was. I was a Methodist. Carl and Gene were shipped out a few weeks later and I moved in with Gene's sister Ella. We got a job in the shipyards in New Jersey. I was a tech welder. They said I was a good one. I loved it. I used to go high in the air, in small areas, hard to get places. We were laid off, though, and I went back to Chicago.

It was in New York that I met John Golden, Betty's dad. John was in the military and he came to Betty's once while I was there. A small world. John Golden would, years later, become my third stepfather.

Virginia Ruth

Mom was married to Paul and living in Chicago at that time. Ella and I stayed with them until I got a different place. Then Ella went to Danville and Betty and little Dale moved to Chicago and stayed with Mom and Paul until they got their own place. Bede and I lived together at different addresses until we finally moved over on 19th Street. Betty, Bede, and I got jobs in a screw factory, but we quit after several weeks. Then I started waitressing work again. About that time Carl and Gene came home on leave and we all went down to Danville, Illinois. Gene's aunt owned a big hotel there, and she roomed and boarded the guests. We all ate at a table about twenty or thirty feet long. It was quite an experience for me. It was in that hotel that we heard that President Roosevelt died. We all cried and felt so bad.

Carl and Gene went back to New York aboard ship after that. Gene and I never seen each other that much and when he was gone away it was like we wasn't married. I did go out with other guys and I'm sure he was not 100% pure, either, when he was away from me. When they came home again, Gene and I were strangers. We talked a bit, agreed on a divorce, and he left. But Gene was a good guy and I saw him off and on. Gene and Carl remained good friends and Gene stayed around Chicago. He got married and had several children. He used to be a cab driver and he would stop in the restaurant where I was working and occasionally say hi, but I never had a chance to talk to him because I was always busy, and that was the size of it. Now, he's deceased.

Carl said that when he and Jess boarded the *U.S.S. Arkansas* Jess never told anyone that he had ten sisters and he kept our picture down at the bottom of his clothes and personal things, but Carl told all the boys that he and Jess had ten sisters and they kidded and kidded Jess about it. It wasn't that Jess was ashamed of us—it was probably that he didn't want to be bothered with talking about it. I think Jess and Carl both were really torn up about our family life at

home when we separated. They came home on leave together once and were very upset about it.

After the war Carl stayed with me, Irma, Bertie, and Gene's brother Bob. Carl and him were close friends. Bob never married.

Bede was living with me when Chet Brniak came home from the war. I will never forget that meeting for the two of them. It was true love, for sure.

Then Mom and Paul moved to Arkansas and I eventually went down there to live with them. Jess' wife, Betty, her boys, Margy, Phyllis, Vera, and I all lived in Arkansas right on top of a bluff. We cut down trees, put one end into the fireplace and let the other end stick out the door. As it burned down we kept pushing the tree into the fireplace until we could get the rest of it into the house.

That was where I met Clarence. I met his brother Herbie, first, at our house. He used to come over when we had dances and things like that. A lot of men used to come to our dances. We really didn't know what they came for because some of them was so damned old, who'd even think about having an affair with them. But there were a lot of young guys, too. We had a lot of fun at those dances. We were the talk of the whole county, believe me.

When Mom and Paul moved back to Chicago, Clarence and I helped move them and then I returned to Arkansas with him. We got married about five or six months later. Our marriage was one more disaster. When we went to get married that night, I had a nice suit on and Clarence's sister Lola was dressed real nice, too. Well, we went down this muddy road and it was raining like hell and Clarence slipped off into a ditch. We were in a truck and there we was! I asked "What are we gonna do?" Clarence said, "Get out." So we got out. Clarence went ahead of us with the flashlight. But it wasn't very bright and we didn't have a light, so we didn't know where we were. By the time we got to the preacher's house we looked like pigs. Our hose were torn and our hair was straight.

Anyway, when we got there the minister's wife, who was an invalid, never got up—just laid in bed and acted as the witness. They had a lot of kids and they were spying on us. Their little heads were sticking out in every direction. And the preacher couldn't find his pants, so he only wore his long underwear. He couldn't find his bible, either, but finally found a little Testament. He thought Clarence was marrying his cousin. He thought I was Clarence's sister and that Clarence's sister was his cousin and that his cousin was our witness. It was really funny—later.

The preacher finally sat us down on a bench and then Clarence smoked all through the ceremony. It was a wedding that sure-in-the-hell was not made in heaven, I'll tell you that. I often wonder that it ever happened because it was so traumatic to me. Nothing romantic about it at all. Today, weddings are so romantic. But ours has lasted for forty-nine years.

Well, this was hell for Clarence's folks, for I don't know how long it was until Clarence allowed Lola to tell them that he and I were married. Clarence was funny like that. We went to live with his family and that's where I finally got to know them. They were all very good to me after we were married.

Clarence and me went back and forth between Arkansas and Michigan to work, and we worked, and worked, and worked. Margy and Richard was very close to us. We even worked for them as they had a lot of land. We lived in some huts in Michigan. One place had no floor. I used to water the ground, sweep good, and put throw rugs down for Carol to play on.

I learned to pick cotton in Arkansas, and learned how to raise and catch chickens and other things I had never done in my life for a living. Of course, I had helped Mom plant seeds, but we didn't have a lot of seeds to plant, and Mom liked to do that herself. That was her baby—she loved to do that.

Clarence and I finally settled in Indiana for quite a few years and then moved over to Chicago because he got laid off from his job. Marvin, my new stepdad, had to sign for us to get a stove as we didn't have any accounts. We owed nothing, but we didn't have any money. We finally got that paid for and got our credit established.

We were with Chet and Bede a lot in Chicago. They were our right-hand people. We seen a lot of Mom and Marvin, too. Our daughter, Carol, was born in Chicago at Chet and Bede's house. I went to the Maternity Center, there, like Bede did when she had her Ronnie. Carol only cost me $25.00. We had great doctors. They came right to the house and delivered the babies—staying right with us until the end. It's a good thing, because when Carol was born I was sick a long time. In fact, they had almost given up on my having her, I think, because I started labor one night and didn't have her until the next day.

Clarence and I eventually went back to Arkansas and lived for quite awhile. But we still went back and forth from the cotton patch to Michigan. I got pregnant with our daughter Doris when we lived in Michigan. But by the time we got back to Arkansas, which was in the fall, I had a really bad spell. Down there, they got up really early in the morning so the cotton would be wet and weigh more. O Jesus! That cotton. I was not a cotton picker and that was all you could say for me. We would pick all day and have about forty pounds in the big bag. I hated it. Anyway, I had this spell and got the hives real bad and almost died. Clarence's mother probably saved my life. She poured a wash tub of water with Epsom Salts and made me sit in there. Believe me, I was not too big then, and I could sit in a washtub of water with no problem. I'll never forget it as long as I live. I thought my life was over.

We stayed in Arkansas through the winter because there was nothing else to do and we had this house there. One night I told Clarence I was probably going to have the baby. I had been sick all day. So he said to wake him up if I thought I was going to have it.

About midnight, I woke him up and told him to go get the doctor. It was really cold and Clarence stopped and told his mother to come up there, too. She came up and brought a neighbor woman. When the doctor got there he told me to go to bed so he could examine me. He never even took the sheet off me. He just reached in under the sheet and examined me and then sat back in the chair and said it wasn't ready to be born yet. A couple of hours later he examined me again, the same way, and said to Clarence's mother, Lettie, and the neighbor, "You better get me some water. I think it's about time for it to be born."

Just before I delivered Lettie said, "The doctor won't leave until he eats. It don't matter what meal he's closest to, he stays until he eats." So Mrs. Rackley and the neighbor lady, after Doris was born, cleaned her up. The doctor examined her, cut the cord, and then sat down to wait for a big breakfast. We had no coal for the cook stove so we had to get some extra wood, and the wood stove was in the living room where Doris was born, but Mrs. Rackley made that doctor a *big* breakfast.

When he got ready to leave, I asked him, "How much does the baby weigh?" He came over, picked little Doris up by the feet and hung her up in the air and said, "Eight pounds." So I said, "How long is she?"

He squinted and said, "About eighteen inches."

Lettie brought the scales up later that day and Doris did weigh exactly eight pounds and was exactly eighteen inches long. The doctor had charged $10.00—a baby—for ten dollars!

In the spring, after Doris was born, we went back to Michigan and picked fruit as long as we could pick. And we did that year after year until Clarence got a full time job and the kids had to start school. I went to work, too, as a waitress. I loved it. I worked at David's, Batts, and a couple of other Chicago restaurants.

By this time we lived on 31st Place. Our apartment was in

the basement. It was a nice little place and we liked it there. Carol and Doris both went to school there. Carol had already started school in South Bend. We lived there for awhile then moved farther west on 31st in a different district and closer to Holden School. I done lots of sewing at that time. In fact, I made most the kid's clothes. I really wasn't back into quilting yet. I thought about it, but I just never got into it. I had done some quilting in South Bend, using Mom's quilting frame, until she move away and took it with her.

After the girls graduated from junior high they both went to high school, and we moved over to a place on Archer Avenue to an upstairs apartment. It was very bad, but the kids caught the school bus right there and Carol finally graduated in the summer—after only three years. Doris graduated later on, after we moved over to 34th and Wood. We bought the house with my sister, Bertie, and her husband Bob, and they lived on the 2nd floor.

After the kids grew up and married I really got into the quilting. Mom would come over and help me. Mom had a very good stitch. They were much smaller than mine. But she's the one who taught me—her and Mrs. Rackley.

When our grandson Heath was born, he was very sick right away. We got telegram after telegram from the government telling us that he had a brain hemorrhage that he was not expected to live. Finally we went to Germany to see him. Later Heath was brought back to the states and Fred and our daughter Doris lived at Ft. Sheridan until Fred came out of the service because his father was murdered in his shop in Chicago.

Heath spent the biggest part of his short life in Children's Memorial Hospital, and from there to Misericordia, and finally to the Deaf and Blind Home. Heath was what kept us going. My heart went out to him and to our daughter. Doris carried a very big load then, and it was a very dramatic time for all of us—a stressful time—sitting up late in those emergency rooms all night long, waiting to get Heath examined to see if they would admit or release him. Carrying him around. He could never walk or talk and couldn't hear or see. It was something I will never get over. Much as I hated to see him die, I was relieved when he did. But Heath will live forever in my mind. I loved him so much and he was such a treasure. He knew what he wanted. He was no dummy and he gave us many laughs as well as tears.

Since 1981 I've had some serious physical problems and some death-threatening times of my own. Many because of Rheumethoid Arthritis. But God has answered all the prayers and I am still hanging in there.

Clarence and I have two daughters—both married—and five granddaughters, one step-granddaughter, and one step-grandson still living. We don't see them much. They're all busy people. But I love them all and I don't ever want them to think otherwise. I think the thing that was missing in our home was the word love. We used to get hit on the head a lot when Dad was mad. Carl, and me, and Dodo got it the most. And we kids had fights, but we love each other today, and that's the main thing.

Tracing back over my life, I have no regrets. I feel like I've experienced a lot of things that some people never experience. And I love all my sisters and brothers very much. Unfortunately we lost many years with Jess, but when he did come back we had good times and happy years until he passed on. Jesse Dale Waggoner was born October 2, 1922. He was the oldest of us twelve Waggoner kids. He was a twenty-year veteran of the service, having served in both World War II and the Korean War. He had five children: Dale, Paul, Zoe (Mary Lou), Stanley, and Lynn. He left a widow, Shirley. Jesse was a Shriner and was working as a dietitian in the Swedish hospital in Rockford, Illinois, when he passed away with a heart attack, November 20, 1978.

Last summer we lost our brother Carl. He died suddenly of

a heart attack. Losing Carl was shocking, really shocking.

Memories of home will never leave me, and I'm fortunate that we had Dad for many years and Mom for eighty-nine years. She was a very good person. She had her faults, but I think anyone of us kids would understand what she experienced when she lost all the kids. I don't think there is one of us in this family could ever say that we ever faced any of that trauma in our life. I can't imagine someone taking my kids away and it was something Mom had to face—and without money. Her hands were tied in lots of ways. I never have held any bad feelings toward Mom or Dad. I know they both loved us all and showed it throughout our lives. They were very poor but managed for many years. We never knew how poor until we grew up. I loved Mom and Dad very much. Since I have lived seventy years, I look back and know why we split up. No money—no help. Not like people get today. But nothing can erase the sixteen years I was with Mom and Dad in that small house. We all learned to love and stayed out of trouble. God alone knows the answer to it all.

Deloris Maxine
(Dodo)

Dedicated to my children

Ten Sisters

On November 10, 1993, I started this chapter with a pen Mom bought for our reunion in 1991. It says on it—Grandma Golden Reunion 1991. Mom passed away April 18, 1993. She would have been ninety on the 6th of June.

My name is Deloris Maxine Waggoner Hart. I will be sixty-six in August of '96. I'm next to the oldest of ten girls, and fourth from the oldest of our family, as we had two older brothers.

When I was seven I had typhoid fever. I missed out on a year of school. Dad also had typhoid when I was a child. Mom took care of both of us. She made me clothespin dolls to play with. I lost my hair and had to learn to walk again.

Around eight years old I was in a car accident. Got my nose hit hard. When the insurance money came, $25.00, Mom bought Jess a guitar and me a small toy cookstove. She also bought Christmas presents for all the kids.

As we got older we climbed trees—all of us girls did that was big enough. We would come down head first. The boys could swing from limb to limb. Us girls never tried that!

We had a branch of water that ran just east of our yard. We made good use of it. Took baths, washed our hair, went swimming in summer, and ice skating in the winter. We also used the front yard in winter to skate. With so many kids we never had any grass in the yard. We had a road that ran east and west by our house. It had a small bridge. We would run out and hide under the bridge when a car went by and rocks and dirt would fall in our hair. We didn't have toys like most kids. We would take sticks and dress them up and name them. Two of the names I can remember—Mrs. Iggely and Mrs. Jomely. We would always find things to do like pulling thorns out of Dad's boots—then they would leak! I can remember taking screws out of the inside of the car just to have something to do, but I always put them back. And we made leaf houses in the fall.

Mom and Dad were always fighting. I wondered why they had so many kids. Each time a baby girl was born we would say, "Mom, please name it Shirley." She never did. Later on in life my brother Jesse would marry a woman named Shirley.

After us older girls got to where we could take care of the younger girls and babies, Mom and Dad were able to go out and be with friends. While they were gone we would clean house and play beauty shop. We would make the small ones sit on the bench and stay out of the way and wait their turn to have their hair fixed.

When the boys got sixteen they left for CCC Camp. That gave us a little more room and the teasing stopped. Dad wanted Mom to go to work to help out on the money part. Dad started asking people to take one of us older girls as it would help him on the grocery bill. Sally Ann Bakery gave us many loaves of bread. Dad added them up for one year, but I can't remember how many it was.

The first time I was sent with some people to room and board, I couldn't have been very old. Anyway, I was so homesick so the woman had to take me home. She walked me across the field. The next place Dad made me go was to a big house. An old lady lived there. I was so scared, but I did learn to use a telephone. I stayed there about two weeks.

The next place belonged to good friends of Mom and Dad. They took two of us, me and my older sister. We liked it there. They were nice to us. We worked for them. They had a blind pony which I rode a lot. I can't remember how long we stayed. The people took a trip out west. They had three boys of their own. They kept my older sister and I went back home. One boy was older than us and we tried to get him into trouble. That may be why we left there!

There wasn't any money and very little food at home. I used to wait for the old hen to lay an egg and I would get it, take the white and beat it, add sugar, and eat it. To this day I still love beaten egg whites! Dad towed—where you take a wash-tub, put a hole in it, and drop it over the fish. So did Mom. We ate lots of fish.

Dad was a good shot. He killed many rabbits for winter. We always dressed out rabbits hanging on the back of the house. Dad used to say of Mom, "She could make a meal of anything." In the summer we had chicken every Sunday. Lots of people came.

When I was twelve years old, Mom, Dad, and an uncle put up a boxing ring east of the branch and lots of people came by to watch the boxing. This is where I remembered first seeing the man that I would marry. Him and his cousin came and stood around and watched. He was going with Jenny at that time! When he was twenty and I was sixteen we got married.

It was about this time that Dad used to go out alone and then we could get the car. Mom would take me and my oldest sister to square dances. We enjoyed that! Coming home one night we ran over a cow. We were lucky the car stayed upright.

Not long before Dad and Mom split up, my oldest sister went to work in town and Mom went to work for sick people. I quit school, took care of the babies, and sent the rest of the kids to school. When the eighth sister was born, Mom and Dad gave her to my grandparents on my Mom's side of the family—and to this day we don't know why. She got to come out and see us often. But Grandpa said that we taught her things that were bad for her. One thing was running and jumping across the branch of water. He said it gave her "stone feet." I never did like him!

My oldest brother Jesse joined the navy in October 1940 when he was eighteen. My youngest brother was still in CCC Camp. The oldest brother came home on leave and we all got to visit with him, but when he left it wasn't long before everyone started getting sick. My younger brother didn't come home from CCC Camp, but we got word that he and my oldest brother had the measles. We all remembered that Jess wasn't himself when he was home. One by one all of us girls had the measles—even little Vera. My Dad got them, too. Mom and Grandma took care of all of us. It was a big job.

When Dad and Mom went visiting, sometimes they would take the small girls with them and make the older ones stay at home. We would be mad so we would climb the trees in the driveway and hide. Mom and Dad knew we wouldn't be far so we would stay in the trees 'till dark then start singing. I bet they knew we were up there all the time!

Us three older girls used to sing at Dixie School. That's the school that most of us went to. I don't know why we didn't keep on singing. Seems like we just forgot so many things for a long time.

When I went to school I never had clothes to be proud of. We were made fun of at school because of it. Today I have lots of clothes. Once in awhile Mom would get busy and make a mess of dresses for some of us that went to school. People gave us clothes, too, and Mom would make them over to fit. If they still were too long, we would pin them up on the way to school. The girls that went to school had high-topped shoes. When they were worn out we put cardboard in the insole. It would hold up for a day. The small girls didn't always have shoes. When Mom went to Chicago to work it was the first time we had new store-bought underpants. We let the small kids run around with only their pants on. We thought they were so pretty and it was summertime.

We were just kids. We would do things we shouldn't have like slide down a slick hill and tear up our clothes. We went to Grandma Waggoner's who lived a hill from us. She left biscuits on the table and as soon as her back was turned we took them. She knew we would! She said to us: "Go and get all the apples you want, but stay out of the peaches!" We always got apples *and* the peaches. Once it had stormed and Grandma said: "Don't go into the peach yard as a storm has broke a tree down." Well we went anyway and Bede slipped on a limb and broke her foot. No one took her to the doctor. She used crutches until she could walk again.

As we got older we picked gooseberries and blackberries and Mom and Dad sold them to people. They would come by our house and give us a little money. We would walk a mile to get ice cream and then be so hot walking home!

When I was twelve or thirteen, Dad got me a cleaning job washing windows for a couple at Lake Paradise. At Christmas time they gave us a large box of boys' toys. They knew I came from a large family. I never told them that we were all girls, but we didn't mind. We could play with any toys! We never knew for sure, but at Christmas time a big box was always at our mailbox. But when the mailman stopped bringing mail, the big boxes stopped too!

Dad built a long bedroom on the south side of the living room just for beds. Three beds fit in there, but it never did have real walls. Besides, there were cracks in the temporary walls and in wintertime snow came across our beds. I liked to take care of my hair, so I always wore a stocking cap to bed. One of the girls—I don't know which one—wet the bed. With so many in the same bed, we could always blame it on another one!

We had hills on the south and west of our house. One person would take turns getting into a tire and the other one would push the tire down the hill. One time it went right down into the spare room and through to the living room—leaving a big hole in the wall.

When free movies were shown at small towns around Mattoon or Paradise, Mom would take us. Sometimes us girls would have to fix a flat tire before we could go. Once, Mom took us girls to a town south of Paradise where me and Jenny entered the dance contest. We did the Jitterbug a few minutes and won $5.00! Then, I don't know how it happened, but Mom got all of us up on the stage.

We had our own home movies when Mom and Dad were gone. We hung up a sheet and got between the lamp and the sheet and we would dance and sing. Mom found out when she discovered the holes in the sheets!

Deloris Maxine

In the spring people would drop lots of cats off at our house and we were run over with cats! Mom would run them under the house, get a gun, and she would kill them. Us kids had to go under and pull them out!

Dad was the kind of man who thought if he bought you something when you were sick you would get well. My sis, next to the baby, had the flu. Dad bought her a new dress. We tried it on her, over her old one, and she wouldn't let us take it off—but she got well. Mom was working away from home at that time.

The county gave us food once in awhile—bags of cracked wheat, cereal, and bushels of grapefruit. We peeled the grapefruit and ate them like oranges. Mom made vinegar pie, water gravy, and washtubs full of donuts! It was a lot to keep food in the house. With no icebox we dropped our milk down in the well on a rope to keep it cold. Mom used to make *Argo* starch. I think most of us took a bite of that thinking it was vinegar pudding.

Mom had pictures taken of all of us but never did take one of our little house. It was a good little house. I am not sure when he built the back room. There were no clothes closets or dressers, except for one small dresser in the living room. I think it had three drawers. I always liked to have my own things together. Mom let me have one drawer. I was twelve then.

About that time my brother wanted to do something for us girls. He was at CCC Camp. For Christmas he bought dolls for all of us girls. I was too old for a doll, so I put it on the shelf 'till the smaller girls needed it. Another time my brother Carl wanted to get all of us girls a Christmas gift. He was in the Navy at that time. He went to the store and bought underslips for all of us. I would have liked to have been there when he picked out the sizes!

When I was fourteen, we all left home. We never got any of our things, no clothing, nothing—just what we had on ourselves. Dad had never finished the back room, only the outside walls with

2 x 4's. We had no stove in the bedroom. Thinking back—I don't know how we lived past the winters! We had a small, pot-bellied stove in the living room. One day in winter, Mom and Dad had a fight and one leg of the stove got knocked off. There went the stove onto Mom's arm. Sure a wonder the house didn't get on fire. Mom's arm was burned so bad. Dad took coal oil and poured it up and down her arm. It helped take the burning out. There were lots of fights. Once a gun was pulled out; sticks were thrown around the room. It was lucky none of the children were hurt. So you see, I was glad when Mom left home. There were no more fights. But I was young and I just didn't know that Dad was trying to put us girls in a home.

I can't remember getting ready to go to court. I must have helped with the little ones. We all looked well-dressed in the picture.

Even though I don't remember how we got to court, I sure do remember how we left! I recall how upset I was when I was the only one called into the courtroom. They asked me if I was pregnant. I told them "No." I remember crying in the halls at the courthouse. All of the girls were crying. And Mom was mad. Dad just stood there. I believe Dad was mixed up with a woman at that time and just wanted to get rid of us kids and Mom. Not that Mom didn't have her fun out. But we forgave both of them, even though they never told us why. They both died not telling us anything!

Anyway, someone asked my Mom and Dad to stay in the hallway and all of us girls to stay in the room. Once the people in the courtroom knew what they were going to do with all of us, someone asked us to stand on the courthouse steps and they took a picture of us. I never saw the picture until I was fifty-five years old!

I never knew it, then, but when Mom died April 18, 1993 we took all her pictures and there was a copy of that picture, a small one, in some of her things. But by then my youngest sister Doris had already had copies made, from one given to her foster mother right after it was taken. Doris had 8 x10's made of it for all of us and it hangs on my wall today!

After we had the picture taken some people took us across the street, on the south side, to a restaurant. I don't remember what I ate, but afterward we returned to the courthouse. They asked my Mom and Dad to stay in the hall and they took us all out the other door. I remember Audrey and Doris screaming when the couples took them away. Vera, the third youngest, went with Grandma Coen. They had had her since she was very small anyway. From the courthouse, they took seven of us and left—not even a goodbye to Mom and Dad.

They took some of us girls in one car and the rest in another. As we started back to Mattoon, I listened to the people talk and overheard names, so I was sure of where my older sister went, and also Bede. They dropped me off first because it was on the northeast side of Mattoon, just off the old Route 16. I was crying and the lady said: "You can forget you have a family." I guess she was good to me. Because we left home with only what we had on our backs, she took me to the police station to get clothes. In the basement there were rows of clothes. She asked me to pick some of my sizes. Then we went to slippers and socks. It was the first time I remember having nice clothes.

There were three people in the house—a nice house. My room was in the basement. I fed chickens, scrubbed potatoes, and stayed with one of their mothers as she wasn't well. I hated it. I didn't mind taking care of the chickens, or helping with the work, but they went out often. I don't know who's mother it was, but I had to sit with her at night. I was afraid of her. I can't remember her talking to me. The man in the house was an Army man. They were good to me, but I was going on fifteen and had a mind of my own.

While I was staying with these people, I remembered the name of the people where my sister Jenny might go, and where my sister Bede would be. I called and got Jenny and we made plans to meet and find Bede. The lady I lived with would often drop me off at the Times Theater to see an afternoon movie. She would pick me up two hours later. One morning when the lady and her husband were out Jenny borrowed a bike from the lady she was with so she could find Bede. I think Jenny had been in the car when Bede was left off so she kind of knew where to go. We sure were glad when we found out that the Webers, who had Bede, were nice people. They had two little girls. I found out later that they had asked for me, but there was a mix-up.

I missed the girls so much I couldn't stand living at the peoples' house that took me. I asked the lady to take me to Mrs. Caton's house—she was the Probation Officer in Mattoon. She did. The lady let me take all my new clothes, too. Mrs. Caton asked my Grandparents to take me to their house. By this time my sister Jenny was also there. It was almost a mistake going there. Every time we left the house Grandma ran out and called Mrs. Caton. We were sure that Grandma and Grandpa had something to do with the family splitting up!

We began to have some fun, anyway. We went to Weber's skating rink a lot. These were the people that Bede was with. They were so good to us, and we had a good time while it lasted. For some reason, though, Mr. Weber said that he was too young for us to be around, although he never did anything out of the way, and the State took Bede from them.

Now, Jenny, Bede, and me were all at Grandma Coen's. Vera was there, too. It was too much for Grandma Coen. She didn't want us anymore. Now that I'm older, I can understand her not wanting to be responsible for us teenage girls. Mrs. Caton wanted all three of us girls to go to the doctor and have some tests to see if any of us were pregnant. I had a smart mouth, so Mrs. Caton didn't like me! She wanted to send me to a Girl's School. I was fifteen. I said she could come by but I wouldn't go. My Grandpa said he would see me behind bars! I didn't like him!

Because my Grandparents didn't want us there, Mrs. Caton had to find other places for us. She put me and Jenny to work at the Old Folks' Home—now called the Rebeccah Home. We got twenty dollars a month and our room and board. They nicknamed me "Sunshine." I cleaned rooms and set the tables. Jenny worked in the kitchen. But it was good to stay in the same place with my sister.

Bede was put in another home with people by the name of Fox. There were already two of the other girls there. But when my Mom found out that the girls were staying with the Foxes, she wanted them moved away from there—so five of the girls were moved to the Cunningham Home in Urbana. By then Mom and Dad lived in Chicago—Mom on the west side—and Dad on the south side.

After Jenny and I had worked just one month at the old folk's home, Mrs. Caton gave us Mom's address, told us to buy a new dress and a train ticket to Chicago. So Jenny and I did this, but first went out and got our picture taken, "posed as if we were going to hitchhike," and sent it to Mom. We got back with her after my 15th birthday, August 16th, 1942.

Mom and a friend picked us up at the train station and took us to a very small apartment. The man thought he had a right to put his hands on us girls, so I was watching him close. We did move to a bigger apartment and Jenny and Mom went to work. I was still fifteen and couldn't work yet. I tried to go back to school, but that didn't work out. Mom wanted her man-friend to come to the apartment when he pleased, but when they worked I put the chain on the door. I didn't like him! That was trouble! Mom got mad easily. She told us to pack and go live with Dad. We would get to Dad's, then she would call, talk to Dad, and would tell him "Send those girls back or I'll send the police." This happened about every two weeks.

Mom sure was a mess! She never talked about the rest of the girls. I never thought she had anything to do with us girls being taken away from her and Dad. I thought Dad made all the plans. But today, I know that Mom knew all about what was happening. We found a book in her things after she died—all wrote in 1941, a year before us girls were taken away from them.

When I was sixteen I got a job on the south side of Chicago. I guess I was living with Dad then. I worked in a restaurant a few months and had to go back to Mom's again. I had been writing to Don Hart, the man that I eventually married. He had lived in Paradise—the same as I did. He was in the Navy—went in January 1942. He sent me the money to buy an engagement ring. I bought one for twenty-five dollars.

Don came home in May 1944. I was living with Mom again. We made plans to marry on May 20th. Because Don was only twenty, we took a train to Mattoon to have his parents fix the papers for him to marry. Only Don and I, and Mom, and Paul (her new husband) was there. But trouble didn't stop!

Don went back to the Navy—he had four more years to serve. Mom was a very jealous person. She always thought her husbands couldn't be trusted, but none of her husbands ever did anything wrong. I trusted all of them. It was only the first boyfriend she had when we came to Chicago that I didn't trust.

Don and I were married, but he left two days later. Jenny had moved to New York and in 1945 Mrs. Caton had let Bede come out of Cunningham Home. She was told to go to Dad's, then asked to go back to Mom's again. I was sixteen and couldn't get a job only in a restaurant as a waitress. I didn't like it, but it got me a little money.

Things were the same with Mom. She never was happy. She never had any money, either, but she would never ask for help. After a lot of fights, I went to New York in August 1944 to be with my husband. He was stationed in Washington, D.C. I was still only seventeen years of age, but I worked for my landlady so I got my room for nothing.

Deloris Maxine

By the end of October I took sick. I had been going to a doctor about my ears and throat and was thinking about having my tonsils taken out, but that wasn't the problem. When my husband came home the landlady told him an ambulance took me to the hospital. He couldn't understand why they would take me for a sore throat—he missed a telegram the doctor sent to him and to Mom in Chicago.

Mom came to New York, as the doctors wanted her to sign for the surgery, but they couldn't wait for her to arrive. It was all over when my husband and Mom got there. I had acute appendicitis, but I did fine.

My husband and my Mom didn't get along. She went to the Bronx to see my oldest brother's wife and to see her first grandchild. While there, she met John Golden. Forty years later, he would be her fourth husband.

I stayed in New York until after Christmas. My husband went out to sea. I was going to have a baby. Jenny had left New York so I went back to my mom in Chicago. My brother Carl was stationed in New York and he put me on a train and sent me home.

Mom was moving again. She didn't seem to be able to get along with anyone. We moved a lot—but Mom was still married to Paul. We moved to an apartment on Blue Island Avenue and got the rest of the girls out of the home.

The war ended in August and my daughter Donna (Sunday) was born September 16, 1945. My brother Carl came home and my sister Jenny came home. The apartment was getting a little crowded, so I got me a little place. Bede got married just after Sunday was born, so her and Chet got an apartment in the same building that I was living in, and Jenny had a little house that she lived in.

We all stayed put for Christmas, then us girls that were married took the younger ones. I took Irma; Bede took Phyllis; and Jenny took Bertie and Margy.

It wasn't long before my mom had to go to court in

Chicago. Some State people were going to try and take the girls away from Mom again. So we all went to court. All of us older ones said that Mom was taking care of the girls, so the judge dismissed the whole thing.

We all left the court. No one had a car in those days. Mom and Paul took the streetcar one way and each of us girls took the girls that was staying with us and went the other way. Mom didn't have any of the girls with her at all. But if any of the girls were sick and had to see a doctor, we would call Mom to take them and she always would. As I write this, I have found out more about my Mom and Dad than I ever knew in all the years I grew up. For instance, my mom would not let my Dad come to my wedding.

My husband came home on leave in 1946. It was the first time he got to see Donna. He had been gone for sometime. He was like a stranger, but we made it. I had made up my mind that I would try to make a go of my marriage after he left.

By that time, even though Paul was a city man, Mom and he bought a small farm in Arkansas. They all packed up—I don't remember where they got the cars or truck or whatever they had—but my sister-in-law (Jesse's wife, Betty) and her son Dale went with them. There was also Jenny, Margy, Irma, Bertie, and Phyllis that went. I was never down there while they lived there, but I understand my sister-in-law got checks from her husband (my brother) and it was the only thing they lived on. Finally Paul went back to Chicago to go to work.

I left Chicago and went back to Mattoon. I lived with my Dad. I had my daughter Sunday with me. By this time Dad had left Chicago and had moved our little house up to the next road east of where it had always been.

Dad was working in town. I wanted to go to work again, but had no one to watch Sunday. Then Mom sent my sisters Bertie and Irma back to Dad's. Bertie had ran a nail in her foot in Arkansas.

Deloris Maxine

When she got to Mattoon Dad took her to a doctor. They wanted to take her leg off, but Dad said "I have a grown daughter at home and she can take care of it." So for two days I used hot towels wrapped in bread wrappers on her leg and it got well. She may have been taking some pain pills. I don't remember. But she's fine today!

Mom moved back to Chicago with some of the girls. I stayed in Mattoon with Dad, Bertie, and Irma. I was nineteen years of age and the sisters were too young to work out, so I had them watch Sunday and I went to work. We lived at least eight miles southwest of Mattoon. I don't remember how I got there, but I went to work in a Wood Factory. The money sure helped, even though we didn't get paid much in them days. Dad was not a big eater, but we still didn't have much to eat.

My sis Bede moved down with Chet from Chicago. It wasn't long before Mom wanted the girls back and Dad didn't want to take care of them any longer, so I quit my job and everyone, except Dad, went back to Chicago. I went to work in a restaurant and lived with Bede and Chet as I needed to have someone to watch Sunday.

My husband came home in 1948. He didn't like Chicago and he didn't have a car yet, so he went back to Mattoon to work with his Grandpa cutting wood. But I found out I was pregnant again. I could stay in Chicago and have the baby for $15.00. I worked up until my seventh month. My husband returned on May 20th, our anniversary, and he stayed for a few days but went back to work in Mattoon. We wrote often.

The baby was due in June 1949, so Don came back and took Sunday with him so I wouldn't have to worry about her (but I did worry anyway!). The baby, Audrey, was born on June 9th. Don came back again and stayed ninety days and then we all packed up and went to Mattoon.

Good jobs were hard to find, so Don took a job with a farmer in Hindsboro, Illinois. We got the house, milk, $100 a month, and

Don went to farm school, so that gave us another $200 a month, which kept us going. We lived in this house, so cold and big. We stayed in just two rooms for the winter 1949. In the spring we moved into a little farmhouse, there. I liked the house, but it was hard work. The well was clear across the yard and there was lots of water to carry and it had an outside toilet. I could put up with that! But when the spring storms came I was scared half to death. We lived there two years. We had a son, Don Jr., born on February 11, 1951.

We made plans to move to Gary, Indiana in January 1952. It was cold and snowy. My mom was married to Marvin Roberts by now. I had been in touch with all the family. The sisters were beginning to get married. My husband got a job in Indiana at a cement plant. We stayed with friends until he got paid, then we got a nice apartment. My dad and Don's Dad moved our things up to Gary. Things went well for awhile. By 1955 we were able to buy our first new car. My husband said the first year he worked in Gary he earned $3000.

We made lots of trips to Chicago. All of us girls had families, but we always tried to keep in touch. Because Don made a good living, I didn't have to worry about the rent or what I would eat.

Our daughter Sunday married in 1963 and we bought a home in Crete, Illinois, the same year. Sunday and her husband moved to themselves and Audrey and Donny started at a new school. Don still worked at the cement plant. After graduation Audrey got married to Paul Byrnes, and Donny married Debbie Flamm, and they all moved away. Don and I stayed in Crete until 1983. We sold our home in just a few weeks after we put it up for sale. By this time our older daughter, Sunday, had lost her first child but went on to give us two granddaughters and one grandson. Our daughter Audrey gave us one grandson. Sunday divorced the kids' father. Our son Don never did have any children, and he and Debbie divorced after ten years. Sunday married again—this time to Paul

Bradley who had two daughters. I baby-sat with my grandchildren for eleven years. When they all got in school, I didn't know what to do.

By this time my mom had lost her husband and had just renewed her driver's license. I thought if Mom can drive at her age, I can too! I was fifty at this time. I called a place to teach me. Now I drive all the time!

Dad died April 19, 1983. He hadn't lived in our old house for a long time.

In September of 1983 we left Crete and moved to Mattoon. We now live back in Paradise. We bought a mobile home just south and across the lake from where we lived when I was kid. There was nothing here on this land but trees. We had them all cut down so we had to put a new yard in again. Lots of work! After all the work, we were on the go every day, seeing new people, old people, aunts, uncles—everyone we knew. My Mom had moved to Charleston after she married John Golden, who she'd met forty years earlier.

Our old house was moved again, to the lane in behind another big house being built there. I go over there often. The lady that lives there saw a picture of all of us girls in the paper in April of 1993 and called me to tell me that they were going to tear down our old house and we could come and take any of the boards we wanted. We were glad to hear that!

Until his death, my brother Carl lived in Paradise, too, right on the lake. Two of my sisters live nearby on Lake Mattoon.

I keep in touch with all the girls. We started having yearly reunions years and years ago—in the sixties. Every year, eight or nine of us girls make up a dance and do it on stage for the rest of the family.

Things went well for Don and me until May of 1992 when my husband took sick with the emphysema he'd had for many years. Life has changed. I do most all of the running! He can still drive and helps me cut the grass on the riding the lawn mower, but he would just as soon stay home these days.

I took sick on the twelfth of February 1994, suffering from painful headaches. I went to the hospital on the nineteenth. My sister Phyllis took me and I had surgery on the twenty-first. They operated on the right temple. I came home on the twenty-second and went back to the doctor's office on Wednesday and had surgery again—in the correct spot this time. I am doing okay—the headaches stopped. The doctor says I have Templearteryitus.

Despite our problems, I feel very good about my life. We had three good children, four grandchildren of my own, and five step-grandchildren. We have three great-granddaughters: Ryan Marie, Ashley Elizabeth, and Casandra Lynn, and one great-grandson, Joshua Dillon Ellis, born January 19, 1994. We also have six step-grandchildren and three step-great-grandchildren.

And there's something new in my life—I started back to church—the Zion Hill Methodist. We went there when I was a child. I enjoy it—I wish I had gone back ten years ago when we moved back to Mattoon. My sister Phyllis and I go together. I get to see some of the kids I went to Dixie School with.

Rhita Jean
(Bede)

Dedicated to Mom, Dad, Carl, and Jesse—
the ones who are no longer with us

Ten Sisters

I'm the fifth child from a family of twelve. There were two boys and two girls born ahead of me, so I came along to break the tie. I was born on October 4, 1928 in Dorans, Illinois. We moved from Dorans to Mattoon when I was two. We continued to live in Mattoon with the rest of the family—seven more were born—until the family separated in 1942. I attended the Dixie School House, a country school located about a mile-and-a-half from home. It wasn't too bad walking to school in the warm weather, but the winters were pretty rough. We never had the proper clothing—boots, hats, or gloves to wear. Mrs. Hyland was our teacher and many a morning she would rub our hands and feet to warm us up when we arrived at school.

All eight grades were in the one classroom and so Mrs. Hyland would start one grade going with a project and then go to the next grade up and so on until the end of the day. Some grades only had a couple of students, but we were all taught well. She would never pass you into another grade unless you were ready for it. I know because I went through fifth grade twice.

The family used to call me "9 o'clock Bede" as many a morning I would want to stay home because of headaches. And then when I knew school had started, the pain would mysteriously fade away. I got my bottom spanked many a time for that stunt.

I remember the school programs that Mrs. Hyland would put on once a month for the students' families. They were so much fun. Each student would get to perform either through a song or playing an instrument—oh those instruments—the cymbals and the kazoos. They made a lot of noise, but I'm not sure how good they sounded. We did keep in time with them, though. Jenny, Dodo, and I usually sang a song. *You Are My Sunshine* was one of them. We did look forward to the plays and I guess the whole countryside would attend.

Food was a big concern at our house. I always disliked those biscuit sandwiches, the ones made with *Milnot* and sugar that we took for our lunches. Once in awhile Mom would get into town and bring us a great lunch of a bologna sandwich and a banana. We thought we had the world by the tail. It's funny, but the other students would trade anything for those biscuit sandwiches. I think we didn't know to appreciate a good thing.

Coming home from school, we had to pass Grandma Waggoner's house so we would stop to see what we could bum from her. Usually cookies, crackers, or baked bread. There was also fruit trees on Grandma's land so we would always get an apple or peach when in season. Once, when I was twelve, I sneaked into the peaches when I was supposed to be in the apples and I broke my ankle. My sister's boyfriend, now my brother-in-law, came by and had to carry me home—about a quarter-of-a-mile trip. I guess you know I got a lecture on that. Dad built me some homemade crutches, but I kept falling on them so out the back door they went.

Our home was small. Two original rooms. But a bedroom was added as our family continued to grow. A round heating stove stood in the middle of the front room and a cook stove in the kitchen. Never had a sink or much furniture, usually, except what someone gave us. But boy we never knew we were poor. We only knew that we loved each other, had each other, and had great times together.

We had a tree that stood by the road in our yard. We nailed some wood seats to it and spent many, many hours with each other and our cousins in that tree. Sometimes to escape work or just to sing some songs. One time our cousin fell out right on her rump. We thought it was funny, but I don't know how any of us escaped injury.

We didn't have toys so we had to create our own. We would dress the fence posts so they looked like women. We even named them. We were fortunate enough to be living in the country so we took long walks in the woods, playing and picking wild flowers. We lived next to a branch of water, so we would make a dam and create our own private pool along with the dirt, the bugs, and the snakes. We did love to swim. I learned to swim alone when I was seven years old. My Uncle taught me.

On Sunday mornings we would tramp off to Sunday School at Zion Methodist Church. It was about a mile trip. We were thrilled when we could receive a small Bible for thirteen weeks of perfect attendance.

The church and my faith have always been a great part of my life. I have attended several different types of churches with the knowledge that "God" was the head of each one. I have always known that there was an angel on my shoulder watching over me. Later Chet and I and the children were all baptized in the American Baptist Church.

When we were home, Mom made all our clothes and our dresses were all made alike out of some flour-sack material. Dad would cut our hair and we definitely all looked alike—the same bowl-shaped hair style!

We had lots of company on the weekends, especially in the summer. We created our own boxing ring by stretching the rope from tree to tree. Pretty crude—but we had fun. Of course this all came to and end when the family broke up.

We would go to town to Grandma and Grandpa Coen's. My sister Vera lived with them sometimes. We would sit on their front porch because across from their house was an empty lot where the circus and carnivals used to be set up. We never got to attend, but we would sit on our grandparents' porch and see and hear all the activity and that was just as good. I've always had a fondness for circuses, especially the clowns. To this day you will find a number of clowns scattered around my home. I've received many of them as gifts and I continue to enjoy them.

Dad became ill with typhoid fever and he was unable to work outside the home, but he did get a job with the WPA as a bookkeeper, which he worked on at home and it kept food on the table. When we had childhood diseases, it was quite a task. Our old-est brother came home on leave from the Navy and brought the measles with him. That started a chain reaction with thirteen of us in the family getting them, even Dad was very ill with them. Mom was the only one that didn't get them, and she sure had her hands full with all of us.

After twenty years and twelve children, my Mom and Dad divorced. The two older brothers were in the U. S. Navy, but the ten girls were given up as wards of the State. I remember the trying times and the arguing that Mom and Dad were going through, but I loved them both and didn't understand what was happening. I do know they wanted help from the State with our family, but as it turned out, the help they gave was separating us from each other. I don't believe this would happen in today's society. At least I hope not.

The day we went to court for our separation was one that will never be forgotten. They took our picture on the courthouse steps and then we ten girls all went to different foster homes.

I went to live with the Robert Weber family in Mattoon. Their family consisted of two girls and one boy. They were very nice and they did welcome me into their home. They owned Weber's Hardware Store in town and they also had a roller rink above the hardware store. I learned to skate, and I did like the Webers very much. However, all I could think of was—where were the others? We tried to see each other as much as possible and even-tually I left the Webers and Jenny, Dodo, and I all went to live with our grandparents. But we couldn't stay there. They already had our sister Vera, so I was taken to live in the Cunningham Home in Urbana, about fifty miles north of Mattoon. I found out that four of my sisters were already there. Jenny and Dodo went to live in an old folks home where they worked for room and board.

Cunningham was a great place. I spent one-and-one-half years there. Although we lived in different dormitories, according to our ages, I got to visit with my sisters often. I saw them at dinner and when doing our chores or attending school or church. One of the fondest memories I have of Cunningham was attending meals in the dining room. Each morning a different table group was allowed to name the hymn we sang that morning. On Sunday afternoons, in warm weather, we would pack a lunch, sit on the front lawn and watch the cars go by, waiting to see who would be coming in to visit. Mom and Dad could visit us anytime and they did, often.

It was in the Home where I realized how generous people were. We received so many gifts for the holidays and attended so many parties, and different groups would entertain us—something we certainly weren't used to. On Christmas morning all of us children would lay our gifts out on our beds and we would go from dorm to dorm to see what each one received.

I remember the boy that I was smitten with at Cunningham. We would try to work at the same job so we could meet in the halls and talk. He would walk around whistling *For Me and My Gal* so I always knew where he was when he was close by. We would hold hands and goggle at each other. He was a nice young man. He had one leg shorter than the other. I don't know what happened to him as we had to leave the home when we were fifteen years old.

While I was in the home, Mom, Jenny, and Dodo moved to Chicago where work was more available. Mom remarried a man named Paul and took me out of Cunningham to live with them. I remember the day Jenny and Carl picked me up and brought me on a train to Chicago.

In Chicago I attended Holden School. Mom and I had some difficult times so when I found out that Dad was living and working on the southeast side, I'd skip over to his place for awhile. That didn't work out too well, though. I felt like a ping-pong ball. I went to live with Jenny as she a had place not far from Mom's. I got a job at the Museum of Science and Industry and went to school one day a week. I loved my job at the Museum and Jenny was a waitress working not far from where I was, so we would go to work together at five o'clock in the morning. Her work day started three hours earlier than mine, so I would wait around, and then, when she got off, she would wait around for me. A three-hour wait for both of us—every day. I don't know how we did it, but we did—for awhile. After that, Jenny and I got a job together at an assembly plant. I worked there until I got married.

Jenny and I have always gotten along very well—except one time. We were arguing and fighting over a blouse in the middle of the bed. We both began to cry and vowed never to fight anymore—and we never have. I love all my family dearly and don't want to fight with any of them.

I met my husband, Chet, at Mom's place one night. My step-dad Paul had invited him home for a dinner. Chet was in the Army and working part time to earn a few dollars. I liked him, but I think he liked Dodo better than me, but she was already spoken for so she didn't give him a second look. After his furlough, Chet went overseas in the European Battle and spent sixteen months in combat. The biggest battle was in the Battle of the Bulge. He received a Bronze Star for bravery in that battle. He was in the Signal Corp. When Chet came home on furlough we picked up where we left off and we wanted to get married. I was only seventeen so I needed my Mom's consent, which she gave. Chet was twenty and he also needed his mother's consent. She would not go to the courthouse so a deputy of the court brought the papers to her house to sign. She did but was not too happy about it. Chet was raised a Catholic but grew away from it as he grew older. After we were married, she disowned Chet for a year. She just couldn't see him getting married to someone who wasn't Polish or Catholic. I had three strikes against me.

Chet and I were married by a Methodist preacher at Mom's

apartment on Damen and Blue Island Avenues on October 11, 1945. My brother and Chet's sister Eleanor were in attendance. My brother Carl bought my gown and we had pictures taken. Mom's husband Paul had a small dinner for us in the back of a restaurant. Twenty-five people attended. We took a streetcar (we never had cars in those days) and went to a tavern for some fun and dancing.

After that, Chet returned to the Army. He was supposed to be shipped to the west coast, but the war ended in the Pacific so he was discharged. He went back to work at the brewery but didn't stay long. He started working for a truck line and continued to work for truck lines until his death in 1972.

In 1947 we moved to a small apartment on the north side. I became pregnant with twins, but I had a miscarriage and was very sick in the hospital for a week. It was at this time that my mother-in-law wanted to be forgiven and get all the family together again. She spoke very little English, so our communication was somewhat limited. We did, however, become very good friends and I loved her dearly until her death.

After losing the twins I went back to work. The following year we were on vacation in Mattoon and I had another miscarriage. I was three months pregnant and ended up in the hospital, so we stayed in Mattoon for awhile. Chet and I both went to work so we could earn money to return to Chicago and I have been here ever since. This time we moved to an apartment on 17th Street. I got pregnant again and on August 7, 1948 our son, Ron, was born. P. J. was born at the 17th street address on the night of March 17, 1951.

I had both Ron and P. J. at home under the care of the Chicago Maternity Center. I paid the great sum of $25.00 for Ron and $75.00 for P. J. The Center treated me like an angel, like I was the only woman that ever had a baby. I don't believe this kind of care exists today.

We moved from 17th Street to Justine Street when P. J. was

eighteen months old. We didn't live there very long. We had an apartment in the basement, but when P. J. was bitten by a rat, we moved to Eleanor Street and lived there for the next seventeen years. Both children started school at St. Bridgets Catholic School and Ron attended there until he was eleven and P. J. was eight. Then they transferred to Holden Public School—the same school where Chet and I graduated from the eighth grade—but that was before we ever met. Both Ron and P. J. went on to graduate from Tilden High School.

Chet and I lived twenty-seven years together until his death of cancer in 1972. I want to say it was a little bumpy along the way, but there were happy times along with the sad. We had the usual problems like our children, money, and everyday living. We both loved people around us and many a weekend we would be busy with family and friends. Several of my sisters lived with us at one time or another.

I remember our first car—a second-hand one that you couldn't drive over fifty miles an hour or it would shimmy and shake. We did give it a workout though. A lot of trips were made to Mattoon and Charleston to visit with Dick, Phyllis, and family. They were the only family living there at the time so their house was always open to all of us. We had so many good times. Dick and Phyllis had a Pontoon boat and we spent many enjoyable hours on it. Another of our favorite places was Waterveliet, Michigan, where Margy and Richard lived on a farm and raised strawberries. We would spend our vacations in Michigan when the berries were ripe. Chet loved taking in the berries and paying the pickers. He never considered it work. It was fun. When the car wouldn't make it all the way, my brother-in-law Richard would come pick us up. Somehow he could always get it going so we could return to Chicago on Sunday nights.

We would often visit with Jenny and Clarence who only

lived about a mile from us. We would get to playing Canasta and would end up spending the night. We had many laughs over that arrangement. We did visit a lot among the families. Seems there was always someone having a birthday, so we would have a great party.

I was close to my parents, too, so I miss them very much. As I said, Mom remarried shortly after their divorce and took me out of the Cunningham Home. That marriage ended, though, and Mom married Marvin, a fine man. Mom lived with him until his death in 1977. Mom then married John Golden—when she was seventy-five years old. They lived together fourteen years, until her death in April 1993. Dad also remarried and lived with Effie until his death in May 1983.

Some of my fondest memories are going out to eat after church on Sundays with Jenny and Bertie and their families. We would go to places like Bishop's Chili, Toscano's, or Oswald's. The kids loved it.

Sometimes in the summer Chet would get hungry for an Italian Ice. We would all jump in the car (the kids in their pajamas) and off we would go. It was a way of cooling off because those summer nights could be hot. Chet loved his ice-cream and we would get sundaes. He would order three for him and one for each of us. You would hear the kids moan and groan.

Life was good most of the time, but we did have some problems. Chet drank some and there were some incompatibilities that just didn't go away. We even separated once, but with some high-powered talking from Chet and his mom we got back together. Chet was a good man and a good worker. He just didn't know when to be quiet. I guess I was guilty of that, too. When Chet became ill, I learned to drive at the age of forty-three. He never believed that I could. It was one of the wisest and proudest things I've ever done.

Ron joined the Air Force after graduation and took his basics in Amarillo, Texas. He was then stationed at Vandenburg Air Force base in Lompoc, California. He came home on furlough in 1968, just in time for the Democratic Convention. He sure didn't care much for how the city was handling the situation. He and Chet had many differences and disagreements over it. It sure put a gap in their relationship and up until that time they had a great friendship.

Ron met his wife, Guille, in Santa Maria, California. She lived not too far from Lompoc. They were married after his discharge. We attended the wedding and met Guille and her family. Guille is Hispanic and we hoped that she would fit in with our close-knit family. She did, and she has been a blessing to all of us. It was the first ethnic marriage in the family, but we've had others since.

Chet took very sick in 1972 with cancer. Ron and Guille came through to visit when Chet was ill, and they returned to California, but not for long. They moved back to Chicago to be close to Chet. They have lived in Chicago ever since. Ron and Guille have three boys. Brian and Josh came first and then came their little girl, Mandy. She has Downs Syndrome and has had medical problems since her birth, but she is a charmer and a blessing to all of us. Mandy has made us appreciate our lives a little more. Andrew was the last to be born, and he's the apple of my eye. I regret that Chet never got to see his grandchildren. I know he would have spoiled them.

P. J. went to work after graduation. She met Lary, her first husband, through a friend. They were both stationed at Rantoul Air Force Base. P. J. and Lary fell hard for each other and it wasn't long before they were talking marriage, which took place in August 1969. They had a lovely wedding and reception. Ron was home on leave and stood up with them, along with Lary's twin brother, Gary, and some friends. After the wedding, Lary and P. J. moved to Washington State. Over the years they were transferred to several other bases.

They were stationed in Rantoul, Illinois, when Chet became ill. They spent a lot of time in Chicago. P. J. would take her dad for his treatments at the hospital and Lary learned to administer shots to help out.

P. J. entered the army as a Behavioral Science Specialist in 1983. She was separated from Lary at the time. A year later they were divorced, and she remarried in 1985. Her husband, Chris, had a son Russell from a previous marriage. He was a sweet kid and all of us loved him very much, but because that marriage ended in 1992, we don't get to see Russell very often.

I went to work when P. J. started Kindergarten. I had worked at several jobs—waitressing, factory work, and as a cleaning lady, so when I found an office job at Old Rose & South Shore Liquors, I found a home. It was hard at times, but it was better than anything I had ever done. I spent thirty-one years on that job and retired in April 1993. I cannot say I miss work, but I do miss the people. I worked with them and they were a part of my family for so many years.

Six months after my retirement I had a heart attack and had Angioplasty Surgery. I'm doing well now and plan on sticking around for awhile, so I'll try to take better care of myself.

My sisters and I have a family reunion every year which we all try hard to attend. There is plenty of fun and friendship there. It is a very special day for all of us. At one of our reunions, all of us, twelve in total, and our parents—with their mates—were there. It had been thirty-two years since we separated, and it was a great thrill for all of us. The two brothers have passed away, along with Mom and Dad and some of the brothers-in-law. All of us ten sisters are alive and kicking. We stay close, despite the miles between us.

Mary Margaret
(Margy)

Dedicated to my nine sisters
who have shared all of this story with me

I was born in Dorans, Illinois, on August 2, 1930. I was named Mary Margaret, but I was better known as "Margy" or "Little Mom." I was the child of Glen and Ruth Waggoner, the sixth of twelve children. We moved to Paradise, a few miles south of Mattoon, Illinois, when I was still very small. We lived in a little three-room house, there, which sat at the bottom of a hill with a stream running in front and beside the house.

Grandpa Waggoner died when I was quite young, so I don't remember much about him, but Mom always said he had a soft spot for Mom and us children. Grandma Waggoner lived up over the hill. Her property was surrounded by a fence to keep in her horses and cows. Grandma Waggoner was a favorite of mine. She was a real thin woman. I used to spend a lot of time with her. I'd go there in the evening. She read by lamp light and it would get so quiet in the house I could hear the ticking of the clock and the rustle of the newspaper. Quite often I'd get lonesome and would tell Grandma I was going home. And I'd walk through the fields and down over the hill to our little house. Grandma died in 1947. I can't remember ever seeing her after 1942, when we were broken up as a family.

I used to write letters to Grandpa and Grandma Coen who lived in Mattoon, and they used to come see us on Sundays. Grandpa Coen was quite a ladies' man, according to his autograph book, but I only remember him quietly sitting in the rocking chair, his hat perched on his head, and a bucket of ashes by his side. And he always sat in front of the window or on the porch. Grandpa passed away in November 1949, soon after our son, Elmo, was born. I didn't go to the funeral.

Grandma and Grandpa Coen were married when Grandma was real young—thirteen or fourteen. Grandpa was a soldier and Great-Grandma put the soldiers up in her place. That's how he and Grandma met.

Grandma Coen was a little white-haired woman—so quick

on her feet. But she used to sit down and play the organ. Mom and us girls would sing the songs she played. *The Old Rugged Cross* was one of our favorites. I realize, now, I never knew Grandma's name until after I was married.

When a circus or carnival came to town, Grandma would go with us to help with the girls, but she was very religious. She belonged to the Baptist Church and was always faithful to her beliefs.

The last time I remember seeing Grandma Coen was in 1969. She came to Michigan with Mom and our stepfather Marvin to see Elmo before he left for Vietnam. She got so angry, as they decided to stay overnight. I had chicken for supper. I remember she ate three pieces of chicken plus other foods. I never saw her again. She passed away in the summer of 1970, but I remember what she said that visit. She said she "felt like a gypsy—here one night, some place else the next."

Mom always claimed she figured *she* belonged to a gypsy. I really think she just felt she wasn't a favorite of her parents.

I don't remember, but have always heard Mom cleaned house for the dentist to pay for her false teeth. I do know Jess and Carl, our brothers, mowed lawns and did odd jobs to help pay for them.

Mom worked hard. She had no electricity in the house, washed clothes on a scrub board, cooked on a wood stove, and canned what ever she could. Mom always made our clothes. Most of our dresses were made out of feed sacks and looked the same, only made a little bit different.

Dad worked for W. P. A. and, at times, for the Illinois Central Railroad. He cut our hair and he was only able to cut one style. No one could tell us apart.

We didn't have much, but we did have a battery-operated radio and the neighbors used to come listen to the heavy-weight fights.

We spent a lot of time under the bridge that spanned the

stream in front of our house. After a rain, we crawled under and made mud houses and mud people. There were fence posts in front of our house, and we dressed them up like dolls and named them Mrs. Jamalea and Mrs. Leakalea. They were our make-believe friends. If they could talk, they could tell some tales. I remember Irma and I were using the barbed-wire fence for a swing. You can guess the rest. We broke the fence and Irma and I both were cut, Irma real bad. My cuts were from the knee up to my hip, only not as bad as Irma's. I have a light scar. She has a terrible scar. Believe me, we both got a real good spanking from Dad—the only one I ever remember getting from him. But I'm sure I had lots of them. That was left up to Mom to do.

We also spent a lot of time in the large tree that stood beside the fence posts. If we saw Dad's car turn the corner, down we came.

I only remember three beds in our little house. One was a single cot. We heated the house with wood. The earliest I remember was when Mom and Dad went to Chicago for the 1933 World's Fair. I was only three years old. Uncle Nolan came and stayed with us kids. I also remember when we shivareed Uncle Pete and Aunt Virginia when they got married.

We walked to a one-room school with eight grades. I don't remember much about it, only that I was kinda sickly and missed lots of school. I'm surprised I learned anything.

The school seemed miles from home and we sometimes stopped by the neighbor's house to warm our hands. They gave us sweet rolls for our lunch. I also remember the woman making us mittens out of old wool coats. They had a large family, too, but it seemed like they were wealthy and that we were very poor.

We used to go to the free shows and get a penny piece of candy with a ring in it. We also went to talent shows. One year Jenny and Dodo won for Jitterbugging. All of us girls got up and sang *You Are My Sunshine* and won a prize, too. I think it was $5.00.

Mary Margaret

One day when I was getting ready to go to the Free Show, I built a bonfire to heat water to wash my socks, but I tipped the pail over and scalded my foot. That was not long before we were separated, so Mrs. Caton was coming to the house at the time, nosing around. She wanted to know what happened. She gave me $5.00 and said to have Dad take me to a doctor. The foot was in bad shape with third-degree burns. Once, Dodo and Jenny were dancing, and my foot was hanging off a chair and they stepped on it and busted the blister.

1941 was our last year together. The boys, Carl and Jesse, had both gone off to the Navy. Mom was working in Chicago. She used to hitch-hike home on week-ends and make our clothes for the school year—our last one before separation. Mom often dressed me in yellow. I can remember us breaking the ice on the creek to use to make home-made ice cream that winter. Jenny and Dodo did most of the housework and Dad worked in town.

I remember Mrs. Caton and a Mrs. Allen coming to the house a lot, too. We thought they were there to help us. We didn't know what was in store come spring.

The next thing I knew, we were in court. I don't know how we got to Charleston and to the courthouse. I remember all ten of us girls, and Mom, and Grandpa and Grandma Coen were there. I can't remember Dad even being there.

I didn't quite understand what was happening—mostly recesses and us singing, and standing on the courthouse steps. I remember when Doris and Audrey were picked up by some strangers. I remember them taking us across the street to a restaurant to eat lunch as the trial was dragging out so long. I don't think any of us ate much as it was a very sad day.

Bertie and I were taken to Mr. and Mrs. Harold Fox's home. They were neighbors and friends of Dad and Mom's. She was a big, fat lady and I hated her when we were home and I hated her even more that day. Her husband was real nice, and she tried to be nice to us, I think. She got both Bertie and me a permanent. I remember her having our picture taken. I don't think we stayed there very long. We let the case worker know we didn't like it. Seems we cried a lot. Soon we were taken to the Cunningham Children's Home in Urbana, Illinois. I was so happy when we found out some of our sisters were already there. Just knowing we would be together was so much better. I don't remember the date, sometime in 1942.

Irma and I were in the same dormitory. I was so happy. Cunningham was a wonderful place for children. We had everything we would ever need—only we were no longer a family.

We were taught many things while living at Cunningham, and I remember walking across the field to the public school. We also attended the First Methodist Church in Urbana.

There were large brick dormitories at Cunningham and a kitchen and dining room. One building was just for laundry. Children were separated by age and sex. Boys were all in one dorm, babies in the nursery, and I ended up in the Illinois Dorm before I left Cunningham.

The University of Illinois and many different organizations used to put on parties for us at different times of the year. I mostly remember Christmas and Easter. Every child was given a very nice gift by Santa Claus and a big dinner. At Easter we had an Easter Bunny and egg hunts.

While in the home, most everyone old enough had jobs to do. The children took turns asking the blessing and cleaning the table and helping with the clean-up in the kitchen. At times we had to help in the laundry. The older girls had to do the ironing. Everyone had to make their own bed and there could not be a single wrinkle in the covers. If not made right, it was torn completely apart and you remade it, until it was done right.

All in all, it was a wonderful place to be, but I didn't want to be away from my family. I adjusted very well at Cunningham though. I think one reason was that we were taught a certain amount of discipline there. We were always taught to respect our elders. We were given a small allowance every week and on week-ends we could go to the roller rink, which was just a short distance from Cunningham.

Sunday afternoon was for visitors, so some Sundays were very sad. Mom and Dad would come see us whenever they could. Mom and our stepfather Paul took me out for a week-end. She had found out where Doris and Audrey were living. She took us to see both of them. Doris was skating out on the sidewalk. Her adopted mother took her into the house and cleaned her all up before we could visit. When she came back out, Doris was dressed so pretty. I don't think she knew we were her sisters.

Dad visited one time and brought Irma and me a new suit and Bertie and Phyllis new dresses. Then he took us to a photographer's studio and we had our picture taken with Dad. I was so sad when my sister Bede left. I don't remember just when I left Cunningham, but I know Mom took Irma and me out of Cunningham at the same time.

After moving to Chicago with Mom and Paul, Mom set me up with babysitting. Then Jessie's wife, Betty, came to Chicago to live and I started sitting with my nephew, Dale.

When Jesse came home on leave, we all took a train down to Mattoon and Charleston to visit our sisters, Doris, and Audrey, and Vera. Doris and Audrey had been adopted and Vera was awarded by the State to Grandma and Grandpa Coen. After Jesse went back after his leave, he didn't come home for several years.

Irma and I attended Marshall High School in Chicago, but neither of us graduated. By 1946 Mom and Paul bought a farm near Drasco, Arkansas. Oh, how I remember that trip. A friend of Mom's had a large truck and moved us down there. We had our mattress in the truck bed so we could sleep while traveling to our new home.

We arrived in Arkansas in the middle of the the night. There was no electricity and we slept in the truck until morning. It was so exciting.

There was a fence, I think a rail fence, that ran in front of the house. The house was made of logs and had a fireplace. It was just three rooms with front and back porches.

Mom and Uncle Nolan decided to build on to the house so our back porch was built into two bedrooms. Mom sent for some kind of heavy wallpaper and tacked it to the log walls. Mom had bought a wood cook stove and all the things to use with it. Our only transportation was a wagon, so Mom bought two horses to hitch to it.

We lived back off the main road amidst the pine trees. There were a couple of other houses but not so far back.

After getting moved and settled in, it was still exciting—so different than Chicago. But money was in scarce supply. Eventually, Paul went back to Chicago to find work and Uncle Nolan moved in to help out. Then Mom and Uncle Nolan moved back to Chicago, too, and my oldest sister Jenny came down to live with us. When Pauline run a nail in her leg, she and Irma went to live with Dad in Mattoon. We lived mostly on Betty's allotment check from our brother Jesse, and Paul and Mom sent money when they could. Brother Jesse's second son, little Paul, was born in Heber Springs, Arkansas.

We used to go to the neighbor's houses for square dances down there. That's how I met my first love. I had gone to the dance with a neighbor boy. On our way home we had to cross a little creek. I didn't want to get my feet wet and asked him to carry me over the water. He would not. Then Dean came by and carried me across. He hung around a lot after that, cutting and gathering wood for the fireplace, running into town for groceries, and riding horses with me. He ended up being the father of my first child. When I let

Mary Margaret

Dean in on my secret, he left, and I never saw him again until December 1992.

I did a lot of the cooking in Arkansas. Mom taught me how to make biscuits and I made lots of yeast breads. I did most of the cooking until Jenny came down. Then I let her take over.

While in Arkansas we learned how to cut pine trees and peel post. Soon we were cutting trees and peeling those posts and selling them. One fellow, who is now my brother-in-law, owned a large truck and he hauled them to the saw mill for us. I can remember Clarence taking us to Searcy, Arkansas. The black people would not walk on the same side of the street that we were on. I thought that so odd.

In July of 1947 Mom sold the farm and we moved back to Chicago with her—on 19th Street where my little Billy was born. Mom said I was too young to have a baby and she couldn't afford another child to take care of, so she contacted someone in Charleston and through that contact a couple adopted little Billy. I knew ahead of time that when Billy was born he was going to be adopted, so when I went into labor Mom contacted Mr. and Mrs. Holmes and on September 7, 1947 Mrs. Holmes came to Chicago and stayed with us until Billy was nine days old. They had made a promise to me that I could come to Texas to visit Billy. They even sent Mom and me a picture of him in a buggy when he was about nine months old. We exchanged letters until I asked if I could come and see him. I never heard from them again and my letters were returned. One time I said to Mom, if it hadn't been for her, I would not have given him away. She knocked me to the floor, so I never talked to her about it again—not until I met my husband. Then Mom said I had to tell him before he and I left the house—and I did.

In 1948 Jenny called me and said Clarence and her were on the way to Michigan to work for the summer and wanted me to go along. So off I went. We rented a small house from a family Jenny and Clarence had worked with the year before. That's where I met Richard

Hickmott. I can't remember what month it was, but the following year, on July 9, 1949, we were married in Chicago. Sis Bertie, and brother-in-law Chester, stood up with us. We went back to Michigan to live and farm. Our son, Elmo Edward, was born on November 3, 1949. I was so happy that I had a little boy. Fourteen months later we had another little boy who died at birth. Sixteen months after that, Gloria was born on Mom's birthday, June 6, 1952. We were so happy to have our little girl, the first girl in the Hickmott family for twenty-one years. So what a joy for Richard's family who had lost their only daughter when their house burned in the early 1930's.

Richard and I had a quiet life, except for raising our children. And although I now had two children, I never forgot little Billy.

Richard and I bought a farm with a two-story house. There was a lot of work to be done, though, to make it livable. The property needed a lot of work to get it ready for farming, too. With Mom and our new stepfather, Marvin, helping us a lot, we made the house ready to move into. I had my very own house and Richard had his very own farm. Dad used to spend lots of time in Michigan on our farm in strawberry time. He loved working in the strawberries. I always felt Dad did a lot of suffering for what had happened to our family. He was a very private person.

When Elmo started his first year in school he had to walk a little way to get there. Coming home one day he was hit by a pickup. It threw Elmo quite a few feet. He went into a coma and remained in one for ten days. When he came out of it I went to visit him. He looked up and said "Hi Mom!" but he had to learn to sit up and walk again. The Doctor said it was the "Good Lord that saved Elmo."

For the first fifteen years of our lives Richard farmed and worked at Whirlpool, so the kids and I didn't get to spend much time with him.

Once I put Gloria in the hospital to have her tonsils out. She had to stay overnight. I went to the hospital the next morning to find she had been quarantined. No visitors! She had hepatitis. She spent four weeks in quarantine, so I couldn't even get close to her. Another time she was in the hospital because Richard dropped a fire cracker on the sidewalk and Gloria was standing beside him at the time. It hit her in the ankle. She was in the hospital for three weeks as the wound had gotten infected and wouldn't heal.

Our house burned in 1960. The next five and a half years were spent in a 30´ x 8´ house trailer. In 1966 we sold the trailer and we moved into Richard's grandma's house. In 1968 we lost the farm that Richard had worked so hard on. Our world fell apart.

Soon Elmo married and joined the Navy and was off to Vietnam. Seven months later his son, Kevin, was born. Gloria married the same year and a year after that, our second grandson, Robbie, was born. Elmo spent a year in Vietnam and then settled on the East coast where a baby girl, Paula, was born. Five years later, Gloria and John had another little boy, Tim.

In 1967 I went to work in town—five and one-half years at Voice of Music, where record players were made. Then in 1972 I went to work for Joanna Western, where I did many jobs in the factory and office. We manufactured wood shutters and woven woods.

In April of 1980 we found out Richard had cancer of the tongue. He was operated on and was told they had gotten all of the cancer. Now, fifteen years later, he is still free of the disease.

In 1992 I retired after nineteen years with Joanna Western. But soon we were hit with some bad news. I got this call from the Chaplain at the hospital saying they had our son Elmo and we should come there right away. When I arrived at the hospital I was so sure as to what I was to hear. Soon the Doctor came in and said Elmo had had a cardiac arrest and they could not revive him. He was forty-two years old. He died October 21, 1992.

Through the years I had been trying to find little Billy who I had allowed to be adopted in 1947. In 1974 I had heard that my youngest sister might know something about Billy (whose name had been changed to Steve) but she could not tell me anything.

Because I was so torn up about losing Elmo, my sisters, Phyllis and Pauline, got their heads together and decided they were gonna find Billy. Phyllis started the calling. She talked to Billy's father on the phone. He was very upset and did not want them to contact Billy. He said "*Steve* was their boy." and I had "given him to them."

Pauline made the initial call to Billy. His wife answered. I think she knew right off Pauline had the right Holmes. She said Steve was home sick and she would give him all the message Pauline gave her and Steve could make up his mind if he wanted to call back. She did mention this was something he had always wanted to know—who his mother was. In a short time he called Pauline. She called me and wanted me to come up to her house. I don't know why, but I had in mind she had found out something about him.

When I got to her house, sure enough, that's what it was. She said she had talked to Steve and he wanted to come up and that he would let her know later in the evening.

He called while I was there. He told her he was leaving and would be up to see us on the 19th of December. When Steve arrived in Michigan I told him he looked just like his natural father, but most people say he looks so much like my brother Jesse and a little like me.

Steve asked me to go to Texas to meet his family. I decided to ride down there with him and bring a train back. We talked of many things on our trip. He said when Pauline called he knew what it was about—that he had been thinking about who I was. His mother had died when he was in the Navy. He had been told that he was adopted as a young boy, but at that age he did not really understand what it meant. His parents adopted another boy a few years after they adopted him. Pauline asked him if he wanted to meet his natural father. He said he did.

Mary Margaret

Dean had been informed by this time and had agreed to meet Steve. On the way to Texas, we stopped and met with Dean, his wife, and one daughter of Dean's sister.

It was an experience, meeting Dean again and Steve's family. And I found out that I had two more grandchildren, Ann and Kevin, and a great-grandson, little Stephen. I told Steve that Elmo's son Kevin had married Suzie just three weeks before Elmo's death, and within the next two years had given me two more great-grandchildren, Emily and Seth. Most of all I have the satisfaction of knowing that my little Billy was in a loving family who took good care of him.

In 1995 my four sisters and I attended the celebration of the Cunningham Home's 100th anniversary. It was nice to see the old pictures they had on display. The building that used to be the dining hall still stands, and the Illinois dormitory where I lived for a short time is still there, but most of the other buildings have been torn down and have been replaced with small individual cottages that house just a few children. Each cottage has two parents and the meals and laundry are both done in the cottages. We only saw one family of the many that shared our houses when we were there. I didn't remember them until I saw old pictures.

Richard and I have now been married for forty-seven years. We have six grandchildren and three great-grandchildren. After living for several years in Benton Harbor, Michigan, we have recently moved back to the house that belonged to Richard's grandmother. We are both retired, trying to keep ourselves busy, still raising a garden, and taking trips when we can. Richard is very handy and helps his brothers at various odd jobs. Writing this little story has absorbed much of my time.

Irma Joan
(Irma)

Dedicated to my sisters who pulled me through it all

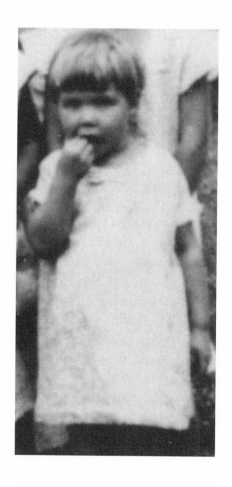

Irma Joan

I am the seventh child born to Glen and Ruth Waggoner. Brothers Dale and Carl were born first. I was born December 21, 1931, a whopping twelve pounds. I was delivered by Dr. Richardson. Mom said although I was the biggest, I was the quickest born—only two big pains. I was born at home like the ones before me. There would be five more girls to follow me, all of us about fourteen months or less, apart.

I learned to climb a tree not too long after I walked and spent the better part of the next eight years sitting in a tree singing at the top of my voice. The tree was next to the driveway by the road at the bottom of the hill that was to one side of our house. The hill curved to the back of the house. A small branch ran on one side of the house and a forest was across the road. A pasture was on the other side of the branch. A wooden bridge with iron railings spanned the bridge on the road. The iron railings were about 2˝ wide. I was pretty good walking across on that railing, as were most of us. I would pretend I was walking on a high wire in a circus. As I recall, I never fell in the creek.

The road was dirt and gravel. When we saw a car coming we would hurry down from the tree, sometimes head first, and run under the bridge. We liked the tiny stones raining down on us through the boards when the car went over the bridge.

We didn't own any toys but we had the trees, the branch, the hills, the woods with all the wild flowers. There were Blue Bells, Boys Britches, Bleeding Hearts, Violets, and many others. The "Umbrellas" were all through the woods, too. And we had each other. We also had the electric fence Uncle Pete put up to keep the cows in the pasture, as well as to try and keep us kids out, I suspect. We used to hold hands in a long line and then the first one would touch the fence and the last one, usually an unsuspecting cousin, would get the jolt.

Sometimes my uncle would plant watermelon in a garden in

the pasture. We would break the riper ones open and eat out the delicious warm, seedless middles. I'm sure he knew it was us kids, but he never said anything.

Our house was 10 ft. wide and 20 ft. long, consisting of two rooms. A pot-bellied stove stood in the middle of one room and a wood-burning cook stove was in the other. A pot of beans or something was usually sitting on the pot-belly stove in cold weather. Mom and Dad shared one bed. The boys shared a cot. All ten of us girls slept in one bed, unless the baby went in with Mom, five on one end and five on the other, layered in quite comfortably. If someone wet the bed, you never knew who it was.

We had cousins that visited often. I don't know where they slept. There were no inside walls, just tar paper. We would tear little pieces of the tar paper off to chew as gum. Unfortunately, that left holes in the walls through which the snow came in during the winter to end up on our bed. We also looked forward to the oiling of the roads. The black tar would harden just a little and we dipped that in sugar and chewed it also.

There was a porch built on the back that was used a lot, I'm sure, for sleeping in the summer. We didn't have many clothes and shared whatever there was. One shelf on the porch held the clothes for all of us. Even shoes were shared among the younger of us. We were barefoot most of the summer and some of us would get new brown high-top shoes for winter. Sometimes I had to take turns with Margy wearing the shoes to school. In later years I'd go shopping with her for shoes and hide my size eight feet gracefully under the chair while she tried on size 4's and 4 1/2's.

The older girls did most of the cleaning while Mom did clothes and cooking. They would clean house and would make us younger kids sit on a bench so we wouldn't get dirty. It didn't take long for them to clean, we had little furniture except beds, a table and some benches. The floors got the attention.

Irma Joan

Flour and livestock feed used to come in bags of pretty cotton material, so mom made our clothes from them. We all dressed alike, but they were pretty. We didn't have many clothes, so it was a treat when she made new ones. I think Mom had a pedal sewing machine, but I certainly can't remember where it was in the house.

I had thick hair and one time the oldest brother, Jesse Dale, was going to cut it. He kept getting the sides uneven, so he put a bowl on my head and cut anything hanging below it. The kitchen had a table and benches and a pile of wood behind the stove. The oil lamp was our light and the outhouse was a place to read the catalog until it ran out.

The house had two doors to it directly across from one another, which proved to be very convenient for my brother one time when he was rolling a tire down the hill in back of the house. It got away from him and went through one door and out the other.

A favorite game for us was to roll up inside a tire and hold on to the inside rim. We'd start at the top of the hill on the road. Someone would give us a push. The object was to see how far we could go without falling and we were quite adept at going right across the bridge. Sometimes we'd end up in the creek, or the ditch, or even in the yard. It took a little skill to turn to the right and go between the fence posts. I don't recall anyone getting hurt, though.

The barbed wire fence in front of the house had two posts, one on either side of the driveway. We dressed the posts in old clothes and gave them names. Dad had an old Model A Ford and when we would all go to town or somewhere, three or four deep in the back seat, we would yell, "Goodbye Mrs. Leekalie! Goodbye Mrs. Jomalie!" to the fence posts 'till we were out of sight.

That Model A Ford was a lot of fun, and not necessarily to ride in. When Dad was gone to work, he worked on the W.P.A. and then for the railroad, he didn't take the car. So we would push it to a high point from the road, give it a good shove and climb on the running boards for a free ride. The car was involved in other pleasures, too. We all liked "chocolate haystacks" candy commonly called "chocolate drops." Dad would treat us once in a while. We'd all get a quarter of a piece. This was Dad's favorite candy, too, so he would hide the rest, usually in the car. It didn't take us long to find it. I don't remember him ever punishing us for it, although I did get spankings from him with a nice thin Hickory switch. There must have been a reason for it at the time, but I can't recall any. I just remember the sting and that I didn't get the switch often, thank goodness.

Sometimes Mom would drive the car. We lived in Paradise and we went to Mattoon, maybe to Grandma's. Mom was a lot of fun, sometimes. There was a lively song called *Scatterbrain*, back then. We would hear it on the radio that was run with a battery—a car battery—mostly Dad's car battery when he wasn't around. Mom would go down "Long Lane" to Mattoon and would drive the car, using the brakes to cause the jerky rhythm of *Scatterbrain* most of the way to town. We would sing it in time to the car "is-n't-it-a -pit-y-that-you're-such-a-scat-ter-brain."

Once in a while, on a Friday evening, we would all pile in to the car to go to the neighboring town of Gays to see a free outdoor movie. Gays is a small town not too many miles from where we lived. The railroad ran through the center of Gays and the big outdoor screen would be right along the side of the tracks and we would sit on the ground to watch it. I don't know what movies were shown. I was more interested in the people around me, the grain elevator, and the trains. Trains came by more often in those days and when one would come by while we were watching the movie, they would stop the movie until the train went by. This would happen a few times each show. I loved being that close to the trains and they still fascinate me. One time we went to the show in Gays and my sister Margy had scalded her foot that afternoon. It had a huge blister on the top of it. I accidentally stepped on it and broke the blister.

I can recall once or twice going to Trilla, Illinois, (I think it was on Wednesdays) where they held amateur contests. Now two of my sisters were real good at jitter-bugging, and since most of us spent half the time sitting in the tree singing at the top of our lungs, we got to be pretty good harmonizers. The two sisters, Jenny and Dodo, won the contest the night they jitter-bugged.

I and two other sisters, either Margy and Bertie or Margy and Bede, won the night we sang *You are my sunshine*. We won a cake for first prize but were disappointed. We wanted to win the second-place prize—six sodas.

There was a shed beside the house which wasn't very high and since it was close to the hill, it was easy to jump on top of the shed from the slope of the hill. Once we had a goat and we used to tease him a lot until he'd start running after us and then we'd make a mad dash for the top of the shed. He would butt the shed but never catch us.

We had some chickens and a big mean red rooster, too. I stayed away from him if I could.

I used to follow Grandma Waggoner around when she collected eggs. Since she lived up on top of the hill, we were there quite often. She tried to teach me to get the eggs from under the hen, but I never could. I just knew that hen was going to peck my hands when she started that clucking.

We ate a lot of beans and bread pudding at home, but when company would come Mom would kill some chickens and fry them. She would hold that chicken's head and twist him round and round until its body would come loose from its head and it would flop all over the place. Mom made a circle on the ground. She said the chicken would jump around but would not go out of the circle. I don't know how it knew, but it never crossed the line. Mom would cook up a few of the chickens and they sure did make us hungry. Since company always ate first we never got any good parts, just chicken feet. Mom never wasted anything so she'd take the skin and nails off the feet and cook them for us. I think I was about fourteen and gone from home before I ate any real pieces of chicken, I'm sure that's the reason I always order chicken when I eat out now.

Usually a company dinner was topped off by Dad and Mom making homemade ice-cream. The finished product was delicious, but it was the making of the ice-cream I remember most. Ice was packed all around the canister that held the mixture and that was put inside the wooden bucket. There was a paddle that went into the canister with a crank to turn it and several gunny sacks were placed on the top. While someone cranked, we would get to sit on the gunny sacks to hold everything down. My rear got cold and wet and it seemed to take forever to make, but it was worth the wait. It was delicious.

After a rain there would be water in the creek. We would play in it and make mud slides on the sides. We'd slide down the wet, steep sides and you entered the water in a hurry. While we did spend a lot of time in the creek, I never learned to swim until I was almost fifty-eight years old.

During very heavy rains the creek would flood and would flow real fast. We never tried to go in at those times, but we would chase the rats along the creek bank.

We spent most of our time outside, even in the winter. If the creek froze, we would slide on the ice. We never had skates but our shoes served the purpose. We made use of anything that would slide on snow and hold us, especially the washing machine lid. Sometimes we'd roll down. We had to dodge the trees, which we got pretty good at doing, or use them to stop. When the tall grasses and the stumps weren't quite covered, it was more of a challenge.

Irma Joan

Although we were very active, I don't recall very many injuries, but the insides of my knees were always scratched up from climbing trees. A visitor asked Dad once what was the animal coming down the tree. Dad said it was just one of the kids. I was coming down head first. Bede climbed up high in one of Grandma Waggoner's peach trees. She'd been told to not climb it, but the best peaches are always at the top. She fell and broke her ankle.

Carl was in a car accident one time with his friends. We were all pretty scared. He got a cut on his head but came out of it fine.

I always was in awe of Dale and Carl, even after I was grown. They were in the CCC's when I was young and then they both went into the Navy. Both Carl and Dale served on the ship *U.S.S. Arkansas* together until the five Sullivan boys were lost—all on one ship, so they were separated. Carl went to the *U.S.S. Macon*.

Dale came home on leave one time and when he left all of us girls and Dad got the measles. Dale had brought them home. Grandma Coen came out to help take care of us. We were all quarantined for two weeks. When Dale went into the Navy he came back as "Jesse." Unlike us they used his first name.

Sometimes when the Ringling Bros. & Barnum & Bailey Circus came to town we got to go watch them parade from the train to the circus grounds, which were just across the road from the block Grandma Coen lived on—Moultrie near 33rd Street. The calliope played and all the animals and the performers paraded down 33rd Street. We watched them put the tent up, but we never got to see a circus back then. But a few years later, I did, and a special clown "Emmett Kelly" stuck in my mind. He was a sad clown that never talked, but made people laugh. To me, Emmett Kelly *was* the circus.

When I was young we had a Coen Family Reunion every year in Lytle Park in Mattoon. Aunts, uncles, and cousins would come and we ate, talked, and played all day. A swimming pool was in Lytle Park and some of the cousins went swimming. It cost money, so we never got to swim there.

Grandma's are special people and I think I had two of the best. Grandma Waggoner (Dad's mom) lived up on the hill past our house. I think it was her land our house sat on. I don't remember Grandpa Waggoner. She was thin, always busy, and was pretty. I remember Grandma Waggoner as being tolerant with me and she always had stick candy for us, usually horehound, which my children now bring to me sometimes. I remember an owl used to sit up on the front of her barn and hoot.

Mom's mom, Grandma Coen, lived in Mattoon. She had pure white hair and she was always cooking or baking. She always had big soft sugar cookies for us when we visited her. There was a player piano in her dining room that she would let us play sometimes. There was also a china cabinet with curved glass in the same room. We were never allowed to bother it. It was never told to me not to touch it, I just knew. Grandma would open it every day and wind up Grandpa's railroad pocket watch which was kept in it.

Grandma Coen had a doll made from China sitting on her dresser in her bedroom. It had been broken years before, but was fixed. She said she got it when she was six years old and it came from Europe. We could look at it but never touch. I was content to just look.

Grandpa Coen fascinated me. He never spoke to me very much, but I liked to follow him to the sheds behind the house to see all the things he collected in barrels. He had several barrels. He would never let us look close, but I saw in one he collected match books. I don't know why, and I don't know what was in the other barrels. He used to carve things from wood. Grandma told us how he had been a cowboy once and had killed a man and pleaded his own case and won. He had worked on the railroad laying track in the early days. He had a banjo hanging on the wall that he used to play, but I never heard him play it. He also had a long rifle hanging on his bedroom wall. We weren't allowed to touch either of them and we never did. Mostly, though, Grandpa would sit in a wooden rocking chair by the window smoking his pipe.

While Grandpa would just tolerate us, Grandma would bring out a big box of pictures and let us look at them. If we asked, she would tell us who they were. We spent many hours looking at pictures, and I suspect, keeping us out of Grandma's hair.

We used to get company often, usually aunts, uncles, and cousins. A lot of the time the cousins would stay a while with us.

The "foundation" of our house was four big rocks the house rested on. That left a pretty good space underneath the house to play in. When Uncle Jess and his family came to visit, he used to tell us he was going to cut our ears off. I believed him, so when he would come, I would go under the house and stay there until he left. His wife, Aunt Blanche, was real nice.

Another Aunt and Uncle lived in Etna. Since they seemed to live the closest to us, we visited them more. The train was up high, right behind their house. They always had a big hog or two and chickens. Our aunt did a lot of canning and made the best jellies and apple butter and she always had some in the center of the table covered neatly with a clean towel.

When they would visit our house, they always left before it got dark. "We have to go home and feed the chickens" was Aunt Freda's reason. Years later she gave my own child a little black chick we carried all the way back to Chicago. We gave it the baby's formula to keep it alive. We lived on the second floor of a two-story house, then, and the new owner of the baby chicken carried it gently up the back stairs and promptly threw it to the ground.

Christmas at home was just another day to me. Dixie School, where we went, would give us a bag with an orange, nuts, and some candy. Zion Hill Church, which we attended regularly, and where we would give a penny for Sunday School and a nickel for church, gave us about the same thing. It was a special treat for me. Zion Hill Church sits on a hill in Paradise about one or two miles from where we lived. It wasn't a big church, but I liked going there. Sunday School was at the front of the church, near the alter. I can't remember who taught us, but I still remember all the stories, and especially the church bulletin that was given out each week with the beautiful picture on the front.

I only remember having one Christmas at home. Dad went out and brought back a branch off a tree (not a pine tree) with a few stems on it. Gum drops of different colors were stuck on the stems. It was a beautiful tree. I don't ever remember presents at Christmas, but this time Mom put faces on clothespins and put a bit of material around them and gave them to us girls for Christmas as dolls. I thought it was great. The clothespins went back in the bag after Christmas, but it didn't matter to me. That was the first doll I ever had. My sisters tell me an Aunt and Uncle Donald Coen brought goodies to the house at Christmas. I wish I could remember that, but I don't.

I went to the Dixie School from the first to the fifth grades. We would have other students join us as we walked past their house. Sometimes we'd throw hedge balls around as we walked along. Sometimes we'd get to school a little early and sit under a bridge near the school until the teacher rang the first warning bell.

I think I had an advantage going to a one-room school. I listened to the lessons of all grades. One year we had a man teacher. His punishment, if we needed it, was to make us hold our arms up in the air for a long time or make us kneel on a broom. I don't remember Miss Hyland ever having to punish me.

Lunch was usually a biscuit with jelly and any apples or pears we could pick off the trees on the way to school. Sometimes we would stop at one house and they would give us sweet rolls.

They got them for their hogs, but they tasted good to me. I was always surprised when some kid would trade lunch with me. I was able to get a sandwich or cookie for my biscuit and jelly. Once a month, Mom would bring us our lunch. We made sure everyone knew we were getting something special. At noon she would be there with 1/2 of a baloney sandwich and 1/2 of a banana. Delicious! And I took my time eating it to make sure everyone seen it.

For a while Dad had a boxing ring in the pasture next to the house. If we had any arguments Dad would make us fight it out with the boxing gloves. We would box even when there was no reason to. One day a cousin was there and I knocked him out. He has never talked to me since.

One time Mom was pretty sick and everyone seemed to talk in whispers. Mom had lost a baby and Dad put it in a box and left for out back of the house with one or two of the girls following him. He buried the baby under a tree somewhere away from the house in an unmarked spot. In those days that was what was done.

All was not peaceful at our house. Mom and Dad had a lot of physical arguments. The big scar on her arm, still visible years later, was a result of being pushed against the stove. A lot of the fighting and arguing I have tried to erase from my mind, but that one I witnessed is still very clear today.

The fighting got so bad at home when I was nine or ten, Dad wasn't around very much. It was when I was ten that Mom dressed us all up in new dresses and we went to Charleston.

Mom and Dad decided to divorce. We didn't find out until years later that Dad had asked the State for some help with the kids. The "help" the State gave was to take all us girls away from both Mom and Dad and give us away.

I don't know how we got to the courthouse in Charleston. I remember sitting on the floor in the hallway. A lot of people came by and were talking about us. I didn't understand why. We were put in a group and someone took a picture. We had all been crying. They wanted us to sing *You are my sunshine*. I don't know if I did. I didn't know where Mom or Dad were. The people who had given us the sweet rolls on the way to school told, in court, that they had to so we'd have something to eat. That was the first time I knew of grown-ups lying and I never quite got over it.

My first memories of Mom were of her washing clothes by hand outside, summer or winter. I also remember her wringing the necks of chickens and I remember her always nursing a baby. I'm glad I didn't see her sitting in a courtroom waiting for her kids. It almost drove her crazy and she did try to commit suicide a few times. She was very bitter for a long time, but gradually, as she began to get her kids back, it changed. She never got all of us back, but she settled for being able to see them once in awhile. I don't think I could have been as strong under the same circumstances. I think Mom liked to do things for people, especially if she thought you were struggling. I think, if she had ever won the lottery, she would have tried to help every person struggling in the family.

Mom was hurt so bad, even by close friends, but she was able to rise above it and enjoy the times she could spend with us. Mom and Dad were divorced after twenty-one years and Mom did marry again, the second time so she could try to get her kids back. She had some success. Her third husband was the one most of our kids called Grandpa and lovingly so. He was much closer to Mike and I and our children than my real dad, who we never saw much. Mom's fourth marriage was when she was almost eighty years old. Mom died when she was almost ninety, and she cherished each and every one of her very large family.

My memories of Dad are good ones, too. I did get spankings, but not often. Dad used to say if someone didn't like me, just stay away from them. I go to great lengths to do just that to this day.

Dad was also a believer in doing a job right and being there on the job. He said the employer signs your paycheck and everyone can be replaced. After I was bigger, Dad bought me a Christmas present, a box of cherry chocolates. He gave all of us the same thing. I never learned to like them, except the cherry in the center.

Dad surprised me while I was in Cunningham Home by buying four of us girls nice suits, taking us out to dinner, and having our picture taken with him in a studio.

Looking back, I only vaguely remember Carl at home except to know he was once in that car accident and Jenny and Dodo writing a song about it. I knew he was in the CCC's and then went into the Navy, but he was gone from home when us girls were split up, so I didn't see him again for several years. After the war, he was discharged but stayed in Chicago.

Carl said he never really knew what happened at home while he was gone, but looking back now, it must have been hard for him to come out of the Navy and no home to go to. He kind of wandered from Mom's, to Jenny's, to Dodo's—just like the rest of us. I remember him coming in early in the morning at Dodo's when I stayed with her. He drove a cab then, in Chicago.

Later Carl drove a CTA bus in Chicago for years. He was a very safe driver and was commended for it. He married Bea and I remember the nice meals we would get there when we visited. Carl always had a ready laugh, I can still hear him now. He was a very special person to me. The Best!

I don't remember too much about Jesse, or "Dale" as we called him when we were young. He was around sometimes and I remember he was stung by a bumble bee. He got a real big lip from it. I also remember him being sick with Rheumatic Fever when he was younger. We weren't allowed to touch him while he lay in bed.

Jesse was in the CCC's, too, and he joined the Navy and came home on leave. While home they would march in their uniforms all over the yard and pasture. I thought they were both so very special and I was proud of them.

Jesse was gone, too, when us girls were split up. I didn't see him again for many years. I received a couple of letters from him and they read like a travel brochure. I always felt Jesse was a very special, but a distant person. I have remained in awe of him.

After the hearing in court, Miss Caton took Phyllis (a younger sister) and I to a car, and I think Mr. Bidwell or Mr. Kincaid was driving it. We got in and I didn't know where all the other girls went to. I later learned the rest of the girls were dropped off one by one. Phyllis and I had never been on a long trip before, so impatient to see where we were going, we kept asking "How much farther?" After, it seemed to me, a very long time, we turned into a lane that had one big brick pillar on each side of the entrance. I had never seen such big buildings and we stopped in front of one of them. I didn't know where we were, but I knew I was not going to go there.

They took Phyllis out of the car first, but I decided I wasn't going to get out. When they reached in one side, I'd go to the other. When that no longer worked, I jumped back and forth over the seats, throwing every cuss word at them I could think of—Phyllis standing out there pleading with me, "Come on, Irma. I don't want to be alone." After some reinforcements, they finally caught me. Phyllis, at least, was glad.

We were taken to this big building we had pulled up in front of. I was taken to the second floor and I didn't know where Phyllis was, but I heard her crying and followed the sound upstairs where there was another big room almost like the first. I saw her but they wouldn't let me stay and took me back down to the first room, called the Hummel Dormitory. There was no kids around, except one, and she was in bed. Miss Gustafson was the matron of Hummel Dormitory and she told me the girl was home because she had broken her leg, but she could show me around. Now I went to school with a girl at Dixie school who had broken her leg. It was in a cast and she sat at the front of the room with her leg resting on a chair. But when this girl jumped out of bed, she had only one leg, the other was gone below the knee and I stared. I had never seen anyone with one leg. I was ten years old and Cunningham Children's Home in Urbana was to be my home for the next three and a half years.

Cunningham Children's Home was pretty frightening at first. The substitute matron was an older lady who stood very straight and was stern looking. When it was bedtime she would tell us stories about Abraham Lincoln as a boy and as a man. I heard just enough to know I wanted to know more. It made a lasting impression on me.

At home, the Doctor came to the house if he was needed—although it was mostly to deliver another sister. If I got sick at the home, it was usually something minor and I was given castor oil, milk toast, and bed rest. I took my first trip to the doctor's office at Cunningham, also to a dentist and to a barber.

There were a lot of girls in my dormitory. There were three or four rows of beds with several beds in each row. There were built-in dresser drawers along one whole wall. The bathroom had two tubs and several sinks. For the first time in my life, I had my own toothbrush, and comb, and brush. We had an outhouse at home and bath time brought out the round wash tub filled with water heated on the stove. After using catalogs or corn husks in our outhouse, the toilet paper was a real treat.

We made our own beds at Cunningham, and if they weren't made right the matron would take them apart and we'd have to do it over and over until it was right. It took me a while, but I learned to make a very neat bed that I still make today.

The meals at Cunningham were eaten in a big dining room with round tables. Once a month we changed tables so we never sat

113

at the same place all the time. I liked serving. We would get to bring the food to the table in big bowls and the matron at each table would dish it out on each plate and it would pass around the table to you. Dessert was brought by certain girls to the persons at the table.

The different jobs were assigned to different ones each month, except when we were old enough to iron, and then it seems ironing was a permanent chore. The lady that ran the laundry was real nice and was the wife of the maintenance man and bus driver. The washing machine was a big wooden tub, about five or six feet long, that went around and around on its side.

The ironing boards were lined up against one wall. We went to iron after school. The first ones there got their choice of which board to work at. One iron had a loose handle that would cause the iron to turn and hit the wrist and cause a burn. That iron was never fixed while I was there, I suspect so we would hurry to work faster so we wouldn't get stuck with that iron. It took me a long time to learn that, and only after getting burned over and over on the same wrist.

Shortly after coming to Cunningham I was given the job of mopping half of the kitchen floor. I was told to use "elbow grease" and I spent the greater part of the afternoon looking in the store room for it. The boys at Cunningham raised sheep and I remember watching them shear them.

Phyllis and I were at the Home for about two months when three other sisters came there. It was so good to see them. Two of them were in my dormitory and the other one went to the Illinois Dormitory which had rooms with only two beds in each. Later Margy and I would live in Illinois Dormitory.

Washington School in Urbana, across the pasture from Cunningham, was where we went to school. We walked there and got to go over a stile on the way. After the one-room school house I was going to, Washington looked huge. I guess I did alright there.

114

We played jacks and marbles a lot. I got to be pretty good at both games and had the skinned-up knuckles that were a necessary part of the sports. I also remember one teacher. Miss Fry taught Geography. I liked Geography, but I spent a lot of time looking at her legs that looked like the knees were bent backward. She would write sayings on the blackboard every Monday and put up different ones the next Monday. I've remembered many of them, but it took me a long time to know what "When you sit down, sit up" meant.

I never had toys at home, but at Cunningham I had plenty of toys. Each of us had our own drawer in the play room and mine was filled with my favorite toys, paper dolls. My imagination knew no bounds when I played with them. In later years it was quite a disappointment to find my own girls didn't care for them at all.

While Christmas was just another day at home, at Cunningham it was like a fairy tale come true. There was a room in our dorm. We could only guess at what was behind its big double doors. All year we never used it, but Christmas morning after breakfast we would come back to the dorm, the Matron would open the big double doors and upon entering we would see a huge tree decorated with colored lights, and ornaments, and garland all around it. There were wrapped gifts under the tree in all sizes. We each got several gifts, which we laid out on our beds so everyone could see what the others got. The best part was the unwrapped gift hanging on the tree. Each of us had one with our name on it. It was always a piece of jewelry. I don't know why that gift should stand out in my memory, but every other gift has paled compared to it.

During WW II the Navy was stationed at the U of I. At Christmas we went there by bus and the sailors had a party. With all of us and them away from home, it was probably as special to them as it was to us.

After the Navy left we were invited to a Christmas party at the University of Illinois given by the sorority sisters. We had a very good time at both of these parties.

Getting on the old bus and riding to church wearing my best clothes was special to me. Our Sunday clothes were for church only. We changed as soon as we got back. It was a Methodist Church. The bus was used only once in a while other than for church.

I remember one time a couple wanted to adopt Phyllis. They took her out to eat, but she wouldn't go without me. We went to the Lincoln Hotel to eat and they bought us each a bag of candy. Phyllis wouldn't go with them, though, and they certainly didn't want us both.

Sometimes we took walks with our matron. We would walk to a small cemetery to watch the swans, or to the little airport north of the Home, and sometimes we got to go shopping in Urbana. We got a small allowance each week. Some was used for church and we saved the rest in an envelope, which our matron kept for us. We could spend some when we went shopping.

There was a small hill at Cunningham we liked to roll down or try to ski on in winter, but I never learned to keep the skis forward. Before we would go out to play, the matron would give us some candy or an orange. The candy was usually left over from a holiday so we got a gooey chunk of it. The first time I got an orange, I was told not to throw the peelings down. Seeing no where to put them, I just ate the orange like an apple. It wasn't so bad after a while.

Each fall Cunningham would have an Octoberfest on the lawn. Home-canned goods and other foods were set up in nice displays. The food was donated to Cunningham by the people who raised it and canned it. The food was then stored in a big room with lots of shelves beneath the kitchen. That was the food that was served to us over the year. We had to eat everything on our plates. We got two glasses of milk a meal. I learned to like all foods except one—prune fluff. After gagging trying to get it down, I finally learned to ask the servers what was for dessert. Sometimes several different desserts were served to use up leftovers. We never knew which dessert we would get then, but I learned to save all my milk 'till dessert time because if there was just one dish of prune fluff, I was sure to get it. I drowned it to get it down.

Mom came to see us, but we didn't always get to see her, partly because she had words with the superintendent or because I was being punished. If I was punished at all I had to sit on a chair beside my bed and do darning. Darning is an art I never learned to do well. I ran out of patience with it in a hurry, which left a rather unusual looking weave. I don't know where all the socks came from to be darned. I suspected they belonged to the ones who never got punished.

The bottom drawers in our dormitory were filled with pretty dresses all laid in them nicely. When I would need a dress, the matron would go through them and pick one out for me. There were a lot of pretty ones I would have liked, but I would end up rather disappointed. Of course I never knew they had sizes on them. One dress I got I didn't like until I wore it. So many people said it was pretty. My mind was easy to change, then.

I didn't want to be in Cunningham Home, but looking back I know it was the best thing that happened to me. We were taught discipline and to do a job and do it well. When I went to Thornburn Jr. High in Urbana, we went by Cunningham bus. That was when I moved to the Illinois Dormitory.

After I had been at Cunningham home for three and one-half years, Margy and I got to go on an Eighth-grade graduation trip to see Mom. We would never go back to Cunningham. Mom kept us in Chicago.

We had never been to Chicago and had never been on a greyhound bus before. I was fascinated by everything we saw along the way. The bus stopped in Gilman to let the passengers eat, but I can't remember getting off at that time. When we got to Chicago the buildings started getting bigger and taller. We were trying to see everything and got right on the floor of the bus to try to see the tops of the buildings. They are even too tall for that. The tallest building at the time was the Wrigley building. I'm sure the rest of the passengers were amused by our enthusiasm.

Mom met us and we took our first ride on a streetcar. It was on tracks that ran down on both sides of the street. It was noisy until it came to a stop and then it was very quiet. You could either sit down on the inside of the streetcar or stand on the back or the front. When it came to the end of the line, the motorman would just go to the other end of the car and start back again. It had controls at both ends. A conductor on the back would call out the next street and would make sure you paid your fare. I really liked the streetcars and you could get a transfer for another car and ride all over for 6¢.

We went to a house where Mom and our stepfather Paul lived, on Throop Street in Chicago. A brewery was just down the block from there and that's where Paul worked. The whole neighborhood smelled like Beer. That's probably part of the reason I don't drink. I couldn't get past the smell.

I don't remember anything else about that house. I remember living on Damon and Blue Island Avenues after that, in an apartment up over a restaurant—later made into a tavern. I sold papers at a stand on that corner. Streetcars would come down both streets but it was the end of the line for Damon Avenue. The streetcar men would come in the restaurant before they started back.

Mom and Paul didn't get along well at all, but Paul liked to surprise us girls and, with Mom, would take us places like Riverview, "Jew Town," or Maxwell Street. Eisenhower jackets were coming into style and he took us to the stores there and bickered with the store owner over the purchase of some suits for us, that had that style of jacket. I loved mine. It was gray and had a pleated skirt. We went to see the Sonja Henie Ice Show at the stadium and to Ringling Bros. & Barnum & Baily Circus. We never knew just where we were going until we got there.

Margy and I learned an important lesson around this time. Margy and I heard on WJJD radio about a *Mr. Walker*. We pictured a little doll that would walk downstairs. It sounded great to us. We pooled our money and sent for it. It was my first experience of misleading advertising. It came, but it was only a coiled up wire that was real flexible and really did "walk" downstairs. We had a good laugh about it and hours of fun with it. Today it's called a *Slinky*.

I went to live with Jenny, I believe. I moved back and forth so many times between Jenny, Dodo, and Mom that I don't remember actually moving to any of the places. I was just there.

I went to Harrison High School in Chicago. It was so big and I hated it. When I moved again one-half year later, I went to Marshall High School and liked it even less. I started skipping school. I was living with Dodo. I would just go to the park and sit most of the time. I hid my books in the bushes. One day a lady came by and started talking to me real nice. She turned out to be the truant officer. Mom was trying to get all of us kids back from the State and the State said I needed to be put away. Luckily the Judge understood I never got into real trouble, just skipped school, so the case was dropped and Mom got most of us kids back again. Ironically, none of us went home with her that day. We all went with our older sisters.

Altogether, I only went to one year of high school, but when I was sixty-two, I went to the Mattoon Area Adult Education Center and earned my GED.

Mom and her husband, Paul, bought a farm in Arkansas about the time the case was dismissed. One day we helped load up a truck with our belongings and moved there. Paul had asked the man who owned the truck to take us all down. There was Mom, her brother Uncle Nolan, our oldest brother Jesse's wife Betty, and their son Dale. Jesse was overseas in the Navy. There was also sisters Marge, Bertie, Phyllis, and me. Before we got started, Dale fell and got a big bump on his forehead. We went anyway. I was excited about crossing the Mississippi River because I had read about it, but had never seen it. I knew nothing about tolls, but much to my dismay, Betty, Dale, and us girls were told to hide in among the furniture and they covered us up with a big tarp in case the truck was checked before going over the bridge. We stayed under there until we were told it was safe to come out. It worked, but I had missed my chance to see the Mississippi.

The farm was in the foothills of the Ozarks. The location was pretty, with lots of small pine trees out in back of the house. There were lots of tall pines on the rest of the property which had steep bluffs on two sides. One side was a drop off of about 100 feet and the other bluff was passable. The farm itself was a rock farm, at least it seemed that way to us girls, who had to pile the hundreds of big rocks up. Mom bought two horses. One looked like the horse of *My Friend Flicka* movie fame and so we named him that. The other was a stocking-footed Roan with white down the middle of his face. He was pretty. We called him Roanie. We used to hitch Flicka up to a plow and try to plow up a place to grow corn and a garden. The soil was reddish and looked nothing like Illinois soil. We had to stop all the time to remove some more rocks. There were far too many rocks to move, so we started leaving some of them there and worked around them if possible. We did plant corn and a vegetable garden. The soil was real dry and we had to carry buckets of water from the stream two pastures over, so it was pretty much a total flop.

The house was a real log cabin and a good sized one. The heat was a fireplace in the living room where we would stand on cold days and half cook the front of our leg and turn around to do

Irma Joan

the same to the back of our legs. That's probably why I've never had to shave my legs. Our "frig" in Arkansas was a wooden box about two-feet long and not very high with a lid but no bottom. It would sit in a small shallow stream running out of the rocks. The water was always ice cold, even in the hot weather. The cold water would run over the bottoms of the containers and the lid would keep the sun out. Cheap and very effective. Besides, we didn't have electricity anyway. The logs showed on the inside of the house so we nailed wallpaper on to the logs. Didn't do much to keep it warmer, but it looked a whole lot better. Uncle Nolan was the supervisor and made sure we got our work done. Because there was no electricity, we went to bed early. There was also no running water and the outhouse was out in back of the house. We carried buckets of water for drinking and for bathing and washing clothes. The clothes all had a reddish look to them after a while because of the soil. It could not be washed out.

One day a guy came by and sold Mom a mule for $5.00. It turned out half the county had paid $5.00 for that same mule. You couldn't get it to work, but he was good for some laughs. He would turn the feed sack upside down and empty it out and eat all he wanted. Sometimes we would ride him to Drasco, the tiny town nearest us. It had two groceries, a filling station, and a post office. You couldn't buy soda to drink, but the ice cooler was filled with #303 cans of juice. Just take one out of the ice. Nothing tasted better. We could get to town from two different directions. The mule would choose the one he wanted to take. Trying to get him home was a whole new adventure. He would go around and around in circles until a lumber truck would come by and then he would take off after it, hopefully in the direction we wanted to go. Most of the time I could get him to turn into our road, but not always.

My brother Carl came down to visit us once and he rode the mule to town. He had trouble getting back home, due to it's stubbornness, and he came back riding with his feet up on it's back. We didn't have saddles, only my uncle did. Carl was sore for awhile and passed on the next chance to ride the mule.

Us girls learned to drive a wagon in Arkansas, pulled by Flicka and Roanie. We didn't have a car, so our transportation was the wagon or on one of the horses. The mule didn't stick around long. He ate his fill and left one day. We never saw him again.

Margy, Bertie, and I would go down in the woods at the bottom of the bluff and find trees that were down and bring the long logs back for firewood. We would fasten a chain around the log and have the horse pull it up the slanted bluff. The chain kept breaking, but we would finally get it home. Margy was always a frail, sickly girl so Bertie and I would let her sit sometimes while we got the logs ready. We would all sing and laugh while working. One day our stepfather Paul came down from Chicago. We didn't know it. We were kind of scared of him. He caught Margy sitting and he really gave us hell. He never did seem to like Margy.

Paul sent money down to Mom once in a while, but it was Betty's allotment check that really kept us going. She would splurge when she got it and treat us all to some cookies. Once, she bought a whole bin of them.

Betty was pregnant when we first moved down there. Since we lived about thirty miles from the nearest hospital and had no car, she had to stay in Heber Springs, where the hospital was, for about one week before the baby was due. I got to go with her and it was really a treat for me. We stayed in a hotel, ate out, and did whatever she wanted to for the week, and we got to take the brand new baby home. It was a very special week for me.

We used to cut tall pine trees and cut them in certain lengths and then strip the bark off of them. I think Mom sold them for posts. One time a man came to cut the trees in back for Christmas trees. He was supposed to sell them and give Mom the money. He was never seen there again.

I never went to school in Arkansas. I should have been in high school, but it was thirty miles away and too far to walk to catch the bus on the main road. There was always work to do at home, anyway.

We didn't have much furniture in Arkansas. Uncle Nolan made us a bunk bed. Mom made mattresses out of dried leaves. A little noisy, but not too uncomfortable.

We went once to a "swimming hole" in Arkansas. The neighbor boys wanted us to go. So Uncle Nolan put them to work helping us build a fence in front of the house. It was getting dark by the time we were all done, but the lights on the pickup trucks belonging to the boys, gave us light to swim in the "hole." It was a very deep section between the rocks. I couldn't swim and panicked when I couldn't touch bottom. Uncle Nolan saw me bobbing and pulled me out. I had almost drowned one time before, in a city pool, but was saved by the guard.

We had a couple of pigs, a male and female. The sow had a litter, but they were stolen from us. The horses got sick and died and the vet said they had been poisoned. One of the hogs disappeared so Mom butchered the other one. We weren't very popular down there in Arkansas because Paul was from Chicago and the rest of us had lived there. They thought we were gangsters. Once, coming back from Drasco, we looked up on the hill toward our house and the whole mountain was on fire. The fire stopped when it got to the young pines in back of the house and the plowed field on the other. After we all left there, the house was burned to the ground.

I didn't care much for Arkansas, except for the music and the square dances. Mom had a couple dances at our house and they lasted two or three days. I liked the fiddle and guitar playing, which was done by neighbors. I never played an instrument, then, but I wished

I could. I used to sit out on the bluff with a broom and pretend I was playing a guitar and I would sing. It sounded good to me. I bought me a cheap guitar when I was fifteen and my future husband gave me a dobro when I was seventeen and living on 19th Street in Chicago. I was proud of the fact that all our seven children played an instrument of one kind or another.

I didn't live in Arkansas long. Bertie and I left there to go and live with Dad south of Mattoon. The evening before we left, Bertie was sitting on the arm of the old couch when the couch broke and Bertie fell down and a nail went into her knee. It was bathed and wrapped and in the morning we set out to catch the bus to Batesville. I was about fifteen and Bertie a year younger. Our clothes were in cardboard boxes tied with rope, and we had very little money. From Batesville, Arkansas, we took a bus to St. Louis, and had a three-hour layover there. We had a candy bar to eat, but Bertie was getting sicker and lamer. By the time the bus loaded, she could hardly walk. Dad picked us up in Mattoon and took her to the doctor. The leg was infected and gangrene had set in and the doctor told Dad the leg would have to come off. Dad said no and asked what we could do to help. My Sister Dodo lived with Dad at the time so she put hot compresses on Bertie's knee constantly until it finally got well.

When we were sent to Cunningham Home, Dad had the little house moved up closer to the main road and this is where we went when Dodo and I lived with Dad. I went to work in Kresge's Dime store in Mattoon. Bede and I both worked there. We made 50¢ an hour working behind the lunch counter. We were told if we worked extra well we would get a 2¢ raise. Oh Boy! did we deserve that raise.

I had a fight with Dodo while we lived with Dad and worked at Kresge's. I had a pretty, grey pleated skirt and Dodo wanted to borrow it. I wouldn't let her because she had nice clothes that I never borrowed. I was wearing that skirt one day when I accidentally tore it climbing over a barbed wire fence. Dodo laughed and said, "That's good!" because I wouldn't let her wear it. I got mad and we started fighting. Dad interrupted and said it was time to go to work, so we put off the fight until the evening—when we finished it. Dad just stood back and laughed and said it was the "damnedest thing he'd ever seen." I've never fought again.

Eventually I went back north.

I first met my husband, Michael Stanley Swierk, on the street in Chicago. I was walking from the house on Damen and 19th, where I lived with Mom, to Bede and her husband Chet's house on 17th and Wood. I was carrying a cheap guitar I had bought at "Jew Town" in the Maxwell Street Market. I liked to go over to some neighbors of Bede's—two men who were somewhat crippled and liked to play the guitar. I would jam with them.

I didn't like Mike when I first met him. He was riding around in a car with a couple of other guys and three girls. They stopped at the corner I was crossing and one of the girls jumped out and took my guitar. I was too dumb to know what to do about it so I did nothing. She finally tired of that game and gave me back the guitar and they drove off, but Mike started looking for me in the neighborhood and I finally agreed to go on a picnic with him.

I went with Mike for a year and a half and he surprised me with a ring shortly after I turned eighteen. It was January 1950. I was living with Mom at the time and our troubles pointed to another move soon for me. Mike's mother agreed to take me in and Mike decided we would be married January 28. I was so grateful he was offering me something permanent, I agreed. I liked Mike. He was easy to talk to and treated me very good. I felt comfortable with him, but I didn't know what love was, so I can't really say I loved him, then.

Because I wasn't a Catholic and Mike was, we were married in the Rectory of St. Roman's Church January 28, 1950. Bede and Mike's friend, Frank Janacek, stood up with us. Mike's mother had a reception for us and we honeymooned at the U. S. Grant hotel in Mattoon.

I knew from the first that this marriage would last because I would do all in my power to make it so. And Mike taught me to love. Not just right away, but he was patient and kind and made me feel special. It grew deeper as the years flew and we shared the birth of each child and the loss of one. Mike could be short-tempered sometimes, but not with me. He handled all the bill paying, but I knew everything that was spent. He was a firm believer in insurance and planned for our future. I also helped by working, taking time off only to have the children.

My husband was Polish. His mom and Dad had come over to America from Poland about 1927 or so. They were not married at that time. My mother-in-law, I called her Ma—she called me Norma—made chicken soup every Sunday and would then bread the chicken and bake it. She always made home-made noodles and lots of Polish dishes. She was a very good cook. She also ran a little grocery store in the front half of the house she lived in. When we got married, we moved in with her for awhile and then, when it became available, we moved upstairs to another flat. It was in Chicago—on the west side. The elevated tracks were over the alley behind the house. When we were in the backyard talking, we'd have to stop when the El went by. It was so noisy. I used to wave to the people on the El and a lot of times, one or more would wave back. Over the years, we got used to the noise and rarely noticed an El going by, unless it slowed down. Five of our children were born while we lived there—three while upstairs. The girls were born after we moved downstairs behind the store into three rooms, with a pantry and bath, when we bought the business from Ma. We kept the grocery for about seven years. I ran the store from 5:30 a.m. to

126

9:30 p.m. while Mike worked in a factory. I cleaned after we closed. When our first girl was born, we waited until the store closed to go to the hospital.

I was always a little anxious if a stranger came in, but most of our customers were neighbors or the regulars that came at lunch time for sandwiches. One day there were two men sitting in a car across the street. They sat there for a long time and Mike had to go somewhere, so he told me to keep our little gun handy. We had kids and I was afraid to carry the gun because of them. He finally convinced me to keep it in my apron pocket. After he left, I pinned my apron pocket closed to keep it away from the kids. I guess if I had been held up I would have had to say "Just a minute. I have to unpin my pocket." I hated guns and I still do.

Mike turned out to be a very serious and dedicated person. He was a good family man and provided well for his family. He had a happy side to him, but he would show it more if he knew you for a while. He would never discuss his intimate life, except with me. He treated me like I was special.

Michael Elliott was the first born on January 30, 1952. Clifford Douglas followed him July 12, 1953, Curtis Lee followed almost four years later, on August 23, 1957, the day before his Dad's birthday. Mary Lorraine was our first girl. She was born May 5, 1962 and slept a lot in a bassinet in the store or was held by customers while I waited on them. Iona Louise followed on November 1, 1963. She also slept in the store while I waited on customers.

We lost one child between Iona and Jerome Allen, who was born November 5, 1972. Patrick Anthony was born on June 28, 1975. This completed our family, except they have multiplied now and I have twenty-three grandchildren and eight great-grandchildren.

All of our children were planned and all of them looked alike at birth. We could pick ours out of a full nursery. When I would come home from the hospital, Mike would have the house spotless and a meal ready. When the first two boys were born, I didn't know much about raising them, especially the first. I could take care of him, but when he reached the terrible two's, I lost my temper with him a lot.

Once in awhile Mike gave me a special gift. My favorite flower is the Bird of Paradise. He looked all over for them and surprised me with a big spray. They were expensive for our budget so he only got them twice, but once would have been enough for me.

We always had lots of company in Chicago and we had every Holiday Dinner at our home, usually with guests.

I used to do spring cleaning and Christmas cleaned for Ma. She had a big pantry-closet combination. Everything had to come out, be cleaned, and put back in the same way. The bigger items and the special vases were wrapped in newspapers to keep them clean. They were never used, but they still had to be washed and wrapped in fresh newspapers and tied back up. She kept a container of leeches in that closet. She would put them on her feet and let them, she said, draw out the bad blood.

The furniture we owned was used, but appliances were always new and were usually replaced about every five years, especially if it started giving us trouble. Of course, we didn't get everything right away. I washed clothes in the tub for a long time.

We moved to Brookfield in 1968 or 69. We bought our first home, a brick house with a big basement and attic. We had saved twenty years for a down payment and we borrowed the rest from Mike's sister. Mike and I cooked and canned together. We went on fishing trips to Wisconsin or Minnesota and we went to see Margy and Richard in Michigan. Mike knew my family was important to me. He got along well with all of them and encouraged me to see them. He was delighted for me when my sister, Doris, and her family visited our home after I hadn't seen her for thirty-three years.

Irma Joan

We finally remodeled the kitchen in Brookfield and Mike came home one day and said he'd found the perfect clock for it and wanted me to see it. We went back to the store and he pointed out, in the store window, this little black cat clock with glittering eyes and a tail that moved in opposite ways with each tick. It was the ugliest thing, but I couldn't tell him that. We went on in and found they had those clocks in different colors. I told him I liked the bronze colored one best, so we got it. We had that clock for years, and Mike was so proud of it. I figured, for all the wonderful things he'd done for me, I could tolerate a small thing like an ugly clock.

We were sailing along, and then Mike came home early from work one day—which he never did. He looked terrible. His eyes were white. I was babysitting three little kids. Mike never did believe in Doctors much so he didn't want to go this time, but Mary and her husband, Dave, convinced him to go. Mary took care of the kids while I took him. The Doctor sent him straight to the hospital where a few minutes later Mike had a cardiac arrest. His trouble turned out to be heart fibrillation. They pulled him through, but sent him to Loyola Hospital because he needed something special. They gave him a test to check his heart rate and when he came back to the room afterward, he grabbed my hand and told me they had killed him twice. I'd never seen him so emotional before. He was given an Automatic Implantable Cardiac Defibrillator. Patches were fastened to the heart with leads on them and were connected to a battery pack sewn into a pocket inside his stomach area. He called himself the Bionic Man. If his heart went into fibrillation, it would shock him and cause the heart to beat normal again, but he could no longer climb the stairs at our house and we started looking for a different place.

One day, when I was in Mattoon to see Mom, who was in the hospital, my sister Phyllis and her husband Dick took me to see a house on Lake Mattoon. As soon as I saw the land, I knew it was what we had been looking for and Mike made the trip down to see the place and loved it. We decided to take it, but Mike said we would have to move before the cold weather set in. This was early October. We put our house on the market but didn't expect it to sell so quick. It sold in four days. Because of the weekend, I had no chance to tell the parents of the kids I was babysitting with that we were moving and it was a shock to them to see the sold sign in the yard.

I got busy packing, mostly alone because Mike was unable to help. He had to make a trip to the hospital because of the A. I. C. D. going off too many times.

I cried a lot, thinking of the way things were going, but it was too late to change our minds. It was especially difficult for our son Jerry who was seventeen. Whether it was because of the uncertainty we were going through with Mike or just a period of adjustment through the teen years, Jerry and I were having a very hard time communicating. I was worried about Mike, and Mom was in and out of the hospital so much, I was very short fused. One day, it went too far and Jerry packed a bag and left home. Mike insisted I go get the key from him. It was the last thing in the world I wanted to do. I was mad at Mike and hated myself. We didn't see Jerry for a couple of weeks, but I knew he was at his friend's house. When he came walking down the street shortly after and saw the "sold" sign he never told us how he felt, but I knew by looking at him that he felt we had pulled his home right out from under him. I have regretted it ever since. It seemed so final.

We did move to the lake. It was beautiful and Mike loved it. Our brother-in-law Dick helped get the place into shape as Mike would get a shock every time he tried to do something. He made it for a couple of years, but he was so depressed. I would take him for rides at two and three in the morning to try to help him relax. The last few months, he didn't want me out of his sight for more than an hour.

130

Irma Joan

He had to go to Loyola to see what they could do for him. I drove up and he started getting the shocks, but they weren't putting his heart back into rhythm. I thought, "Oh, dear God! Please let me find a policeman just in case he passes out." I kept watching where the hospitals were and figuring how quickly I could get there. Mike asked me to hurry on to Loyola, but when we got off the expressway, he wanted to make a quick trip past our old home in Brookfield. It was as if he had a premonition. He never came out of the hospital.

I still had Patrick at home and it took a little adjustment to cope. I thank Mike for keeping me informed. It made it easier to be thrust into taking care of everything. I found I could do it and very well. We had almost forty-three years together and I don't regret a day of it. When Mike got sick, he told me how to do things he used to do. I tuck-pointed, fixed the sink, and put in a sidewalk and floors. I wouldn't tackle electricity, though.

I've worked most of my life. I started selling papers on a street corner in Chicago not long after I left Cunningham Home. I liked the job. I worked in Dime stores, as a window decorator, and behind the counters. The first factory job I got was Bell Electric in Chicago. They were just getting started. Bertie started there first, but since she wasn't old enough to work in a factory, she used my birthdate. I started there shortly afterward and used my own birthdate. We had some anxious moments, afraid it would be found out. It never was. I worked days until the children came along and then I worked nights for years.

I've had a whole slew of jobs in factories from punch presser and lathe machines to coil winder, rubber and plastic modeling machines, and from drill presses to conveyer lines. There was something interesting about each job. If work got slow, I wouldn't hesitate to pick up a broom and clean or scrub up the sinks. Mike worked days and I worked nights so we didn't need a sitter.

Ten Sisters

Sometimes Ma would watch them if Mike had something to do. When I tired of full time factory work, I worked a couple of months in the summer at The Farm. It was a farm stand in Westchester, Illinois, where fresh vegetables and melons and pumpkins were sold by the family who raised them. I worked hard there and loved it. The owners worked equally hard. Then I started baby-sitting.

The only time I didn't work was when Mike was sick. After he died, I went back to work, trying different jobs and ended up working for Max Market IGA in Mattoon, Illinois—in the Deli.

For awhile, I had three grandsons living with me. Now I have two. I work and I take one day at a time. I love the challenges and the sunrises, and I hope to be around until I'm 101.

Roberta Pauline

(Bertie)

Dedicated to The Cunningham Children's Home,
especially Ms. Miles and Ms. Gustafson, for giving me security
and teaching me responsibility in my formative years

Ten Sisters

I don't know why I'm writing this chapter of my life. Following my years spent in the children's home, life was pretty much like anyone else's. I guess the important thing to me is that after being separated and going in all different directions, it was a wonder that we all were able to find each other and get together again.

I don't remember much prior to my family breaking up. I have no memory of being at home with my parents. I can remember watching my brother Jesse carving his initials on a big tree. I can remember Grandma's house up over the little hill and I can remember the small bridge in front of our house. We used to get under it just to hear the cars. We would receive a face full of dirt as they rumbled by. Some people say I have just blocked it out of my mind, as I was nine years old when the family broke up, but I don't even remember the day in court when we were all taken from our parents. Most of my memories are from after the break-up, starting with the foster home where my sister Margy and I were sent.

Our foster mother was a big, heavyset woman who had to sit on a washtub. Her husband was a tall, slim man who was very quiet. Margy and I only stayed there a short time as we wanted to be with our sisters and the State placed us in the Cunningham Children's Home in Urbana, Illinois, where three of our sisters were already residing.

I loved the Home. I was in awe of everything. Most of the children, like us, came from broken homes, but some were orphans. Each child was placed in a dormitory-style setting according to their age. Each dorm had one matron, except for the boys', which had two.

I made a lot of friends in the Home. I loved the dormitory style. Our beds were all lined up in rows, and I could talk to the girls next to me after lights were out. It was nice to have a bed of my own. At home most of us girls slept in the same bed.

Roberta Pauline

At the Home we were taught to make our beds and we were given a doll to place on it. These dolls weren't ours to keep, but we could play with them. I had never owned a doll.

Each child's name was sewn into his clothes. The socks were marked with your name on the bottom in indelible ink.

Chores were assigned once a month and you would get a different job to do for that particular month. I might be working in the laundry folding and sorting clothes, or working in the yard or in the kitchen doing dishes or setting the table. But most of all, we were taught to take care of our things and to respect other people's things.

We had to attend church, and we attended public schools. We wore regular clothes, most of which were donated, but we learned to take care of them as they were handed down to other children—after changing the name tags. At the home we were taught responsibility, manners, and respect for others, but we were never spanked—just punished.

Many parties were planned for the Home children. We always looked forward to them.

My sister Phyllis and I spent almost every summer in various foster homes. As we were wards of the State, we were candidates for adoption. It was always Phyllis they were interested in, but she would never go without me. The foster home that I remember most vividly was with a family in Iuka, Illinois. They owned a small cafe with a couple of gas pumps. Phyllis and I flipped hamburgers and prepared Blue Plate Specials. We also pumped gas when no one else was available.

Across the street from the cafe was an old spooky-looking abandoned house that had windows reaching from floor to ceiling. These windows were shuttered to close off the entire light. We used to make up stories of what might have went on inside. Many years later, Phyllis and her husband, and my husband and I were on a trip and went to see the old house. It was still there and the shutters were hanging on their hinges. It brought back memories.

We also were in foster homes in Villa Grove and Salem, Illinois. We never cared for the foster homes and were always glad to return to Cunningham Home.

My mother remarried and she and my stepfather took us out of the Home and moved us to Chicago. I still did not live with Mother, though. I was sent to live with my older sister, Virginia, who was married and whose husband was in the Navy. I was far ahead of the other children in the eighth grade and they double promoted me and I graduated after one-half semester.

I was very impressed with the big city. I loved to ride the streetcars. Chicago seemed so safe, then. My sister Virginia worked nights at a restaurant. I used to go to the movies by myself. The theater was a few blocks from our house. One night after returning from a movie, finding my sister not home, I walked about two miles to another sister's house on the north side of Chicago. Needless to say, they were both very upset with me.

About that time, my mother and stepfather bought a timber farm in Arkansas. They moved four of us girls down there. My sister, Virginia, followed. Later, my older brothers' wife and their two small boys went down there, too. There was no school for me to attend, as the local school only went to the sixth grade.

Things were pretty tough in Arkansas as we lived on what little money my stepfather and mother, who had moved back to Chicago, were able to send us. My sister and sister-in-law had been left to take care of us, and my sister-in-law received an allotment check from my oldest brother for her and the boys. Many a times, that was all we had to make ends meet. The winters were rough. The log house had a very big fireplace in it and we would cut down a pine tree and stick it in the hearth and as it burned down, we would push it in farther and farther.

Because no school was near, and maybe because we were

extra mouths to feed, my sister Irma and I were sent to live with Dad after a few months. I had run a nail in my knee prior to taking the bus to my father's home in Mattoon, Illinois. By the time we arrived there, it was all swollen up and I was running a high fever. The doctor wanted to remove my leg when he saw the wound, but my father talked him into trying to treat it. The doctor came out to my dad's house every day to give me a penicillin shot. The gangrene that had started cleared up, but my father said he could not keep Irma and me, so he sent us to live with our other sisters in Chicago. I moved in with Rhita [Bede] and her husband and Irma moved in with Deloris [Dodo], whose husband was in the Navy.

I did not go back to school in Chicago, either. Instead, I got a full time job working in a factory. I was only fifteen, but I told them I was sixteen. Jobs were pretty plentiful then, but didn't pay much.

I was the world's worst job hopper. I have worked for several big companies that were located in Chicago. I have worked for Cory Coffee, Eastman Kodak, International Harvester Press, Cook Chocolate, Coach and Car, Rolland Electric and Bell Electric. I guess I was trying to find my niche. I have been a punch press operator, power sewing machine operator, wired television tubes, soldered, worked on many assembly lines, and done bindery work. Most of these jobs were held before I had any children.

At the tender age of sixteen I married a neighborhood boy who had recently been discharged from the army. After two years, our son Jimmy was born. We had been living in a small furnished apartment and we decided to move to a third floor walkup. My husband was an apprentice lather and the work was seasonal so money was very tight. Most of our clothes were bought at a second hand store and we never went out to eat. We played cards for amusement. We did buy a 3-inch T. V. that had to have a big magnifying glass in front of it to enable us to see it from a distance and the only thing we could get was wrestling and *The Milton Berle Show*.

When my son was two, my daughter, Karen, was born. We still lived in the big apartment building and I fought roaches and bed bugs, as there were many apartments in the building and the landlord wasn't able to get into some of them to treat for pests. Because of this, we decided to move. This time we took up residence in the old neighborhood where I had lived with my sister when first coming to Chicago, but every six months the landlady would raise the rent, so we decided to move again. By this time, my husband had landed a job on the south side of Chicago building a new school. The job was to last for awhile, so we found an apartment near where he was working and moved again.

When my son was seven, he developed very bad bruises on his body. Once he was hit on the arm by a small rubber ball, which left a bruise so bad it appeared that he'd been beaten. I took him to our family doctor who admitted him to the hospital to undergo tests.

After many tests and a dozen specialists, it was determined that my son had a rare blood disease, called Thrombocy Topenic Purpura, perhaps caused by the DDT that was used in one of our prior apartments. His spleen was damaged and he had a 75% platelet loss—a blood clotting factor in the blood. My husband and I were in a trance. They told us they could give him transfusions, which might help temporarily, and they gave him high doses of the wonder medicine, Prednisone. This kept him from bleeding internally, and other than the bruises, he had no other symptoms. Never a nose bleed. No gum bleeding. No fever. And he had plenty of energy.

After treating my son for about seven months with transfusions and the Prednisone, they could see no real improvement. A specialist from Children's Memorial was brought in on the case. So many doctor's looked at him that it scared me. They didn't seem to know what steps to take. My son was in a local hospital and our hospital bills were huge. One day the specialist mentioned a case he was treating at the Illinois Research Hospital. I asked him if he could get my son in there. He was able to and we were very glad because Illinois Research is a learning hospital and doctors discuss similar cases, adding to their collective knowledge.

It was decided that they would remove the spleen. They told us it was a 50/50 chance of success, but without the spleen removed, Jimmy could not live. Besides, the transfusions were only good for a day and he was still bleeding internally.

It took quite a while to prepare him. They had to increase the Prednisone and feed him megadoses of vitamin K and vitamin C so he would not bleed too much during the operation. I remember asking the doctor how soon they would know if removing the spleen would cure him. He said they would take a blood test right in the operating room and would know immediately as other small lymph glands would take over the job of the spleen.

That had to be one of the longest days of my life. I don't even remember how long he was in the operating room. The waiting just about killed me. Finally, one of the doctors came to the waiting room and gave us a "thumbs up" sign. I broke down and cried. He said the platelet count was going up. That was the happiest day of my life. They had to keep Jimmy in the hospital to wean him off slowly from the Prednisone. I visited him every day, traveling from the far south side to the hospital on Taylor Street. I would drop off my little girl at my brother Carl's house and continue on to the hospital. After a month, it seemed like Jimmy was not getting any better or wasn't recuperating from the surgery. He ran a fever all the time, was very much overweight from the Prednisone, was depressed, and didn't eat very much. The Illinois Research is a good hospital, but it was very hard to catch a doctor to discuss the case. I wanted to know why Jimmy was so sick. One day I was able to catch up to a doctor who I'd seen in my son's room. He said he thought Jimmy had a blood clot in the lung caused by the mega vitamins given prior to the surgery to clot the blood. He told me they were going to take him back to surgery.

I looked at my young son and thought of all he had been through. He'd had many painful bone marrow tests through the breast bone and the doctor had said he'd been so brave. They did n't give him any anesthetic for those tests. And they had given him so many transfusions and taken so much blood from him that his little veins had collapsed and they had to do a cutdown on both ankles to get the needles in, but the transfusions were just of the platelets, and Illinois Research was one of the only hospitals in the area where they separated the blood back in 1958. Now he had to be told that they were going to take him back to surgery. I tried to explain that it was necessary as he was not recuperating as he should. He was so depressed. When any of the family came to see him he hid and did not want to see them. And during this time, his roommate, who he'd become very close to in the ten months in the hospital, died of Hodgkins' disease. That news made Jimmy even more depressed. He wouldn't even talk to his dad or me.

The surgery was scheduled for early morning and we took our little girl with us to wait in the visitor's room. This was another long wait. After surgery the doctor told us they had found the blood clot. He also said they had gone through the same incision made when they removed Jimmy's spleen and that they were not closing the opening. They said they would place a tube in the lung to allow the clot to drain, and he would have to be in the hospital for a couple more months.

In a short time, Jimmy was beginning to feel better, but wanted to know why he could not come home. A classroom was set up for children who had to stay in the hospital for long periods, but Jimmy never wanted to attend after he was able to get up and around. The teacher told me not to worry, that Jimmy was a bright boy and would probably not even have to take the second grade. She was going to recommend that they let him go on to the third grade when he came home.

When I finally brought him home he was still wearing the big bandage and had the drain tube in his lung. I dressed it daily until it was healed. We had to take him to both the blood and surgery outpatient clinics for the next three years, before he was officially discharged in 1962.

Looking back, I cannot tell you what else might have taken place in this world during Jimmy's illness. Those years are lost years. My every thought was filled with him. I'm sure any parent with a sick child must feel the same way. Jimmy is well now, but still has bleeding tendencies. He was in the Selective Service Lottery as Number 18, but was rated 4-F because of his blood problem. He is now married and has two daughters, but he learned a lot early in his young life.

The next couple of years were taken up with trying to get ourselves out of debt. Even though Illinois Research does not charge for the doctors, because we had insurance we still had to pay the hospital portion that the insurance didn't pay, and we were still paying various doctors for Jimmy's care prior to going into Illinois Research. We cashed in insurance policies, borrowed on my husband's insurance, and pinched pennies.

One day my older sister came to me and told me that my husband was having an affair with another one of my sisters. She also told me that our mother was letting them use her house to meet. I didn't believe her. I knew my husband had been staying out late, but he said he was working overtime as it was summer and it stayed light longer. I believed him. I had gone to work part time in a card factory near our house to help out with the bills. A neighbor watched the children. I found out later that he had been taking off work. When I approached my mother, she denied that she was in on the arrangement, but when I confronted my sister, she admitted they were involved and met at Mom's home. My husband and I separated for a time, but went back together when our daughter became ill.

Karen had gotten measles, but had never recuperated. She ran a constant fever even after the measles went away. The doctor came to the house and examined her. He said he heard a heart murmur and he thought she might have Rheumatic Fever. He said I should carry her to the washroom and the table, and not let her do anything strenuous until he could make arrangements to place her in the hospital for tests. She was admitted to St. George's Hospital. Our family doctor called in a heart specialist who determined she had a patent ductus. This is a small channel which short circuits blood from the pulmonary artery to the aorta in a fetus. For many children, it closes at birth or shortly thereafter. Karen's hadn't. And the blood flow had caused it to grow to the size of a woman's little finger, causing an enlargement of the left side of her heart. She was removed from St. George to Holy Cross hospital to be operated on. They cut out the channel and assured me she would be okay, that because she was still a child the enlarged heart should not be of concern and would not get larger. By the time she was grown, both sides would be fairly normal. Persons who have this condition do not live much past thirty if they are not operated on, so we were greatly relieved. She is fine today and is married and has one son.

During that time, with my daughter to worry about, I tried not to dwell on my husband's affair, but it was a very trying time for me. I learned I was pregnant with my third child and the apartment building we lived in was being sold. We would have to move again. This time we were able to scrape together a small down payment on a two-flat apartment which we bought together with another sister and her husband. We had worked things out financially and logistically, but I knew in my heart that I had doubts that we could work out the personal problems in our marriage.

I was about five months pregnant when we moved into the old building we'd purchased. It looked pretty good with the prior tenant's furnishings in it, but with everything out of it, the place was a mess—a real handyman's special.

My second daughter was born in November 1964. I went back to work in a bindery at nights and socked every cent into the apartment. We had to straighten doorways because the house had been raised years before, causing floors to sag. My husband was able to do all of this work. He plastered the hallway, the dining room, the bathroom, and the kitchen. The kitchen floor was taken up all the way down to the floor joists and new sub and finished floors were put in. Our marriage was still pretty rocky. We just tried to stay out of each other's way. Looking back, I don't think the hurt was as much with my sister or husband as with my mother. I had never lived with her since we were all separated and I always felt as if I was not one of her favorites. We were never close, although she told my youngest daughter that I was the only one of her children who had never talked back to her or sassed her.

When my baby was ten months old, my husband and I separated for good. I stayed in the apartment and he moved out. He lived for a time with my mother and stepfather. I received custody of the children and was to get $25.00 a week to cover support of the two girls. I waived support for Jimmy as I knew Bob couldn't afford any more and by this time Jimmy worked part time and paid most of his high school costs. Luckily, my portion of the mortgage was only $50.00 per month. I went to night school at a local high school to learn to type and transferred to Jones' Commercial and took up data processing, keypunch, and office machines. After completing these courses, a cousin urged me to go to a bank downtown where she worked and apply for a job. I needed night work because of the children. Having had petit mal epilepsy since I was about nine, I was on medication and had to tell the doctor who gave me the physical about it. She was sympathetic, as she had a dog who also had epilepsy, and she recommended they hire me.

Having had no school beyond eighth grade, the bank required that I take a test. I scored as high as the high school graduates and they hired me, but I think there might have been another reason. I knew how to keypunch and they had no keypunch operator. That might have had a greater impact on them offering me the job.

After two years of separation, I was divorced. We had been married twenty years. The support quit coming. I worked all the overtime I could to make ends meet. I was away from my children a lot. Jimmy was working in a pizza place and he helped out some. Two years after I divorced Bob, I remarried. My second husband had never been married and did not care for children, but only my youngest daughter was small. We were married for thirteen years and then divorced. I retired to Michigan in 1989, after twenty-one years at the bank, but I worked for four years more in a small oil company.

They say history repeats itself. My youngest now lives in Michigan and is divorced and raising two daughters. It is tough for her. I feel that living close by allows me to help her out if she needs it. I love my grandchildren and my children are good people, who are good parents, who take good care of their children.

My sister and I never have discussed her involvement with my husband again. I love her as much as I do my other sisters. My mother and I never discussed the issue again.

I haven't mentioned my father much. I never really knew him. He was a very private person. He never discussed the breakup of the family except one time when I was visiting and one of my kids was sick. He said, "What do you think your mother and I would do if one of you kids were sick all the time?" He also said he did not know how to take care of ten girls. I know it would have been a tough job.

I never got to know my brothers who are now both deceased. Jesse was in the Navy for twenty years, and came home very seldom. When he came home after his discharge, he didn't know one of us girls from another. He was such a handsome man. We started our family reunion when he came home from the service. Other than the once-a-year reunion, I didn't see much of him. Carl lived with my sister Virginia and I for a short time. He, too, had been in the Navy, but for only six years. After he was married we didn't visit with him much. Before he died, he and his wife had moved to central Illinois, where he lived until his death. I wish I had gotten to know both of my brothers, as well as my father, better.

I was nine years old when I went into The Cunningham Home and came out when I was fourteen. I credit the Home for teaching us to be responsible for ourselves, teaching us manners, and moral values. There has been some controversy recently regarding group homes. I have to state that we may not have had the love of caring parents, but what we learned in the Home has stayed with me throughout my life. I can never remember my mother ever hugging me or kissing me until I was well into adulthood. My father, on the rare occasions he came to visit, never kissed us. He always shook our hands. So there is no promise of loving parents, even if you live with them. I would rule out foster homes, as most of them only want the extra money they can receive and to claim them as dependents. In my opinion, the camaraderie of group homes between children is the next best thing for unwanted or abused children, or children from broken homes where neither parent is able to care for them.

Family Album

This photo may have been taken at Easter. Left to right: Back row: Carl and Jesse. Middle row: Dodo, Jenny (holding Doris) and Bede. Front row: Irma, Bertie, Phyllis, Vera, Audrey and Margy. Spring, 1940. Mattoon, Illinois.

Family Album

Back row, left to right: Jesse, Jenny, Dodo, Bede, and Carl; Middle row: Irma, Bertie and Margy; Front row: Vera, Audrey and Phyllis (holding Doris). Summer, 1940. Mattoon, Illinois. Below: Jenny and siblings.

Waggoner family in 1930. Glen (Dad), holding Jesse is at far left behind Grandpa Waggoner. Grandma Waggoner is in center behind man. Ruth (Mom) is standing second from right. Mattoon, Illinois. Date unknown.

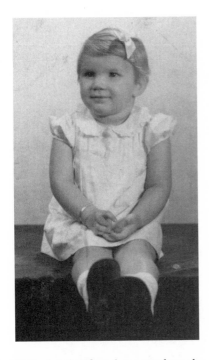

Doris shortly after she was adopted
by Dale and Amanda Replogle.
1942. Shirley Tremble Studio.

Our dad, Glen Waggoner, about
nineteen years of age. Probably
taken shortly before he was married
to Ruth Coen.

To the left: Margy and Richard
(holding Elmo). Chicago, Illinois.
Date unknown.

The Waggoner children in 1935.
From left to right: Back row: Carl (holding Phyllis) and Jesse;
Middle row: Jenny, Bede and Dodo; Front row, Margy, Bertie
and Irma. Taken at home near Paradise Lake, south of Mattoon,
Illinois. This location was not seen by Doris until the summer of
1996. She had visited the old house before it was torn down, but
it had been moved to a different location.

Family Album

The two (sometimes 3)-room house near Paradise Lake where we and our parents lived for more than a decade as it looked in 1993. South of Mattoon, Illinois. The building was torn down in 1993.

Side view of the house at Paradise as it looked in 1993. This building was moved several times. Sometime after the break-up of the family, our dad, Glen Waggoner, lived in it for awhile.

Carl and Jenny. Location unknown. About 1943.
Of the two brothers, Carl maintained the closer ties to most of the sisters throughout his life. He was known to help emotionally and on occasion, financially, when time and money permitted.

Grandma Lillie Coen was to play a significant role throughout our lives. She became Vera's guardian in 1942. This photo was taken at her home in Mattoon, Illinois. Date unknown.

152

The Coen children. From left to right: Back row: Aunt Bessie and Aunt Bonnie; Front row: Uncle Arthur, Uncle Donald and Mom (Ruth).

Carl and Jesse (Dale) with Grandma and Grandpa Coen at their Moultrie
Avenue home. Probably 1941. Mattoon, Illinois.

While both brothers maintained some contact with various sisters and their
parents, there were long gaps in communication—in some cases from eighteen to over thirty years. Bertie felt she never knew them well and virtually
all of Doris' rare contact with her brothers came in the last few years of their
lives. In fact, she remembers seeing Jesse on only two occasions.

Dixie School. Mrs. Hyland is the teacher. From left to right: Margy is in the front. Dodo is directly behind her in the third row; Bede is directly to the left of Dodo; and Jenny the second girl on the right (in front of four boys). Paradise. 1935.

Audrey with her new mother,
Lotta Belle Cole. Fall,
1942. Charleston,
Illinois.
Their's would be a
stormy relationship.

Billy at nine months old.
Margy gave birth to Billy in
1948. This photo was the last
contact she had with him for
forty-five years. This photo was
probably taken in Texas in 1949.
Dale and Amanda Replogle had
been asked to adopt Billy, but
thought it would be too confus-
ing for Doris. Instead, Doris
learned many years later, he was
adopted by a member of the
Frommel family.

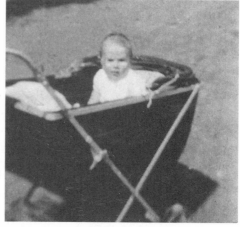

156

Family Album

Grandfather Robert Waggoner (son of Robert Waggoner and Margaret Armontrout) and Grandmother Iona (called Ona) Harrison Waggoner. The baby is Walter and the little girl is Faye. Our dad, Glen, was not born when this photo was taken. Date and location unknown.

At Left: Vera and Audrey in 1944, two years after Audrey was adopted and Vera went to live with Grandmother and Grandfather Coen in Mattoon, Illinois. These visits were rare.

At right, Margy meets her son for the first time in 45 years. Margy in center with grown-up Billy (Steve) on her right and her daughter Gloria on the left. Benton Harbor, Michigan. Photo by Carol Knapp. December 25, 1992.

Ten Sisters

From left to right: Phyllis, Vera, and Bertie in coats made by Mom, Ruth Coen Waggoner.

Probably about 1940 or 1941. Mattoon, Illinois.

Below, left: Doris and neighbor Jerry Walker in her playhouse on Division Street. The building was not much smaller than the house in Paradise. 1946. Charleston, Illinois.

Below, right: Phyllis at about three years of age. At Paradise, south of Mattoon, Illinois.

From left to right: Bertie, Dodo, Margy and Bede. Probably taken in Chicago in early mid-1940's. Notice that three of the girls appear to be dressed alike.

Dixie School with Mrs. Hyland. Left to right: Fifth row: Jenny is far right at end of row; Fourth row: Dodo is fifth from left; Bede is seventh from left; Third row: Bertie is at end of row by boy; Irma is fourth from left, and Margy is second from right between tall girl and girl with hands crossed.

Carl, his wife Bea, and little Carl.
Date and location unknown.

Carl spent his retirement years with Bea at Paradise Lake, south of Mattoon, Illinois, not far from his original home site. Fishing and gardening were his avid hobbies. His sudden death, in the summer of 1995, was a motivating factor in writing this book.

Carl, Dodo, Jenny and Jesse. Probably about 1942 or 1943. The girls were helping a lady clean house and they stopped long enough to take this picture. Mattoon, Illinois.

Bede, Jenny and Dodo. This photo was taken in Mattoon just before Bede
went to the Cunningham Home in Urbana, Illinois. 1942.
This photo of Bede is often mistaken for Doris—even by Doris!

Carl, Chet's sister, Eleanor, Bede and Chet at Bede and Chet's wedding.
October 11, 1945. Chicago, Illinois.

Bede. About 1944 or 45.
Chicago, Illinois.
Below Jenny about 1943.

Audrey in 1942, shortly after she
was adopted by Jess and Lotta
Belle Cole. Charleston, Illinois.

Irma, Phyllis and Margy. Date and location unknown. Note the matching suit, a common custom.

Vera, playing
Indian at Grandma
and Grandpa
Coen's.
About 1944.
Mattoon, Illinois.

Below, left to
right: Doris and
her cousins, Janet,
Carolyn and
Roberta. 1993.
During her child-
hood, Doris spent
many weekends
and most holidays
with these three.

Doris and doll, Mary,
About 1947. Charleston,
Illinois.

Below, right: Vera in
black-face miming Al
Jolson. About 1950.
Mattoon, Illinois.

Family Album

Doris with new parents, Dale and Amanda Replogle at their home on Division Street, Charleston, Illinois. February 11, 1946. The table was made by Audrey's father, Jess Cole.

Vera and Audrey. 1946, possibly taken at a fair.

Left to right: Phyllis, Bertie, Irma, Margy and Bede (?) at Cunningham home.

Grandma Iona Harrison (Waggoner) front row center. Date unknown.

Family Album

Chet and Bede, friend and Dodo. Chicago, Illinois. Date unknown.
Below, left: The dress Doris wore to the courthouse in 1942. To the right, the
first dress her new parents, Dale and Amanda Replogle, bought her.

Thornburn Junior High. Miss Ewald's 7th Grade. Margy is in front row, fourth from left. May 1944. Urbana, Illinois.

Dodo and Don's wedding. May 20, 1944. Chicago, Illinois. They were married in the church office on Halsted Street by Rev. Floyd Hoover.

Below: Jenny and Clarence Rackley in front of the fireplace at the Arkansas farm. About 1947.

Margy is at far right in back row. Thornburn School. 1945.

Family Album

Dodo and Jenny jitterbugging on the roof tops of Chicago, Illinois. About 1944.

Below: From left to right: Phyllis, Jesse's son Dale, Sam Endsley (neighbor), Margy, and Jesse's wife Betty. Arkansas, 1947.

Uncle Nolan and Grandma Coen.
Mattoon, Illinois. Date unknown.

Doris with "Ruth" on a rare visit.
About 1955 or 1956.
Charleston, Illinois.

Photo at right is Audrey at 14.

Family Album

Thornburn Junior High Minstrel Show. Urbana, Illinois. 1945 or 1946.
From left to right: Bertie, Margy and friends.

Doris. In Glen Ellyn. 1978

Ten Sisters

Dad (Glen Waggoner) shortly before his death.

Doris and Harry. In the Lutheran Church, Charleston, Illinois. Wedding ceremony performed by daughter Teresa's father-in-law, Rev. Robert Hackler. May 28, 1988.

Opposite page: Standing: Bede, Mom, Grandma Coen; Sitting: Margy, Dodo Irma; Vera in front. 1946.

Mom and Marvin Roberts. County Fair. Charleston, Illinois. August, 1952.

Five generations! From left to right: Dodo and Don's daughter, Sunday;
Dodo; Mom; Sunday's daughter, Lisa; and Grandma Coen.

Bertie. Probably
in Michigan
about 1994.

Family Album

1957 Reunion. From left to right: Dodo, Vera, Doris, Phyllis and Audrey. Mattoon, Illinois.

Below: Vera and Bill Barber on their wedding day. Alaska.

Margy, Mom and Phyllis.
Date and location unknown.

Opposite page. Paul Kopeck,
Bertie, Mom, and Margy.
Chicago, Illinois.

Below: Standing: Phyllis and
Bertie. Front: Irma, Dad and
Margy. Taken while the girls
were in Cunningham Home.
He took them out for dinner,
purchased new clothes and
had this picture taken. 1943
or 1944.

Dixie School. 1939. South of Mattoon, Illinois. Left to right: Third row: Far left, Irma; Second row: Bertie is first girl on far left. Another girl stands between her and Phyllis, and Margy is second girl from right.

Dad. Date and location unknown.

Jesse. 18-years-old. Mom's diary
verified that Jesse sent money
home frequently, in sums of $3
and $5, to help with the family.

At right: Elmo and Gloria on
Margy's first car.

In Chicago: Chet Brniak, Bede, Carl, Don Hart, and Dodo.
Date and Location unknown. Probably in Chicago.
Below: Dodo and Don on their 50th wedding anniversary.

Family Album

Above: Margy and Dodo. Date and location unknown.

At left: Doris' mother, Amanda Replogle. At Doris and Harry's wedding. Charleston, Illinois.1988.

At right: Margy with Ruth. About 1990.

Audrey in 1949.
Probably taken in
Charleston, Illinois.

Below: Jesse, Betty
Golden, and Jenny.
Probably taken short-
ly after Jesse and
Betty's wedding.
Chicago, Illinois.
Date unknown

Tearing down our home in Paradise. Dodo, Irma and Phyllis helped. 1993. Brother-in-law, Dick Ferguson salvaged wood and made each sister and Carl a momento from it.

Doris and her parents, Dale and Amanda Replogle with home-made travel trailer, on the way to Texas—1948. The trip may have had to do with the adoption of Billy.

187

Jenny and Dodo 1942. Note on back says: "Dad aren't we cute. If they don't hurry up and send us to Chicago, we will get out along the slab and do this, hitch-hike. [signed] Dodo and Jenny."

Presumably written in Mattoon, Illinois.

Doris' seventh birthday party held at Aunt Pearl and Uncle Chalk's on Adams Street, Charleston, Illinois. From left to right: Top: ? Brant, Audrey Cole (sister), Betty Gose; Third row: Joyce Lang and Sandy Calhoun, Betty Blagg; Second row: Mary Sims, Jahalia Cobble, Carol Catron; First row: Rosemary Gordon, Karen Richardson, Doris Replogle and Sharon Brant. 1947.

Family Album

At the 1995 Cunningham Children's Home Reunion. From left to right: Standing: Bede, Phyllis, Margy; Seated: Bertie and Irma. Urbana, Illinois.

Margy and Richard. Waterveliet, Michigan. Date unknown.

Irma and Mike at daughter Mary and Dave's wedding.

Mom with Carl in his CTA uniform. He drove for the Chicago Transit Authority for thirty years. Chicago, Illinois.

Family Album

Vera and Phyllis. A note on the back says: "How Vera and Phyllis looked when I first met them." The note was written by Audrey. March, 1952. Chicago, Illinois.

Doris with her parents, Dale and Amanda Replogle. 1944.

Below: Left to right: Dodo, Bede and Jenny. Early 1930's.

Elmo, Mom, Gloria, Margy and chickens. 1954. Michigan.

Mom and Marvin's twenty-fifth wedding anniversary in Chicago.
From left to right: Standing: Audrey, Phyllis, Margy, Bede, Dodo,
Jenny, Carl and Mom. Kneeling: Doris, Bertie, Irma and Vera.
This was the first time most of the sisters had seen Doris' family.
The only one missing was Jesse. 1974.

A recent photo of
Bertie with Leroy
Hickmott.

Audrey and her father, Jess Cole a
year after her adoption.
Charleston, Illinois. 1943.

Above: Margy, Richard and Elmo.
Early 1950's.

At left: Doris, Ruth, and Grandma
Coen with Jesse's son, little Dale.
About 1953. Charleston, Illinois.

Mom and Marvin at their twenty-fifth wedding anniversary with Doris' youngest, Michelle. Chicago, Illinois. 1974.

Top right: A recent photo of Phyllis and Dick. Mattoon, Illinois.

A recent photo of Audrey and Bob.

Family Reunion. The only time all twelve of us were together after 1940. From left to right: Back row: Stepmother Effie, Dad behind her. Carl, Jenny, Bede, Doris, Audrey, Jesse (Dale), Stepfather Marvin, Mom standing in front of him; Front row: Vera, Irma, Dodo, Margy, Phyllis and Bertie. 1975.

This photo, reproduced from the original award-winning article by Bill Lair published in the *Mid-Illinois Newspapers Inc.* was taken in April 1993. We are in approximately the same formation we were on that day in March 1942. From left to right: Back row: Virginia Ruth (Jenny), Doris Evon Jean, Rhita Jean (Bede), Deloris Maxine (Dodo) and Audrey Faye Lee; Mary Margaret (Margy) is in the center; Front row: Roberta Pauline (Bertie), Irma Joan, Phyllis Ann and Vera Mae.

Again, we thank all those who helped gather photos for this project.

Phyllis Ann

(Phyllis)

Dedicated To Those Who Come After

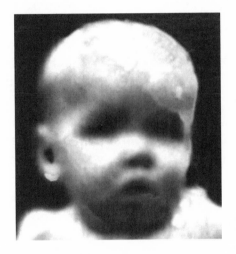

Ten Sisters

I'll tell you about the bad times—and the good times.

I was born the seventh daughter the day before Mom and Dad's anniversary, which was the twentieth of February. I remember very little about home in Mattoon. Just bits and pieces. I remember the tire ride down the hill behind our house, Dad burying a box with a tiny little baby in it, and a fight that Dad and Mom had—and later them embracing. And I remember our fears that in the night someone would get drunk and come down to our house and the time Jesse got a big, fat lip from wasps that he was going to destroy. I recall candy being brought home to us, the kind that had the little initial rings around it and, of course, I always yearned for that initial "P" ring because the first one that Dad brought home, Pauline got. I can remember, too, when the girls were our babysitters. None of us wanted Bede because she didn't know how to fix our hair. Another time, the yard flooded, don't know why or just what happened.

My memory of the Courthouse that day in 1942 is limited to the hallway and the steps, where we had our picture taken. When I look at myself in that picture, I wonder if I was angry or just flabbergasted or bewildered. Attorney Kidwell and another lady took Irma and me to the Cunningham Children's Home at Urbana. During the ride, we just kept asking, it seemed like such an awful long ride, "Are we there, yet? Are we about there?"

When we got there, two of us were to get out, me and Irma. Those buildings looked so big, so scary. I don't know what I thought, but they had a bad time trying to get Irma and me out of that car. They finally got me out and I stood and cried for Irma to get out. She kept hopping back and forth across the seats and using some of her favorite language. I just kept crying and crying. It took four people to get Irma out of the car. I was so relieved when they got her out of there because some others had a hold of me.

I guess it was Margy and Bertie who came to the home next, Now I might stand to be corrected here. I just remember that they

198

came, and Bede was there, which made five of us. We really had a good time.

Everything at the Cunningham Home was done very orderly and precise. We were responsible for personal cleanliness, our beds, and area closets. They took me to the Miles dormitory first, then I was moved to Humble dormitory. Fifty white beds stood in neat rows. We had access to the basement playroom on rainy or bad weather days. There were lots of doll houses down there and, of course, all of us girls wanted to play with them. We were taught to share.

Some of the girls had helpers, by this I mean special people sending gifts at special times of the year. I received a very large valentine box of candy, birthday gifts, Easter baskets, and, of course, Christmas presents. One of my favorite Christmas presents was a dark-haired doll with all pink satin clothes, but I did not get that or other personal items upon leaving the home.

I was selected for adoption many times, but I would not go without one of my sisters. There was one family by the name of Hughes. They sent me the most beautiful boxes of clothes and other pretty things. Of course, it was always intended that I share with everybody in the dorm. And then a sailor whose wife was crippled wanted to adopt me, too. He was stationed at Urbana. Irma and I went there. I would never go without one of the girls. One time a Professor Fawcett got me to go to their house by telling me that Pauline was coming later. All night long I cried and waited for Bertie to come. She didn't, of course. When I got up in the morning, I threw a good fit, cussing and kicking.

Then I was punished. I didn't get to go to any Christmas parties that year. I was put to bed while the other kids went to the different sororities, fraternities, and the sailor's base. It really hurt my feelings. I had to lay there and look at the clouds. That gave me a lot of time to think. I thought about a lot of things. Of course, I was pleased to see the kids return from their Christmas parties and I was eager to see what they got. I really never felt any envy of the kids because I knew it was of my own doing.

I often sassed and would receive bread and milk and then had to go right to bed.

In the Home, to get to Washington school, we had to walk across the pasture, then we walked across the stile. The steps went up over the fence and back down. My favorite teacher was a Miss Irwin. I thought she was beautiful even if she did report my "Honey" note to the matron. One day, coming home after school, the matron met me at the door where she usually passed out candy bars. She asked, "Well, Phyllis, what kind of candy bar do you like?" I said I didn't know and it really didn't matter. She said, "I'll tell you what the teacher tells me. You wrote a honey note to your little boyfriend today, so I'm going to give you a little *Bit O'Honey.*" I hate those things even today. I did have a favorite boyfriend, though.

Dad often visited us and would take us out to eat, or for ice-cream, or shopping. One time he bought us new outfits and had our pictures taken with him.

Mother had remarried during our years in Cunningham and took us last ones, Bertie and I, out of the Home in June 1945. Our first train ride was to the Coen reunion in Mattoon. It was fascinating. I loved that train trip and today I still love a train trip, if I have someone to talk to and to share.

While we were at Cunningham, our sisters' lives were changing. Our sister Dodo had a baby. "Sunday Gal" was born one September, on the nineteenth, which was a thrill to all of us—to see our new little niece. Chet and Bede were married in October of 1945. I remember Bede in a blue gown. We sat back on the side-lines taking it all in and then they left, I don't remember where, but us kids were there for the wedding.

200

Phyllis Ann

Paul Kopeck was Mom's second husband. He was good to us kids. He took us a lot of places—always on a streetcar—which were *looooo*ng rides. He would take us to the zoo and Riverview. Many, many Sundays were spent at Riverview Park in Chicago, up on Diversey and Belmont. Another thing Paul would do was to wash our heads. And then he would beat our hair to death with a towel. He said it was good for us.

But we were afraid of Paul, because he had such big massive hands and he seemed, thinking about it now, like he was two people in one—he was so big, although there was only one time I recall getting a good spanking. I thought it was with a belt, but it could have been some kind of switch. That taught me well!

Paul and Mother's marriage was getting very rocky. Everybody moved away, going to different sister's houses to live. Bede and Chet had moved to Walnut Street in Chicago and I went to live with them. It wasn't easy. Chet was a big and demanding man. He often punished me by having me kneel on my knees or hold my arms in the air for long periods of time. One time, it was as long as two hours. And sometimes he would send me back and forth to the store until he'd made up his mind what he wanted. Somewhere during this time, I lived with Aunt Bonnie, Mom's sister, to help take care of the first set of Scott twins, Aunt Bonnie's grandchildren. It meant another change of school.

Irma was living with Deloris, right down the hall from our apartment. I stayed with Chet and Bede until I moved over to 19th Street with Mother, where she had moved when she separated from Paul. But only for a short time, because Paul and Mom had gotten together again and bought a rocky farm in Arkansas.

The next year, 1946, a bunch of us were together, again, at the Coen Reunion in Mattoon. I remember Vera, and I think she and I were dressed alike that year. We had those little blue navy-looking outfits on. Oh we were proud! We were really proud!

Ten Sisters

Shortly after the reunion, we headed out for Arkansas in a big truck. Us kids and furniture were kept hidden in the back, under a tarp, and they would occasionally switch around and let one of us ride up in the front of the truck, which wasn't very pleasant either, because they had somebody extra to go along and ride with us. To this day, I do not remember who that was. Paul and someone else was driving us down there.

Besides them, there was Vera, Margy, Bertie, Irma, and me. We thought we were never going to get there. We thought the trip from Champaign to Mattoon was long. My God, this felt like it took days. It did take one whole day to get down there.

As a young child, you accept what happens. You don't do much about it. You just enjoy the good times with your sisters. That was the main thing, that I was with the sisters, and I know that we were very glad to see Vera when we got out of the Home, and on this trip, we were together.

We finally got to Arkansas. I think we broke ground back to the farm house. I don't think it had been traveled on for twenty or thirty years. It was called the Old Nash Farm. The bluffs gave way to smaller bluffs, and just rocks and not much else. Carl came down shortly after and he said, "Why these people down here don't even know that World War II is over with, they are so backward and so reclusive."

It was quite impressive. We butchered the pigs when we got down there and then we began cleaning up the yard. The dewberries that grew close to the ground were real good eating. Muskadines (wild grapes) were plentiful. The boards on the house couldn't hold paste. We had to tack things up. But all in all, it didn't look too bad by the time it was all straightened up. A little touch here an a little touch there, and everybody cooperating—and then it began—Chores!

Being a younger one, I probably was able to go into town and it seemed like Bertie and I went every day, walking two miles into Drasco for groceries, and two miles back. And we always needed groceries! Mr. Southerland allowed us credit month to month.

Mom and Paul finally left to go back to Chicago to work. After that, the only means to eat were Betty's allotment checks from Jesse. I thank Betty to this day for sharing with us.

Uncle Nolan came down and Carl was there. When Mom left Jenny came down, too. But before long Bertie hurt her knee and she headed back to Mattoon.

I remember the dances we had. I remember the boys coming and tying up their horses on the fence and Uncle Nolan making them repair that fence because the horses had jerked trying to get away and tore it down. We did have a radio. Thank God for that, because it was our connection to the outside world. It was a battery radio and we could hear the *Grand 'ole Opry* on Saturday nights. That was the only time I remember listening to the radio.

We had a big garden in Arkansas. Mom and Uncle Nolan toiled to get those horses to plow up the garden and work the land. I do remember that, but people there were suspicious of us Yankees. Our horses and cows were poisoned and they tell me the old place burned down after we left and all that is standing is the fireplace.

I don't know when we went back to Chicago. It was sometime after Bertie and Irma went back to Mattoon. "Oh happy day," or so I thought. Joe Bum and Clarence Rackley (Jenny's future husband) took us back to Illinois. I had left my security behind and I began a whirl-wind life until I was married.

I really remember Mom more in Chicago than anywhere else. She had moved to an apartment. I moved in with her and Marvin. She had just met Marvin—barely met him—and some of us had a hard time accepting him. I was with them awhile, but I finally ended up with Chet and Bede. Bertie was in Chicago and she and I were gone too long someplace and Mom set our clothes out and wouldn't let us in. Bertie and I went over to Chet and

Bede's, crying and angry all the way. I know Chet couldn't really afford to keep us, but he would not refuse us. Even after the court gave Mom custody of some of the girls again, we all went home with an older sister. It didn't seem to matter where we ended up, as long as we were in contact with one another. Later in life, when I became a foster parent, I couldn't emphasize that enough to the foster care workers—that it was so important to us kids that we had each other.

From then on I lived here and there. Besides Bede and Chester, and Bertie and Bob, and Aunt Bonnie, I lived with brother, Carl, and his wife, Bea ; at Dodo and Don's; and even over in Michigan at Margy and Richard's—whoever would have me when Mother got upset or moved to a too-small apartment. Periodically, Mom would come and get me and make me go with her. It was back and forth, back and forth. Finally, Mom married Marvin. By this time we were all very fond of him. After they were married, I went down to live with Dad again. I was sixteen the last time Mom came after me. It was at Dad's and he became very angry with her, but I went. It was only for a few months, though, and then I went to live with Bertie and her husband, Bob, again.

Bertie and I had changed schools eight different times in two years. I was in the Longfellow School in Mattoon for the longest period of time. They tore it down and the next time I saw the spot where it had been, it gave me a sense of, "well, there will be no more changes to that old school again; no more questions either."

I went to Mattoon to live with Dad for the final time in the fall of 1952. He still wasn't married. Jenny and Clarence and their baby, Carol, came through Mattoon on their way to Michigan and my life began taking a turn.

My stays with Dad were lucky for me. Dad loved the Coles County Fair, so we went often where we would sometimes see Doris. We always saw Audrey. She stayed at the fair all day long. We had great times, because Audrey and I loved the Carnival rides.

Phyllis Ann

I was able to see Doris and Audrey at their homes, too. Dad seemed to keep in touch with their parents. They were both so cute. It was always exciting to see them—to see any of my sisters.

I met Dick Ferguson on December 6, right after he had just gotten out of service. I was quite impressed with him and I guess he was with me, too. He was a chunky little guy at that time. Dad always said that Dick would never amount to a "durn," but he did in spite of being a motorcyclist. But Dad ended up being proud of him and Mom was very proud of him, too. She often told him how much she appreciated him. He was always kind to Mother and to Dad and never said anything, you know. He would comment to other people that she didn't seem to be satisfied. I think it was just that Mom didn't treasure material things. She treasured her family. I realize that now more than ever.

I was living with Dad when I met Richard. I was dating his friend, so I lined up a date for Dick to come at 7:00 p. m. and Gene to come at 6:30 p.m. That way, I could get rid of Gene and would be ready for Dick. Dad just had a fit, and said I couldn't do that. But that's what happened and from then on we've been an item. Of course, we didn't get married until January of 1954. Dad even allowed us to stay with him for awhile. We paid the electric and food bill.

Vera stood up with me but not without a fight. We had to rise above suspicion that we did not have Glen Ariel waiting over in Charleston. Secretly, they were an item, too.

I had kept in touch with Vera. I remember coming down to Mattoon once when Vera was doing her Al Jolson Act with a little group. I thought it was wonderful that someone took an interest and wanted her to do that and it made me feel close to her again. Vera had gotten involved with Glen Ariel just before I came back to Mattoon. I was disappointed when she got involved, because she and I had always said that we were going to live together in our own apartment. We had visions of sugar plums, but not with the same couples, not with the same person.

About eight months after we were married, we had the opportunity to buy this house in Neoga, Illinois. We tore it down, board by board, hardwood floors and all. We salvaged the good oak wood and rebuilt a four-room house after buying a third of Dad's acreage. We didn't have any bathroom so we had an outside GEM. It was alright and we stayed there six years, living behind Dad.

Because Richard was from around this area, we have always stayed in and around Coles County. Deborah, our first child, was born in 1955. In 1961, we sold our little four-room house on Magnet Hill and moved eight miles East to Charleston. Richard's folks lived there. Paula was born that same year. Life was a lot of bumps, grinds and growing pains, and yet we decided to become foster parents. That was a very interesting venture. I look back now and wonder why I ever wanted to do it. Was I wanting to share how important it really was to keep brothers and sisters together? The foster service that had Elaine and Ethyl, our first two foster children, wanted to know how I felt about separating them and I said no, that I thought they should be together. I prayed that everyone would accept each other and they sure did. All in all, we cared for nineteen kids. Within seven and one-half years, we crossed our lives with those nineteen lives.

Dick worked for the General Electric Company for thirty-six years. When it got close to his retirement, we began looking for a place to live on the water. We had a little camper on Mattoon Lake, but we weren't going to live in that the rest of our lives. We began by looking at different lakes in Tennessee and in Kentucky. I finally told him: "No. we can't live that far away. Our children aren't wealthy and they wouldn't be able to travel as much as we would want to see them." So we ended up in Neoga, the same town where we had torn down the little house for materials to make one of our own. I remember the very spot!

Phyllis Ann

When I think of Mother, my whole life was wrapped in the one year I was alienated from my mom. In all honesty, I couldn't figure out if she loved me. At times I felt she did and at other times, I felt she didn't. When we lived in Charleston, Mother moved to Charleston, too. She married John Golden and they moved in next door to us. We had a lot of hugs. We had a lot of spiritual moments and I know Mom is at peace, but it still seems to all be wrapped up in that one year. After she died, I ran across these few sheets of paper that Mom wrote. Although it was just written on scratch paper, it looked like she had started writing her life story. Since I never understood her very well—maybe none of us did—I think I should add her own words here.

My first proposal was from a twelve-year-old neighbor at the fair in Charleston. Our Grandma Gee always brought a big basket of food [to the fair] and of course we always were with her and Grandpa Gee.

I used to love going to school. I started in the Teacher's college at Old Main (now Eastern Illinois University) on Lincoln and Fourth. We lived then on Cooper Street, across the street from our best friends, Paul, Myra and Ruth Stites. . . .Their dad made woven rugs. I loved to watch him make them. Ruth Stites used to get under our kitchen window and call for me to come out to play but Dad always made me finish the dishes....

Arthur, Helen, and me used to hurry home on Fridays so we could go to Grandma's...two miles from our place. We would run down Hog Farm Road, which is now University Avenue in Charleston. One time Mom was playing the organ and Dad was playing his "squeeze box" so they didn't hear me cry. . . .my shoestrings were in hard knots. Arthur heard me and came to my rescue. Dad and Mom played after supper quite often.

. . . .When I was ten, we moved to Mattoon, and I started to Bennett School. Our Principal was Annie Johnson. She was my mother's teacher when she was a little girl in a school south of Charleston. Dad worked for Grandpa Gee and that is where he met and married my Mother (Grandma Coen). She was only 15 and Dad was 26 years old.

I remember one time Dad came home at noon and asked us kids what we would rather do, go to school or go to a circus that was in town—Ringling Bros. . . .Well, I guess you know what we did! We were so happy that he took us! I never forgot that he worked so hard and didn't have time to show much affection to us kids. Mom, though, relied on Dad's advice for everything.

Bonnie and Arthur always thought Dad favored me, but he never did. They would tell him I did something and I got sent to bed with no supper. We laughed about it after we had grown up.

A girl at our school always pissed on me. So Dad told her he would give me a quarter to whip her—and I did. Arthur missed his promotion at school and I went home crying. Momma asked me didn't I pass, and I said yes I did, but Arthur didn't.

I thought, when I was little, that Grandma Gee never washed her dishes. But she always did them right after the meal and set the table and put a table cloth over it.

Phyllis Ann

. . . .My cousins lived near Grandma Gee. One time I was sitting on Grandpa's horse and Donald threw a corn cob, hit the heel of the horse and I took a wild ride. No saddle. No bridle. I hung onto the mane and stayed on until we reached Gramp's barn. That horse ran right into the barn and stopped, after a run of about a mile or more.

. . . .After we moved to Mattoon I never got to see much of my Grandpa, but Grandma came to visit us and always brought her sewing. She made lots of quilts (like Jenny does). I used to make quilts and comforters, but I never got to keep anything and neither did the children. Well, I about covered my life to age eighteen. Of course, I worked at whatever I could.

Once I was working for the McNair's on 33rd and Western [in Mattoon]. I didn't draw my wages for three weeks. I expected to go the the Fair in Charleston. I had never been there alone and I had three weeks pay [coming] and figured on having a good time, but Dad said it wasn't safe for me to go alone. I was 18 and knew how to take the Interurban but he made me give him the money so he could take care of it. Well, he did! He paid both our fares over and back and to the fairgrounds. When we got there, he gave me five cents and I never saw him again until lunch time. Then he brought me a hot dog and disappeared until time to go home. I never saw anymore of my $18.00 and never quite forgave Dad for that.

I got acquainted with Glen after I left home and went to live with my sister, Bonnie. Aunt

Ten Sisters

Blanche and Aunt Vivian went to Dixie School and they liked to stop at Bonnie's. They asked me to go home with them. We saw Glen [Waggoner] on the road and now the rest is history.

When I look back on the Home, I believe it was the salvation part for us kids. We had good memories from there, more good memories than we did otherwise. My sisters and I went back to the Cunningham Home for the 75th Anniversary and the 100th Anniversary. We saw the Zike kids from Mattoon and the Henderson kids. When we were at the home, it was was run by the Methodist Church. Now it's run by the State of Illinois. It has become so liberal that it's almost sad. I do think regimental living is good. I think that is why guys can come out of the service and be so disciplined about their own lives, most of the them, and they can carry on through life, because it's not what happened yesterday, but what happens today and tomorrow.

Now Dick and I have been married for forty-two years. Besides our two daughters, we have nine grandchildren, two step-grandchildren—among them a set of twins. Dick and I both enjoy crafts, fishing, and sightseeing. We are in retirement, but Dick, of course, went and got himself a part time job. I asked him how come. He said. "I've got to have something to do in the winter."

We now live at Lake Mattoon. I'm very glad for most of the experiences up 'till this time in my life. But there were some very bitter times—including the alienation I felt from Mom—an alienation that went by the wayside in the last year of her life when she was so sick. It came from my closeness to Dad and so often having to defend my love for him.

I thank God for my family, and for sweet little Grandma Coen, and for my sisters and their husbands. And I thank my sister Vera, for the little initial "P" ring.

Vera Mae

(Vera)

Dedicated to Mom

Ten Sisters

My name is Vera Barber, born Vera Mae Waggoner, the tenth in the family, and eighth of ten sisters. My birth took place on the "hottest day of the year" Mom said. A scorching July 20, 1936. I understand I was named by my grandfather Coen (Mom's dad), and for many years I didn't like it. I always wondered why he named me Vera, but as I grew older, I've learned to love my name. I understand that in Greek it means truth. I like that.

I grew up in my grandparents' house, although I can see from pictures and hear from my sisters that I was at home often. The story I heard from Grandma was that I caught the whooping cough at nine months old and that they took me home because the doctor said I should be closer to town. My sisters say that my grandparents were fond of me and would keep taking me home with them. I choose to believe that both stories are true.

I was six years old when the family separated. I don't remember anything of the picture taken on the courthouse steps in 1942, but I can tell by the look on each of our faces that the circumstances were out of our hands, that this was an unhappy event. I did not have the trauma of total disruption some of my sisters talk about it, probably because I came to the courthouse with my grandparents and left with them. But the separation was real to me. Emotions are a strange thing—they can lay buried for a long time and reveal themselves unexpectedly like they did for me the day we returned to the courthouse for a second picture-in 1993. All I could think of was how happy I was to be there and how ironic that it took Mom's death to bring it about.

I don't recall the house in Paradise, either. But I do know that when everyone came down with the measles, I was right there to catch them, too. Mom kept a little diary in 1941 and she named who got them, and when. It reads: "Saturday June the seventh 1941, Margy, Bertie, Vera, Phyllis, and Audrey broke out (measles)." So it was never like I was an only child. I always knew I came from a big family, I don't remember seeing my sisters much. Not until I went to live with Mom and Paul, my stepfather, in Chicago. I saw my sisters at the Coen reunions. One year my sister Phyllis and I wore look-alike outfits. I have a picture of us with Bede, her husband Chet; Dodo, and her husband Don at the park on the swings. Reunions were a regular part of growing up in a small town.

I seldom saw my dad. He worked in town and dropped by to see me once in awhile. He talked with my grandparents and with my Uncle Nolan. I hung around, but we did not have too much to say. Our conversations improved as I got older when I visited him when in town—after I had a family of my own.

Mom was not only in and out of my life pretty often, she was always bringing people here, or taking me to visit others. When she was married to Marvin, they went somewhere every weekend to see one of the girls, or Carl. She would come to Mattoon on some weekends and I always looked forward to seeing her. Sometimes it meant returning to Chicago with her. Other times we visited other relatives nearby. When we were together sometimes she would embarrass me because she talked so loud and was so frank in public. Mom's voice was strong and she used it to defend herself and others if she thought it was necessary. Life was not quiet with her. I am like that, now!

It seemed Mom never let anything stand in her way once she made up her mind. After Marvin died she stayed home a lot more, but then her phone bill went up. I used to call her and she would tell me she was in the bathroom! She had had a phone put in there! That was Mom.

The unusual nature of my family came to me quite obviously when I was in school and had to fill out forms where they asked so many statistical questions: my name, Vera Waggoner, the name of my mother—hers was either Ruth Kopeck or Ruth Roberts—and then the name of my guardian, and that was Lillie B.

Coen. My birthplace was Paradise Township, but my home was Mattoon, except that my mother lived in Chicago. Most of the kids had just one of everything. I had to take time and spell it all out. I hated that. It was just tiresome and a reminder of our brokenness.

The earliest memory of my surroundings is a dark leather couch in the living room of Grandma and Grandpa Coen's house, with two or three chairs pushed up along side of it so I would not fall off. This must have been my bed until I moved into Grandma's bed after Grandpa died. I don't know if that is when I started sucking my two fingers, but despite all the remedies offered and bribes they made to me, I did not quit until I was about twelve years old!

Gram had the same pictures on the walls though the years. One of Jesus in Gethsemane and a portrait of my great-grandmother and great-grandfather. There was always a calendar from our insurance man, Grover something, and later, a picture of Uncle Nolan in his navy uniform.

Grandpa always wore a dark jacket and a hat on his head when he was outside. But inside, he revealed a full head of silver. He kept wearing the same overalls (so Grandma growled), and he never buttoned the whole jacket—just that top button. He sat in front of a living-room window most of the time and chewed tobacco. His chair was a sawed-off rocker and he had a spittoon along side of it. That ugly thing—he never hit it so you can imagine what the wall looked like! (Grandma's mumbling and facial expressions said a lot!).

Grandma—I can still see her sitting at the kitchen table reading the *Upper Room*, a little devotional book. I would listen to her and when I got older, I would read them, too. There were many times when she woke up with a sick headache and would sit in the dining room with a cold cloth on her head. She suffered from gall bladder trouble. I used to comb and set her hair. She had lovely white hair. She was a pretty woman.

Vera Mae

We had no phone. We used to play the radio a lot, especially in the evening. *The Grand Old Opry* and *WLS Barn Dance* were favorite programs of ours. Grandma had a book from the WLS days that showed pictures of Lulu Belle and Scottie, Mac and Bob, and Rex Allen Sr. I loved that book. We had few other books in the house. Gram's hymnal and her Bible were used as often as anything. I was not a reader when I was in school, but I love books now, and read them more than once.

One of my very favorite times was when Grandma would open the trunk and we went over each and every item that she had saved through the years. A porcelain-headed doll that was hers as a young girl, clothes that had belonged to our grandma Gee—like an old grey dress, a dark plaid shawl and high-topped shoes that she had worn. There was a small box that once held a knife and fork for each of her children, an autograph book that belonged to my Grandpa, an old long wallet that belonged to Abraham Lincoln (she would show me what were supposed to be his initials in it.) I believed it! There were old tin-type pictures of Grandpa when he was a cowboy and pictures of Roy, the son she and Grandpa lost.

I was allowed to touch these treasures and we would talk, but I can't remember discussing anything about my folks or my sisters. I'm not sure why. Today I ask about everything—I wish I had then. I got the impression that if I asked about them, it meant I wasn't happy there, or loved my parents more. I'm not sure Grandma and Grandpa had those thoughts, but if they did, they would have been justified, for as soon as I reached seventeen, I did go to Chicago and stay, reaching out for my "own" family.

Gram never did have much, but the things that she did have she kept close to her heart. One was a jewelry box that held what seemed like a hundred hankies. Mostly gifts. She could tell you where each one came from and when. I loved for her to open it up because it smelled like lilac and cedar lining—I can still smell it today.

Ten Sisters

Those early years, before Uncle Nolan came, the house was so dark. It was an ugly, mustard color on the outside. There was no indoor bathroom. We still went outside or used the pot. We had a small kitchen with a water bucket on a table and an old ice-box. A "coal room" was next to the kitchen and there was a back bedroom that no one entered (of course that's the one I wanted to get into).

The bedroom belonging to my grandparents was off the dining room. It had a big, wide doorway and we used it for placing Grandpa's casket later on because of that. The one piece of furniture I loved was the pump organ that belonged to Grandmother. How I loved that! She could play it really good if you wanted to hear hymns, and we did. It gave me an appreciation of music and instruments. I could play by ear, but I never learned to read music.

We had a bunch of old sheds out in the backyard. They tell me that when I was very young, Grandpa used to have me go around the yard with him and pick up burned match sticks. We must have done that a lot because when the sheds were torn down, we found a lot of 12" x 12" boxes with all those match sticks in them!

My Grandfather died in 1949. He was laid out in their bedroom. I slept with Gram that night and Rusty, my cat, kept me awake most of the night. He sat outside our bedroom window, purring and meowing. I was told that cats do that when someone dies in the house.

That same window sticks out in my mind because in the middle of the night Mom would arrive from Chicago and she would peck on the glass and call "Mama, Mama. It's me, Ruth." I waited for that. Every time she came I wanted to go with her, and then every time I got to Chicago I would yearn for Mattoon and Gram's house. Being with Mom and my sisters was both exciting and troubling. The need for attention and stability pulled and tugged at me most of my life it seems.

Living with Grandparents I saw aunts, uncles, cousins by the dozens. The Coen reunion was an annual event, and the neighbors truly were "second family" to me, but I knew Mom and Dad and I always missed them after a visit and wondered about them. We had a lot of visitors. My mother had three brothers, Arthur, Donald, and Nolan; and four sisters, Bessie, Bonnie, Helen and Irma. Aunt Bessie and Uncle Carl ran a farm in Tolono, Illinois. They came the most often. They had this huge car. He always bought Hudsons, it seemed. They were very soft spoken people and good to me. They usually gave me a present at Christmas. Gram seemed to depend a lot on them looking in on her. They always brought fresh produce in season. I know we had very little money for extras.

Uncle Arthur and Aunt Irene came to see us often. They lived many places. I remember Mowequa. They had six children. I used to visit them at their place. Uncle Art was a little guy and Aunt Irene was heavier and taller than him so when a picture of them was taken he would stand sideways and look up at her. She was great— she just laughed. He always made me giggle. I played with these cousins through the years.

Aunt Bonnie and Uncle Elmer lived in Chicago and they came down periodically. When their family grew up, some of them settled around the Mattoon area. I saw my cousin Wanda most often. In fact, it was her wedding that I remember well. We were having our Coen family reunion and right in the middle of the day, here comes Wanda and Wendell Easton, car all decorated and horns blowing, with a bunch of tin cans tied on the back of it. I thought they were the most romantic couple I had ever seen. I see them at our reunions now, and they celebrated their fiftieth anniversary in the summer of 1996!

Uncle Donald and Aunt Bessie were special, too. They lived across town from us, but they would drop by after work. He spent so many years working in a grocery store or meat market. Aunt Bessie was the prettiest aunt, and always laughing and forever doing little things for us. They had a beautiful garden and brought roses a lot to Gram, along with special foods. But what I loved was when they had Christmas Bingo parties. She would wrap up a lot of things around her house that she didn't want or couldn't use and all the guests would win them. That was a memorable time. She and Uncle Donald always gave me a gift at Christmas, too.

Aunt Irma lived close by with two daughters, Judy and Cora Jane. Her husband Norman and she had divorced while their girls were young. I never got along with my aunt. As a child she seemed to me a pious little lady, always carrying her Books (she was of the Christian Scientist faith) and used to tell me constantly that I talked too loud, talked too much and was dirty. She always wanted her little girls near her and sure didn't want me near her. I began to dislike the girls because of her. I knew this wasn't fair. I know they were poor, too. When Aunt Irma came to live with us later on (I was a teen by then) she used to hang a blanket in the living room across one side and bathe, and bathe and bathe in there. It drove me crazy! I guess now it was the only privacy she really had at our house. Anyway, I have a new perspective now and wish that I could tell her. Mom later told me her sister Irma was once a tom-boy and had had a rough life.

An aunt and uncle who was always "present" for my Grandma, but who I had never seen, was my Aunt Helen. She and her husband Asa lived in Mattoon when they had their two girls , but moved away long before I was around. They were missionaries of the Baptist Church in San Paulo, South America. My grandmother missed her awfully! I grew up hearing the stories of her singing, her beauty and her goodness. I missed my big chance to meet her when I was married, living in Chicago, and she came home to see all her family. I recall a time when she sent a tape home talking to Grams and sang her a song about Mother. I don't know her children, although, I know the son they had in South America remains there to this day. When I was in San Jose in 1976, one of my dreams came true. I drove up to Paradise, California, and saw my Aunt Helen and Uncle Asa. She looked so much like Mom, only smaller. They both died soon after that.

And then there was Uncle Nolan, Mom's younger brother. He came to live with us when I was about eleven. He was like a father to me. He spoiled me rotten. I know I loved him dearly and he gave me much to be grateful for. He knew how to play the guitar and taught me how to play well enough to entertain myself. He was an amateur cartoonist. I have many of his drawings. He liked working with wood and made me many things throughout the years. He was a funny guy and could cheer anyone up. But he was also a demanding man, not in a gruff way, but in the expectations he had—mostly that everything would remain the same.

Uncle Nolan had been married twice. His first wife Goldie and he were married for only one year. They lived with Grandma and Grandpa that year. Goldie tells about Mom and Dad coming up there from the country every weekend with the five kids they already had. They would pick up Uncle Nolan and Goldie and take them back to Paradise to visit. I asked Aunt Goldie where they slept. She laughed and said "Ruth had feather ticks that she threw down on the floor and it was no problem!"

After Aunt Goldie and Uncle Nolan's marriage was annulled, they each remarried someone else and divorced again. Then, about twenty-five years later, they got in touch with one another, remarried and moved to Chicago. That is where I really got acquainted with her. Uncle Nolan died in 1993, just after Mom's death. Aunt Goldie remains in Mattoon.

Life in Mattoon was lonely at times and I looked forward to events like the circus coming to town. In the big lot across the street, in the forties, was the circus grounds for Barnum & Bailey. That was great to watch. Carnivals set up there, too. But in the early fifties it was turned into a cornfield and I could no longer watch the traffic on Dewitt Avenue, a highway just a block away. I couldn't see the Amish people going by anymore. Seeing them was such a part of the daily scenery. A Mr. Wittenberg, the owner of a little gas station, was murdered on the corner of 33rd and Dewitt. Scared us silly. Then they built a drive-in and a big gas station there which changed the landscape, too. Life was changing.

This was about the same time that a whole row of houses went up across the street, and Uncle Nolan had moved in with us and was remodeling the house—putting in water, bathroom, kitchen cabinets and tearing down the porch on the west side of the house. When he wasn't doing any of that, he taught me to play hard ball. He set up a tin can on one of the trees and had me practice until I could hit it. He called me muscles because he said I pitched like a girl, but I got them over the base! Once when I was playing with Bubby Hatfill—he loved baseball—I hit Mr. McMichael's rear car window. I thought he was the meanest man in the neighborhood. I was scared and cried, but Grandma made me go over and tell him what happened. I went and he just said to me, "Oh well. Don't worry about it!" I could have kissed him, and I never saw him as an "old meaner" ever again.

The neighbors were good to me. But none of them had children at home until the Hatfills moved next door, and the Reeves and Pyles moved in across the street, about 1947. The Reeves and the Pyles both had little girls. Bubby was the only boy in the block. Red-haired Bubby. He had two sisters, Carolyn and Sandy. I named my daughter Sandy for his youngest sister. But Carolyn and I were "club members." We had a "Lucky Seven Club"—only girls. Every weekend it seemed their family had ham sandwiches and potato chips. I thought that was the cat's meow and I know I "happened" to be there at that time too often!

Alma and John Cole were like another Aunt and Uncle.

They lived in the house on the corner next to ours. They had a porch swing and I felt so close to the sunset. It was beautiful in the spring and summer. She was the most devoted woman I think I ever met. Her husband John worked on the railroad. He got very dirty in his job. I could see her every evening washing his face and hands, back and hair, ever so gently and carefully, and then while he was getting ready for dinner, she would set a nice table and then they would eat. He must have had a very trying job as he looked so tired. She baked a lot and was generous with Gram and I. They didn't have children, but she loved her nieces and nephews and sewed for them all the time. I went to school with Mary Marie. I thought she was so lucky to have cute clothes and all.

Watching these neighbors I could see what being a mother and wife was like. I just wanted to grow up, get married, have children and a little home to watch the sun go down from.

I did stay at least one time with my youngest sister Doris. We rarely saw each other. Doris was adopted out to a family in Charleston, the town next door to Mattoon and the county seat. It was the County Fair season. I was so impressed with her room, bathroom and the entire house. Doris and I took two baths in one day! It was hot and we got to change clothes twice! Doris' mom, Amanda Replogle, had her clothes all laid out on the bed. I thought—what a treat! Amanda was very good to me, but I felt she felt sorry for me. I guess it didn't matter because I enjoyed that stay.

I visited with Audrey, my younger sister, who had been adopted, too. She had this beautiful playhouse in the backyard, with doll furniture in it that her adopted father had made her. Her parents were nice to me. Audrey's house seemed remote—even though it was only one block off the highway. I don't think either Audrey or Doris ever visited me. I can't say for sure.

The first time I remember going to Chicago was after Margy, Irma, Bertie, and Phyllis got out of the Children's Home. I went to live with them for awhile, just after the second grade, but after a time, I went back to Grandma's. I went to Chicago again after the fourth or fifth grade. It's hard to recall exact dates. Anyway, I went to two elementary schools, maybe in the same year, Whittier and Holden. Bede, my sister who is seven years older than me, graduated from Holden when I was going there. Mom was married to Paul Kopeck then.

I can still see the places we lived in Chicago. First the little house on Hillock. It was down the street from the Archer Bridge that went over the Chicago River. I used to run down to the corner to watch the bridge go up as often as I could. I must have looked like a real tourist! There was a bakery on Archer that is still there today. How I loved going there to get fresh bread and rolls. Paul and my brother-in-law to be, Chester, worked at the neighborhood brewery so I used to take Paul's lunch to him. Then we moved to an apartment on Blue Island and lived on the second floor. I liked it! In fact I loved the city, probably because Mom and Paul took us to so many places: Riverview Park, The Railroad Fair, zoos, ice-shows, and circuses. The city offered so much and we got to see so much. The museums, alone, offered something new each time we went.

I know that Paul and Mom had their troubles, but he was good to us and treated us well. We had new outfits, new suits, hats, shoes and purses at Easter time, which was a big thing in the city. Today it is clear, in looking back, that Mom married Paul to get the children out of the Cunningham Home and he helped her do that.

They must have thought that getting away from the city and going to Arkansas would give us a chance to reunite. That seems reasonable. When that was accomplished, there was no more reason for them to be married, so they were divorced.

We went to Arkansas from Chicago, I think. We had a place outside of Drasco, an itty-bitty town. The nearest big town was Heber Springs. Life was very different there. I can't say I liked it very well after leaving the big city. It was too isolated for me. We used to spend a lot of time in the evenings watching the lights from cars as they came out from town. Phyllis and I went to a one-room school house. It was so quaint. A lot of the relatives lived down there, too. My sister-in-law Betty with her sons Dale and Paul. Jenny was there for awhile, and Uncle Nolan came to take me back to Grandma's.

My souvenir from Arkansas is a scar on my leg that I got from a hot, falling fireplace poker. I also took a fall from one of the horses, Ronie. It was raining out and he slipped on some rocks. It was a very rocky farm.

I went back to Mattoon with Uncle Nolan. I was set back in school every time I returned to Mattoon. However, my sixth year at school was the best school year of my life. I had a wonderful teacher. She introduced geography to me and I was hooked. She also made the national, world, and local news prominent in our curriculum. But I think it was her way of handling students that left its mark on me. One time something was taken from her desk. We all saw who did it, but no one wanted to rat on him, so after waiting some time for a breakthrough, she had us line up and walk through the cloak area where she would be standing. She said, "Say yes or no, then return to the room." So this is what we did, and when everyone had gone the route—she sat down and said "We can go on now." The boy's face and our loyalty was saved.

The next few years were to be most influential. The church and the local theater became *big* in my life. The First Baptist Church had always been a home away from home as that is where Gram and I went. I was baptized at nine years old—on Easter Sunday. The congregation believed in full-immersion baptism. The church had a baptismal font that looked like the river Jordan. Rev. Lively was the pastor. I was afraid he would drop me.

When I was ten I had a Sunday school teacher, Margie Freeland, who encouraged me to learn five passages from the

Ten Sisters

Bible. I was so proud when I could recite from memory the "Ten Commandments," all the books of the *Bible*, "The Lord's Prayer," the "Beatitudes" and "The Twenty Third Psalm." She was so proud of me she gave me a letter with a one dollar bill in it. (I still have the letter today—but not the dollar!)

Reverend Dice became our pastor and our church turned into a home for lots of teens. We even had one guy with a car and he would take us out to "the Drive-In" after BYF (youth fellowship). One summer I got to attend the summer camp for the first time. It was great. I had a chance to spend time with the families of our congregation: the Nighswanders, the Dices, the Martin girls, and Mary Giberson. I used to spend Sunday afternoons in Grandma's *Bible* classroom. This group had the distinction of being the elders of the church so they were named "The King's Daughter's Class." They had a nice piano and it was so private. No one said anything. I was sort of adopted by the class.

Besides the church, I became involved in the Youth Entertainers' Guild of the Ricky Theater. I got involved because of Merle Reeves who lived across the street from us. She was working with Walter "Bud" Mullaney who owned and operated the little theater on the West end of Mattoon.

Merle started rehearsing as a minstrel singer and miming Al Jolson's recordings. I went crazy. Could I learn that? Well, I spent hours at her house watching her. For some reason she was giving it up and wanted me to do it. So I did. They had a four-part musical that took in the Gay Nineties, the Jazz Age, the War years, and I can't remember what else. I was also in the Gay Nineties part singing *Dearie, Do you Remember*. We rehearsed and finally presented the show. We went to the Policeman's Hall with the act, and to many old peoples' homes with part of the show. Our big moment came when we were invited to go to Mooseheart—a place in Northern Illinois for youth. We took a bus and I remember that

Vera Mae

Mom and my sister Phyllis knew about this and came up to see the show. Anyway, when I got up on the stage to do my act, the record was broken. I wasn't able to finish. I was devastated. It ended my "show business" career.

It was about the time my grandfather died that I left and went to Chicago, again, with Mom and Marvin. Marvin was Mom's third husband, and the Grandpa that most of the grandchildren grew to know well. Mom and Marvin were married by the same minister who conducted Grandpa's funeral. He was a Baptist and was reluctant to perform the ceremony for a divorcee. I don't know what they told him, but he did marry them. Mom never forgot that and years later, with some research, we found him and he returned to Mattoon and buried Marvin. He said he was glad he'd married them and that he'd had confidence in their marriage from the start.

Even though I went to Junior high school at Hawthorne in Mattoon, and met a lot of great girlfriends, and though this was the period in my life that boys took on a new significance, I was losing interest in school. I felt I was dumber and looked homelier than ever. It was the first time I looked within for my own needs or wants. I began to see, although I was not in the grade level for my age, I could learn if I applied myself. And I knew that all of life was learning something. I looked outside of school for meaning. I wanted to be popular in school, but I knew that the social world took money. I did not have it. I looked to adults to give me attention and the guidance. I feel fortunate today that enough adults were there to help me along the way. Immediate family was not enough.

I had a science teacher who took an interest in me and I ate it up. He worked at the radio station and invited me to watch his radio shows at the studio on Sundays. I did and was fascinated by the smallness of the place and the role he played outside of the classroom. Today I wonder if a teacher could give a child such innocent attention without being considered suspect, and whether a

225

young girl would feel free enough to seek these kind of experiences without being considered naive.

The summer of 1951 brought about the break from my grandparent's place. I was fifteen and off to Chicago and living with my sisters Phyllis and Irma, and nephews Dale and Francis, along with Mom and Marvin. The place was one area but they built partitions making it into four rooms. Mom was never limited by space. She simply altered the space. We were pretty snug! Phyllis and I bought the same style dresses, hers in purple and mine in either blue or red. It was fun to be together, even if I was little sister. I never liked that distinction. I became overly defensive. Someone asked me many years later what kept me so feisty. I didn't give it much thought, so he said, "Perhaps it's because you are short." Hey, if that is what it took to help me be stronger, then so be it.

I went to school at Marshall High in Chicago. It held about three thousand students, about two thousand more than I was used to. I had one girlfriend that I can recall—Sylvia Esposito. Marshall was in an area we now talk about as an 'area in transition,' with many blacks and other cultures that I'd never seen before. I was to move into that part of Chicago in years to come. The experience was an eye opener.

We moved to another section, near south side, and I continued on to school at Harrison High—one semester in each. I found some friends in the Treble Choir that went to a little church in the vicinity—I would be married in it later. School was just something I had to go to—more or less.

When I turned sixteen, my sister Phyllis and I moved in with my sister Bertie, and her husband, and baby. I wanted to quit school and found out that I would have to attend a continuation school one day a week until I was seventeen. At the same time, I got a job at Forum Cafeteria downtown. The Forum was open every day of the week so it fit into my schedule. I was a bus girl. The place was beautiful. I was happy earning my own money and it felt good. After three days the manager called me into her office and asked me if I would change my hours and job. They needed a payroll clerk in the office. I couldn't have been more pleased. The place employed well over 150 people for 'round the clock service. I saw loads of fellows from Tilden Tech! In looking back I think I had a good introduction to the working world. I managed to put away payroll savings bonds, pay for my meals at the forum, and I paid Bertie and Bob $10 out of each check. I still had El fare and money to buy a gift or two. Money went a long way back then.

It was while living in Chicago that I met my future husband. Glen was a brother-in-law to Bertie. He went with her before she married his brother Bob. I used to tease them because her name was on his arm. He was a few years older than me, but he was headed for the service, so our acquaintance was short lived. Glen's family lived across the street from my sister Bede, and her husband, Chester. Glen had four brothers and one sister. To this day I think that my sisters set it up for us to get together because they liked him and wanted me to have a nice guy, too. Even if they didn't, I flipped. We wrote back and forth, but by this time I was headed back to Mattoon. I'm not sure why.

I showed up at the Sears store in Mattoon and asked my uncle if I could come back. He must have said something about returning to school, because the next thing I knew I was registering at Mattoon High School, again. I tried to make the best of it, but I was unhappy. Most of my former friends were two years ahead of me and I had my heart and head in Chicago by then. I attended basketball games a lot. If I had stayed on I might have seen my sister, Doris, as she was a cheerleader at Charleston High and the teams were forever rivals! But she would be in high school a year or two later. The best thing was church and the friends I had there.

My uncle, Grandmother and I would have disagreements.

Ten Sisters

As I saw it, they didn't want me to grow up. They were worried about the influence the big city had on me and wanted me to stay in Mattoon. I tried. I cashed in my savings bonds and bought paint for Grandma's living room and dining room. It did brighten the place, but I just didn't want to be there anymore. I made it pretty miserable for them I know. Finally I left after I got out of school that year. I was seventeen years old.

Glen returned from active service in Korea. I was ready to marry. He had just bought a car, but sold it so we could set up household. We married at the Methodist Church in Chicago on July 31, 1954, just eleven days after I turned eighteen. My sister Jenny was my bridesmaid. We took no honeymoon as Glen was an apprentice in the lathing trade and summer was the time to work. I took two weeks off and then got a job at United Screw and Bolt Corporation. My brother-in-law Mike worked there and told me of an opening. Glen and I settled down in a cold-water flat on the south side of Chicago. We were part of the couples, now. Uncle Nolan and Aunt Goldie lived in Chicago and despite the fact that he had a hard time accepting my moving away and getting married, we had good times with them.

After five years, Theodore Nolan was born on June 14, 1959 (Flag Day). My stepdad Marvin named him "muscles" as soon as he saw him. I went to Lying In Hospital on the East side of Chicago. They kept mothers for eight days. By the time I left there, I was sure this having a baby stuff was "the berries." Both of us had insurance covering births, so my insurance paid for the whole thing and my husband's insurance paid us a flat $150, or something close. So we made money on Ted! This couldn't happen today.

I had no idea of what to expect after I got home with the new baby, or that having the total care for him would put me in such a depression. I called Mom and cried, "Mom, I never thought babies would be so exhausting!" I was up every night. I tried to sleep some, but was worn out most of the time. The only saving grace was the fact that a lady by the name of Irene Mackey lived upstairs from our apartment. She was a pediatric nurse at Mercy Hospital at night and got home just about the time I was sitting up with my son and begging him to sleep. One night I could not help myself—I asked her what I could do. He was colicky. So she asked if she could rock him and to my surprise she put him to sleep. That was the first of many drop-in calls I asked her to make. I am so embarrassed thinking of how I was always whining. She got me through. I wish that I could personally thank her.

When Ted was about nine months old we bought a house in Tinley Park, Illinois. It seemed like life was complete. We had a new home and a new baby. What more could I want?

While in Chicago, we saw our families often, but in Tinley Park it was different. No one lived out our way. Phoning was a huge expense. I stayed home now, getting acquainted with neighbors, doing the things that suburban families did. My neighbors were close and we got together for picnics, parades, and such. We saw the Ariels often and since my sister Bertie was an Ariel, too. They came annually for holidays, like Memorial Day. The guys liked the Indy 500 auto race. We had some fun times.

I also started the family newsletter in 1963 as a way of keeping in touch with everyone. The family reunions were being hosted by each family. Since I was tenth in line, we traveled to many places before it was our turn to host. I remember the one we had at Lincoln Log Cabin State Park. Phyllis and Dick hired a live band who played great country music.

When Ted was still small, I was an absolute "soaps" watcher. My day was planned around *Love of Life*. I didn't drive yet, and for lack of transportation, we stayed home a lot. That awful day when John F. Kennedy was killed was the only time my watching was interrupted, and the funeral went on for four days. The depth of the event made me realize that I wanted to make some changes in my life. The first thing I did was to turn off the soaps. It was then that I began asking what was life all about. I was sure that there must be a meaning to life, but what was it? I felt driven to seek some answers.

Life went on pretty much the same. Ted went to Orchard Hill kindergarten. It was out on a farm with a lamb, and dog, and horse and so many extras that I wanted him to have the experience, so I started working there, my first job after Ted was born. We rode the bus together each morning and came home at noon. There were so many kids there, so many cookies to serve and so many Kool-aids to pour! Anyway it culminated in a big graduation ceremony. We have a film of him in his cap and gown.

When Ted went on to elementary school his friendships expanded. Glen decided to build a hockey rink in the back yard. He spent one winter making the net, goal posts and planning the short season. The weather was cooperating and publicity was out. Everything was GO! We had so many people in our house all the time, it began to feel more like a neighborhood center than a home. I began to resent the wear and tear that our house was undergoing with all this activity. I wanted them all to leave.

On the one hand I knew it was all a good thing and hated how I felt, but I was unable to reconcile my feelings. I talked with Mom a lot. At first she lived in Beecher, Illinois, and then they bought a little house in Joliet. Mom would come over and the two of us would volunteer at the Tinley Park Mental Health Center.

A few of us volunteers worked to get a center off the ground, someplace to take patients to every week for socializing. We had brought a few home to visit our families, too. Paul Franks was a frequent caller. This exposure to the hospital convinced me to go for training and be a nurses' aide. I did that for about two years, until I got pregnant with my daughter.

Vera Mae

1969 was another year of family milestones and personal turmoil. In the summer I decided to spend four weeks living at a summer academy on the west side of Chicago, sponsored by an organization that emphasized practical training for laymen. I had already attended some courses that the Ecumenical Institute had offered and had a growing interest in what they were doing. It wasn't just me, the movement was a social phenomena going on across the land. I wanted Ted to have an experience outside of Tinley Park and be introduced to something new. He was ten years old, not too keen on leaving his friends, but I convinced him to go to camp held by the institute in Canada. First of all, Ted got sick and when he arrived home we found out he had a lot of allergies the campground site had set off.

That was the summer my grandmother died. I was called home from the Academy because Grandma was in the hospital. She had been living with Mom in Joliet. When I arrived at the hospital, I went to see her. Mom was crying, the first time in my life I saw her out of control, and begging me to leave the room because Gram was dying. I wouldn't hear of it. Instead, I was angry that they had all those life-preserving lines attached to her and it seemed to me they were violating her right to live or die in peace. Mom was so distraught. But soon the nurse came in and unplugged everything. I called to Gram. I wanted so much for her to know I was there. This tiny little woman, who was in her last breath of life, bolted upright in the bed. She had the same expression that I'd seen when she woke up in the morning before putting on her glasses. She looked around and said, "Oh hi," and fell back. All liquids were expelled from her body. I was grateful for the experience of being there to witness natural death. I had just read D. H. Lawrence's writing in which he said death was artificial, but dying was beautiful, and it seemed to me it was so.

I decided to go back to the Academy and continue what I

had started. I missed my grandmother's funeral by returning which upset Mom. I didn't give anyone a chance to argue with me or to convince me otherwise. If anyone in my family objected, I know years later they forgave me. The entire set of events changed my life forever. I was not to know how it changed others for some time. I began to plan my life differently, but the changes I was asking myself to make affected me so much.

Nightmares became an everyday occurrence. Once I even dreamed my son was sliding down a hill on a sled and went on in to a body of water. I was terrified and woke up crying. I never got over the feeling those nightmares evoked. I know they were responses to the anxiety I was going through. But at the time I told myself they were omens—that I was going to lose him and I could do nothing about it. I was learning what it means to be separated, and the pain that comes with it.

The final change that year was the birth of my daughter, Sandra Ruth, born October 27, 1969. She had the bluest eyes and was a charmer from day one. Her arrival home was heralded by a constant parade of trick or treaters who wanted to see the new baby. This time I was in the hospital just three days with no afterbirth blues. I began to have hope that all was well.

I began to travel into the city and visit the Chicago Metro House of the Ecumenical Institute. It was on Blue Island near Ashland, an old neighborhood of mine. I recruited other people for courses and events held at their west-side campus. There was always child care for Sandy so I didn't worry. My family resented my time away from them and they complained that I was going "there again." At one point I went to the Prior of the religious house and told him I was going to get a divorce. He quietly but firmly told me to not do that, that they were not about breaking up families but "building a new family order—a new movement of the religious." His attitude postponed my decision. I will say that they never asked me to join, never asked me to stay, nor asked me to leave. The decisions were always mine. People ask me what it was about the E. I. that attracted me. The Ecumenical Institute provided an image of what life could look like that I had never seen before. The institute people had decided to make a difference in the everydayness of life. Their life style was dynamic, to say the least, up at four-thirty to go to daily office, a brand new experience in worship, stressing the drama of life, using drums, clackers, the use of the body and voice. During the day, a portion of the members spent time in the community developing leadership, engaging in projects and training teachers. House Church, the weekly communion service, was held on Sunday. This is such a small view of the E. I. All in all, it was the community that I wanted to be part of. To do that took sacrifice and dedication.

Since my image of myself was first and foremost a mother, I was having a difficult time excepting my new-found commitment. I was tormented for a couple of years, keeping things going and not wanting the criticism that I would get. My struggle prompted my husband to react. One day he said to me, "If you want to go and be a teacher, or whatever, then do it." I had awful doubts though. What was I getting into anyway? What would people say? What if it was a cult? Or worse—a subversive group? These were all questions I had been asked and I didn't know the answers. But the answer was, of course, there was no answer. Everyone would think what they wanted to. What were labels anyway, except an attempt to rationalize the world. I had no fear anymore. I could move on.

After eighteen years, Glen and I were divorced in 1972. Sandy and I moved into the city and Ted stayed with his father.

We moved in Easter week and were assigned to the Academy. After eight weeks I was sent to the west side. I was to be a pre-school teacher with the three-year-olds. Sandy was in the four-year-old class. You cannot imagine how happy I was. I got hands-on practice in using the methodology that had been taught in the Academy.

We spent two years in Chicago and then went to Ottawa, Canada. This was to be the start of several one-year assignments in Bristol, and London, England; San Jose, California; Billings, Montana; Richmond, Virginia; and Anchorage, Alaska. Sandy and I shared the same room in houses across the continent and England for the next eight years.

Life with the E. I. was all that I had hoped for and more. I began to understand what faith was all about. I never worried about my diet or my weight. I was not concerned with getting degrees or being "educated." I was not caught up in the pursuit of material goods or paying mortgages. I was helping to build a new tomorrow. We worked from sunrise to sunset, demonstrating the possible. I loved it, and Sandy seemed very happy. We were getting our education. It was a long time before I realized that I was a single woman with a child.

I met and worked with interesting people of various backgrounds. Many were religious—ministers, their wives and families. We all had one thing in common—our desire to be social pioneers. The structures of the community placed men and women in all the various roles or "jobs" and that was new to me. We were a singing people. Exposure to songs from around the world helped to unite our community. We studied theologians, heroes, pioneers and looked at films in a fresh new way. Time was divided by quarters, days into day one and day two, and weeks into week one and week two. Themes and decor completed the image. And we had some time for ourselves. Monday night was family night. Sandy and I would usually go to the nearest McDonalds. It fit our budget! Then there was extended family time when we could leave the campus and visit relatives and take vacations. I never knew how the other members could afford to do that on the stipend we received for doing full-time volunteer work, stipends that were derived from some of the members working at jobs outside "in the world" to support all of us.

Two of the programs I appreciated the most were the E. G. (Emerging Generation), and the Student House. The curriculum was created by the adults and emphasis was put on being great human beings. At the end of elementary education, the youth were expected to go and live in the Student House and embark on their own rite of passage. It was one floor of the International Training Center in Chicago. Leadership was assigned to them around the clock. The youth had to earn their own money and were given a stipend. All the group took part in home classified deliveries. In the evening they could be found sitting all around the floor rolling these newspapers, then they would be up at 4:00 a.m. the next morning, run the deliveries, return and eat before they tackled their other assignments.

The toughest year that Sandy and I had was in Billings, Montana. It was the coldest place I have ever lived, bar none. Our group included six high schoolers, three smaller children and four adults. We were doing a town meeting campaign, trying to conduct one in every county or prefecture in the country during 1976-77. It was a great effort, but it was a strain on most of the houses. We were living with all these kids, and I held down a shipper's job at a beauty supply house in the daytime and another gal and I led the youth meetings in the evening. Our young people were in dire need of strong leadership. I had no illusions about the commitment that the order demanded anymore. I was at a real low ebb. About this time, the founder and teacher of the E. I., Joseph W. Matthews, died. All the adults in our house were given tickets to go back to Chicago and attend his funeral. I was excited about going home again, and about honoring this man who I really respected.

Lo and behold! When I arrived at the Center in Chicago, I was holding the door for guests and members of the Order, when I looked up and saw my mother and my sister, Jenny. I was speech-less, but so happy. I cannot tell you how much I had longed for any one of my family or friends to seek me out. All those years when I had not attended the reunions due to the fact that I was either not close or too busy, I still heard from Mom. But there was Jenny! That year I received presents from the girls and I sent them, of all things, a carton of bubble bath that I could buy at the beauty sup-ply store. It was so little and they certainly didn't need it, but I was happy. That same year, Sandy and I moved out of the Billings House to an apartment near where I worked. Sandy came down with a condition known as Bell's Palsy. One side of her face was paralyzed. I was worried sick. Our landlord was a big guy who looked like he was a marine (I think that he had been). He always used to shovel every bit of snow all around the apartment so neat-ly. It impressed me so. He used to fix good stews, too, and invite Sandy and I to eat with him. The room he had was so warm. She and I spent Christmas that year at a hotel and it was beautiful. Most Christmases were spent alone at a house when everyone else went home to celebrate with their families. We never had any money for travel. It turned out to be one of the reasons we finally moved out. I felt the inequity more at those times. I realize now that I might have been able to take more control of those situations, but I didn't.

Mom and Marvin Roberts celebrated twenty-five years of marriage in Chicago in 1974. I remember the event because Sandy and I were sent tickets to come to an evening party. Bertie made sure that we were there. Ted also came and we really surprised Mom and Marvin. I had not seen any of the family for awhile and it was the first time we met Doris' family. Marvin died of cancer two years later.

1978 was a bench-mark year. We moved back to Chicago where Mom, who was celebrating her seventy-fifth birthday, was living alone since Marvin's death. My sisters and I put on our first "cabaret" at the reunion and I felt like I was at home again. My sister Bertie got me a job at the First National Bank. She, my supervisor Alice, and I had a lot of good times. I learned to spend money again for us and all seemed well until I went to a summer event at the Institute of Cultural Affairs Center in North Chicago. The year before, the E. I. had expanded and adopted the new name. I walked up to the Assignment Room on the eighth floor and not seeing my name anywhere became despondent. Someone came along and said "Why here it is." and pulled this magnetized nameplate from in back of the big blackboard and asked where I wanted to put it. It made me realize that I still had ties to the organization I did not want to break, and again I realized my family was not enough. I decided to return to the fold and we were immediately sent to Richmond, Virginia.

Mom got married the next year to John Golden—her fourth marriage. I didn't understand then why, but I know now she was looking for companionship. Mom was what I would call a married woman through and through—she needed a husband and would never have just "lived with a man." They settled in her home town of Charleston, Illinois.

After a year in Richmond, we went to Anchorage, Alaska. Ted, who was about to turn twenty-one, came to visit. He moved in and became part of the family. We were so happy to see him, but less than a year later, Sandy was off to the Student House in Chicago and I was reassigned to Japan. Ted got a job with Flying Tigers' Air Freight. When they shut down and Federal Express took over, he moved with the job and remained with FedX in Anchorage.

While I was growing closer to Ted, I was losing touch with Sandy. In Chicago, she was living in the Student House. Some of the parents lived in the same building, I didn't, except when I went there for training or conferences. It became even more difficult for Sandy and I to see each other or to be in contact after I went to Japan. After two years in Chicago, Sandy went off to Tonga for her first year of high school. I began to worry something awful about her. What I failed to see was that it was the beginning of the end of what I thought was a close relationship throughout her childhood. She was becoming a young lady and I was going through the pangs of motherhood all over again. Would it never end?

My colleagues in Japan were so good to me. They loved having new visitors view their temples, see their gardens, and practice the age-old customs of the Tea Ceremony and Ikebana—flower arranging. They took me everywhere and a ride on the Japanese train is quite an experience. Japanese culture is so different, especially the food, which I had to get used to, along with the simple living arrangements. I learned a great deal. While I was there, I had a job teaching English in a Ashiya Girls' school. The school is one of the better known in Japan. The school grounds were huge and incorporated a women's college as well as a kindergarten—spiral education, we would say. The director of the school was very kind to me and gave me all the tools needed and more. My senior high class was very modern and had a huge television in it to show films. I used it to motivate conversational English. I had some struggle with language and custom in the school, but the students made it not only possible, but a wonderful experience. I have many souvenirs from the students and the people of Japan.

I made a life-long friend in Sadako Yoshikawa. She was a senior staff member in the Japanese House. We wrote letters to one another. She visited me several times, bringing students to Anchorage, and gave me two of the most beautiful dolls that she had made—one victorian and one Japanese—that I shall treasure, always. My dream is to return to Japan and see her once more.

In 1983, Ted met and married Kathy, an Alaskan girl who had a son, Noah. The next year they would have a son, Russell. I decided to take leave and go back to Anchorage for the birth at Christmas time but the little squirt, he didn't show until after I returned to Japan.

I loved Japan and thought I wanted to stay there for another year, but I was glad when they sent me home. When I returned to the states in 1983, Sandy was attending school in Washington D. C., and I was sent to New York. The D. C. public schools were not good. The I.C.A. office had about seven youth attending high school there, so it was decided that they would go to a Catholic high school. I did not object, but I didn't have the money. Again, I do not know where other families got it. I became increasingly aware of being a single mother with a daughter. I also knew I did not have the guts to seek help. We left the order so I could be with Sandy. We needed each other. We left our respective houses and drove to Charleston, Illinois. Mom was there to help us.

It was good to see all the relatives again, but it was very hard financially to live in Charleston. Jobs were low paying and I had to go on welfare for the first time in my life. When I saw how little we got and how our whole life was in their hands, I got off. I remember swallowing my pride and asking for help from my family and Sandy's father. Rent was low but utilities were high. I was working at three jobs and hardly making enough for us to survive. It was to be a portent of the future for the next six or seven years. I know now part of it was age discrimination. I had never been without work before. Luckily, we had a lot of support. My sister Phyllis was only a few blocks away so we saw her often. One year, on Christmas Eve, a big, big box arrived. We were so excited! It was a television set from Santa Claus. We tried for a long time to find out who it came from, to no avail. Finally it was told—Bertie had done such a nice thing!

Sandy would graduate from Charleston High School. Ted came down from Alaska and we were delighted. After graduation she wanted to go live with her dad. As much as I would miss her, I thought it would be a good thing. Perhaps she could go on to college in Chicago. As for me, I wanted to renew relations with my son, his wife, Kathy, and their boys. I was proud of them and wanted to get to know them better. I was off to Alaska—ready to settle down. My wandering days were over. It was 1987.

I moved in with Ted and Kathy. The boys were little then. They went to a day-care center. I got a job close by. But the apartment was pretty crowded. I moved out and got an apartment of my own on Government Hill. I liked it, but finding a job was no easier than in Charleston. I was too young (54) for the Older Peoples Action Group to help me and too old for many of the positions. One thing I was able to do was to host my friends from Japan. So Sadako Yoshikawa came for three weeks, bringing with her three young students. We set up home stays for the three of them and then she and I went to senior citizen homes where she demonstrated tea ceremonies and Ikebana. We ended her visit with a get-together with all the host families and friends who participated. It was great. She repeated the visit the next year.

I still needed to find a long-lasting job. I found enough to establish credit for the first time in my life by saving $500 then borrowing back on it, but life was not easy. I got a job as a telephone marketer, doing surveys, and I went to school six hours a day to learn computers and accounting. But the next job turned out to change my life significantly. I read an ad in the paper for a live-in or out housekeeper and cook. I was hired. My lease was up, and I moved into the house where I was working, a short few blocks from Ted and Kathy.

Jessie Barber was a stroke victim and could not feed herself. I would talk with her, but she could not answer. Her husband Bill was devoted to her. I admired him for the care he gave. When I arrived at the house he was then able to run errands and handle his affairs. At these times I would fix her nails or just sit with her. From pictures around the house I could tell that they had many good memories.

One day when I came to work he was alone, saying that Jessie fell and had to be taken to the hospital. She had broken her hip. He would visit her in the morning, afternoon, and evenings. Jessie never came out of the hospital. She died in May 1990.

Bill was a quiet man, never complained and treated me nicely. I was going to school now, the telephone job had ended with the elections over, and so I settled in. He and I would talk a lot. I liked the company and he did too. Things just started to get more serious. It had been years since I considered getting married again. I struggled and felt things were getting better financially. And yet I did yearn to settle down. Bill was so different from any man I had known. His business savvy had been honed as an FAA executive and unlike most men, he had it all, or all he wanted anyway. That was reassuring to me. When we started talking about what it meant to get married, I felt it was too soon, so we set one year to wait it out. On February 9, 1991, we were wed. The following year, May 1992, Sandy married Robert Baggot in Chicago. Ted, Kathy, the boys, Bill and I went down to the wedding. Sandy's dad had remarried. Pat, Sandy's stepmother, had made her gown. It was beautiful! That same fall, Sandy and Bob decided to come to Alaska and stayed for a year! I did not want them to leave.

By 1993, Mom was failing fast and the family had an early reunion in July of that year. Bill and I returned for this special day. I was able at that time to get some of the girls talking on tape about the old days and Mom enjoyed having us around her. I taped her and John one night. I'm grateful for that time with them. It was the last time I saw her alive. She died on April 18, 1993. A better friend I will never have. She knew all my weaknesses, yet loved me. She never turned me down when I needed help, even when she was disappointed.

I returned with Ted for the funeral. We said goodbye, but not without a new resolve. All of us girls were there, and for the first time, in the very place the separation took place. My sister Doris said she thought she could get a photographer to come and take a photo at the courthouse. I did not realize how much that day meant to me—I cried and cried on my sister Audrey's shoulder. After the photo, we all went up into one of the courtrooms and the reporter let us talk away. This achievement, and it was an achievement of Mom and the older sisters who would not give up, was realized. It is now clear why Mom returned to Charleston to live out the rest of her days. Her death brought us together in the place where we parted.

This chapter would not be complete if I failed to mention the battle I have waged against non-hodgkins lymphoma diagnosed in 1995. Other than the fact that I hardly knew what it meant, I was totally unprepared for the next six months of my life. I cannot imagine going through what I did without the love and support of my husband who went to every appointment with me and never left my side. Nurses taught him how to care for all my needs and he did just that. I kept thinking how ironic it was that after taking care of his first wife for three years, he was now caring for another wife. I had imagined things the other way around, but not this!

The following is an excerpt from *Timeless Memories*, a book compiled by sister Audrey from our *Family Newspaper*. She asked me to write about my experience with cancer.

> Having been tested for and diagnosed as having a hiatal hernia, I began taking Zantac. . . . After some months and no relief to speak of, I quit taking it and asked my doctor if perhaps I didn't have a gallbladder condition. She said she would set up some further tests. . . .The Sonogram operator said, "I can identify all the organs just fine, but there is a growth here in your abdomen that I can't name." The Cat Scan proved to be the confirming evidence . . . .I agreed to surgery May 1st.
>
> The surgeon reported that the tumor was

intricately woven around the renal vein and could not be cut out as hoped. . . .to sum it up. . .the tumor was made up of large and small cancer cells. . .it was metastatic (means scattered) and that it was non-hodgkin lymphoma. . . .My general practitioner set me up to see an Oncologist. . . .

This new doctor was just a little lady. . .but this did not let you know just how aggressive she was. . . . After taking an excruciatingly painful bone marrow test, she wanted me to begin treatments the next week! I said,"WHOA! I have not recuperated from the surgery, yet. . . ." As unhappy as she was, she put them off for three weeks. . . .

When I had my check-up with my surgeon, I told him I was nervous with the lil' woman. He said she was known for her thoroughness, but if I was unhappy. . . .I ought to change doctors. . . and not to wait! He said all doctors understand this. . . .Well, the little lady was from India and I began feeling. . .I was being prejudiced. . .so I found myself staying with her. . . . . After the second round of chemo. . . not to mention all the trips to the ER, a serious talk with her in which she stated more than once "I told you all this before,"I decided we could not make it together during this journey! I had already been introduced to another [doctor]. . . .I did like his manner and his decisiveness, so I asked him to take my case. . . .

My medical history consisted of[:] one tonsil-lectomy; two children and one broken bone. I had little context for the "medical world of today." It is a round of x-rays, slurping fluids, injections, blood with-drawals, pills, culture samples and chemo. . . .then all the effects to your system, like nausea, constipation, dehydration, diarrhea, infections and constant fatigue.

A lot of agony came from my own inability to accept the truth. . . .one of the best things I can do for myself is to drink 2-3 quarts of liquids a day, especially during the two weeks of treatment. Well, I just had to be cajoled, begged and finally, "OK...here comes the IV. . . ."

Eating [was] difficult. . . .My food looked utterly gross in anything larger than the size of a peanut, so I cut all my food into tidbits to get it down. . . .this passed, but [I] still have a hard time with large cuts of anything: lettuce, tomato or meat.

The other thing I struggled with was refusal to look at or discuss having a "groshong" which is an outside catheter surgically placed in the left side of the chest to allow IV's and blood withdrawals easier and more effective. But no! Not me! I was going to have my 6 RX's through normal channels as I referred to them. I would be punched with those darn plastic needles in every possible vein until August 19th when I had no less than 12 punches, four nurses and no results, I finally cried "Geronimo" and the doctor said: "No more. The priority for you is the "groshong!" I no longer objected.

I am not a "hair person" and yet losing it was one of the hardest things I have had to face. . . .

But the hardest thing to face was my emotions. I apologize to Bill most of all, and to my family. I know at times I have been unbearable. I felt so "out of control."

Vera Mae

All through my treatment, my sisters kept a running phone line to me. A day never went by without cards and letters in the mail. Because of the family newsletter, even more friends and family wrote. I got a big scrapbook and it became filled in no time. Reading them was one activity that I did over and over. Prayers were said for me from one part of the country to the other. I had visits from some of my sisters, but I knew the rest were with me, too. Sandy got to visit me, and Ted and Kathy were around all the time. My grandsons came to know me in a little different light.

Bill's daughter-in-law, Karen, is a nurse and came to care for me when it was all new and scary. It was reassuring to have someone who knew what to do. She told me that when I recovered we would go to Hawaii. At the time I couldn't imagine wanting to go. How quickly I changed my mind when I began feeling better. We did go in November 1995 and it was wonderful!

Around the same time my friend Yoshikawa San, from Osaka, came for a visit. She had been to a doll show in New York. She made the most beautiful porcelain Victorian dolls as a hobby. The dolls had arrived here earlier in laundry hampers! She gave one to Kathy, Karen, and to me. When I was too sick to get up and around—she sat with me and casually knitted me two hats for my cold head. She was never idle. She is a great lady!

My condition is in remission now. I have returned to work full time. I feel great. I like to say that I have had three good lives and will now, at sixty, be celebrating another, if not more!

I was in an art shop this year when I saw this saying— "Whenever I go on a trip, I think about all the homes I've had and I remember how little has changed about what comforts us." What comforts me is knowing this:

"That life is beautiful. And I have been loved dearly, more dearly, than the spoken word can tell."

The Last Farewell

Audrey Faye Lee
(Audrey)

Dedicated to my children who gave me so much love and happi-
ness that it kept me forever going forward with my life

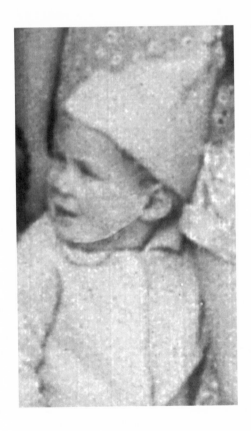

Audrey Faye Lee

When I first started to do this story, I thought of how difficult it was going to be. Now I know that although recalling past events would be difficult, it was going to make me feel a certain kind of cleansing or setting aside the past that was almost too unpleasant to want to remember. There is some debate going on in my head as just how much of the past do I really remember and how much of it is only what I had been told. I will try and tell as much of it that I recall and spare you the details of hear-say.

I know the earliest memory did take place in the courthouse. I still see Vera and me sitting on a step, knees nearly touching our chins, dressed in ragged, worn clothes and singing our hearts out, "Bell Bottom Trousers, coats of Navy Blue, I'm in love with someone, and he loves me too." That's all I remember of the song today, but I'll always see that picture in my mind. At four years old I was quite unaware of what was happening. I can only accept that it did happen and it was not the fault of any one person but the burden and truth lies in the turmoil of the times.

I had the good fortune of being adopted, but having been with nine sisters and my Mom, always having been in the company of females, I was very shy of men. It was a long time before I would take up with my new father.

My new home was very strange to me and after sleeping in one room and sharing one bed with all my sisters, I was afraid of the new bedroom that was to be mine alone! I have been told that my first days with the Coles I cried myself to sleep, wouldn't eat, had nightmares, and refused to talk to them. It must have been a very trying time for my adopted parents, too.

My new home was nice, clean, and another world for me. It didn't take long for me to understand that my new mother didn't share my new daddy's enthusiasm at my being a new member of the family. I found out years later that he had lost two wives in childbirth and wanted to have a child in the worst way. My mother had been an only child and she definitely did not like children. This situation was a no-win situation from the beginning. My daddy was a quiet, gentle man who tried desperately to see that I was kept occupied and out of her way. He would take me with him when he went to town or to visit someone. He used to hangout at the local hardware store where I spent many hours playing with nails and sorting them. I would dust the shelves and look over all the goods they had for sale. Another hangout of Daddy's was a service station where he caught up with all the news and talked shop. I spent my time there just drinking cokes, eating peanuts, and scribbling pictures on scrap paper. Daddy worked as a telegraph operator for the the railroad and worked second shift. I didn't get to see much of him after I started school, but he kept his nights off for me. We would make fudge and popcorn and work a jigsaw puzzle. He would read to me and tell me about his family and his childhood days, growing up in the Ozark Mountains in Missouri. He was proud of his family, and I always knew that he missed them.

I used to play in the wood shop, gluing small bits of wood together, while he built me the most beautiful doll furniture. Working with wood was his hobby and I think it rubbed off on me. My Daddy was a good and loving person, but he always held back in his affections because of Mother. She was a real piece of work, who thought a kiss or a hug was taboo.

I sure did not like Mother very well. I was totally afraid of her. She lacked patience and could not tolerate very much of me. She never allowed me to have friends spend the night and hardly ever let me spend the night with someone else. She continually preached to me the point that I was adopted. I had to be better and do better than any other child. She always thought I was so contrary and compared me to my natural mother and what a loser she was. She demanded perfection yet while I was in school, she never even looked at a report card or attended any activities that I took part in.

Audrey Faye Lee

I was an honor student and that was all she cared about. She consistently told me how she would like to have adopted my sister, Vera, because she had her coloring and small size, and that I was a blond haired, oversized clumsy ox! Well I had my own thoughts about her. She was a liar. She led a double life. During the day she was a housewife, but when Daddy went to work, she was a swinger. Dressing up, perfumed and powdered, she hit the nightspots. I knew this from an early age. I hated her for it. I wanted to tell Daddy, but I was too afraid. I prayed he would come home some night and catch her in her little molting act, but he never did. Looking back, I know he already knew. I'm sure, today, that they were playing out their own little game, and it just didn't include me.

"Susan" she would call me—never Audrey, unless she was mad as old hell. I always knew if I was in bad trouble, and that was all the time. I don't want to give you the idea that I was an angel. I wasn't! I think knowing that I was adopted and knowing that I had another family out there, somewhere, kept me defiant and gave me a sense of independence. It gave me a feeling of security and hope. I did know that Doris and Vera were my sisters and from time to time they got to visit me, and I them. I loved Vera. I wanted to be free in spirit as she was. I wanted to wear blue jeans and a ball cap and feel her zest for life. We got to see each other often and I'm sure she knew we were sisters, although we didn't talk about it.

I don't remember my real grandma and grandpa well, but I remember their house when I went to visit Vera and the funny refrigerator they had, but most of all I remember the love they had for her.

Doris was another issue. I was always jealous of her. We grew up in the same town, attending separate grade schools, but saw each other until I decided to tell her that we were sisters. She didn't want to hear that and cried, went home, packed her clothes, and was going to run away.

I got one of the first beatings in a long line of beatings that night! I really didn't care. I wanted to hurt Doris. She and her cutie-pie ways, her in her ruffles and lace and sweet smile, her and her parents that gave her so much of their time and attention, let alone the attention my own daddy showed to her. Daddy never built me any toy that he didn't build for her, too! I just didn't understand and it would be awhile before I did. It did teach me one lesson, though, that you can't live a lie. It always catches up with you, sometimes in the form of a little nine-year-old girl.

Being raised as an only child can be lonely. I did all kinds of things to keep busy. My neighbors produced some of the greatest pleasures for me. On one side was Mr. Thistle. He provided me with a magic tree that grew peppermint sticks every night that I could pick in the mornings. I would grow up and write for my children the story of the "Magic Candy Tree." There was an elderly couple across the street that had a flower garden and a gold-fish pond. I spent a lot of time playing in their yard and watching the frogs and fish. Sometimes they would invite me to come in and have milk and cookies and let me look around their home at all the odd (antique) furniture and other things they had. I was careful not to break anything.

My favorite thing to play with was the bellows by the fireplace. I loved the swooshing sound they made. I appreciate the trust they had in me, that I would not damage anything. Behind my house was a large two-story house. I became acquainted with the family when I first came to Charleston. The lady was real nice. Sometimes she was my baby sitter. She taught me so many things—how to make hollyhock dolls, color Easter eggs, sew, play cards, how to paint and how a flower grows. She was probably one of the earliest influences into self-production in my life. She gave me self-confidence and opened my mind to the finer things of life. Art and imagination—those were the key!

The neighbors to the north of my house were strictly off limits. Mother said they had a son that had a steel brain (he had been injured in the war) and that he was crazy. I was so afraid of him that one day he brought out the garbage and I went screaming and running into the house. On Halloween, all of us kids would throw corn on his porch and soap their windows, then run like the devil.

School was my salvation. I could have spent every day and night at school. I put my best foot forward. I never had to study, and I excelled in everything I attempted. It just came so easy! I had some very good teachers, one of which was a life-long friend. She was the only teacher to physically correct me for reading a comic book in class. She taught me in sixth grade, was the Principal of the school, and was related to my natural mother! She used to invite me over to her home to play piano for her and her sisters. They were both old maids. After moving to Tennessee, Bob, Rhonda and I went to see her every time we made it to Illinois. We kept corresponding all through the years. She passed away at age 96, mind as sharp as it could be.

In Junior High I had two teachers that come to mind: Mr. Whitman, my English teacher and Miss Watkins, my Music teacher. Mr. Whitman taught me to seek out the answer to any question I might encounter. He taught me to have a sense of humor and to do the best that I could do, to never settle for anything less. Miss Watkins was a wonderful person. She was sometimes criticized for her flamboyant ways. She was very independent and strictly did her own thing—in her own way—but she made lots of friends and had the respect of her students. She taught me that you did not have to be first in anything, but to be a part of something that would make a first. Like sportsmanship, it takes the whole team to win, not just one person. That was one lesson that I learned from scouts. I was a Brownie, then a Girl Scout. I took piano and singing lessons. I really wanted to take dancing lessons, but Mother didn't think I had the talent to become a dancer. What I really wanted to be was a movie star.

I literally grew up in the movie theater. I went four or five times a week. Mother did allow me to use one wall of my bedroom for pin-up pictures and every inch was covered. I would sit in my room at night and pretend to be Lana Turner or Betty Grable, and I'd be married to Clark Gable or maybe Cornell Wilde. What fun those times were for me. I could be anybody I wanted to be—and dream.

It always seemed to me that I was on the outside looking in. I never quite seemed to fit in anywhere. Other kids didn't understand me and I had few friends in school. Maybe it was because I didn't know how to be a kid. Money was never a problem. I received an allowance of $25 to $50 dollars a week and had my own charge card for the clothing store, but I wasn't happy. Money can't take the place of love. I used to take the kids at school for lunch and buy trinkets. I was trying to buy their friendship. It just doesn't work that way.

I was so frustrated at being left alone most of the time that I did the most terrible things. The worst was stealing. The first time I stole it was a lipstick from the 5-and-10-cent store. I got caught trying to return it and did I get in trouble with Mother. It only made me more defiant and so I decided to do the ultimate. I started stealing from my daddy's wallet. At first it was just a dollar or two, then it was ten dollars once a week, and then something every day. Why did I steal from the one person that loved me. I don't really know, except that I wanted to get his attention. I wanted him to accuse me, be mad at me, I wanted an excuse to fight back. Daddy mentioned more than once to Mother that he had some money missing, but neither of them ever mentioned it to me! What had brought me to this point in my life? I was crying out for their attention and as always, I got only silence. It seemed nobody cared.

It all started about the time I was seven years old. Mother had an aunt and uncle that lived in a near-by town. Mother always went there to shop and she would leave me with the uncle while she and the aunt were gone. The aunt was always nice, always smiling and cheerful. She was a great cook, always making pies, and for me, my favorite chocolate cupcakes. Their home was warm and sunny, with a flower garden out back with lots of bird houses and bird baths. The uncle could whistle just like the different kinds of birds, and they would fly onto your finger to eat right out of your hand. I loved watching and feeding the birds and squirrels. I thought this garden and this house had a magic to it and sometimes the uncle would bring a radio outside and I could dance over the grass. But shadows were lurking in this great house and around the man who lived in it.

It all began quite harmless. In the middle of the house was a doorway that hid a stairway leading up to the attic. I used to peek in there, but it always looked so scary, and besides, Mother told me not to go up the stairs. One wintry day while the women were gone on their weekly shopping trip, the uncle asked me if I would like to see the attic and all the treasures it held. I said "yes" without hesitation and up the stairs we went. It was enchanting. It was one of those big attics that you could walk around in and it was filled with all sorts of strange and wonderful things—old toys and trunks of clothes, furniture, pictures, old costumes and a doll! Not just any old doll, but a "Shirley Temple Doll." She was beautiful in her pink dress and bonnet. I loved Shirley Temple and oh! how I wanted that doll. Uncle said, "See I wanted to surprise you. Are you surprised?" Indeed I was. "Could I have her? Was she mine to keep?" I couldn't believe my eyes. The uncle said I could play with her, but I had to be very, very nice to him and that this had to be our secret. At seven years old you don't see or know the underlying reasons for all of this. It was just a game of secrets and children love secrets. That day I started learning about betrayal. I wanted the doll. He wanted a favor. He handed me the doll and I started to caress the tiny curls—so he started to caress me. First it was just a light kiss to the cheek, then a pat on the leg, then he unbuttoned my blouse and caressed my breast. I felt funny and didn't like being undressed in front of him. I asked him to stop and he did, placing the doll back in it's box. We returned to the downstairs and for the rest of the day,

I kept asking him for the doll and he refused to reply. Once my Mother was there, I kept quiet, too.

The next trip over to Uncle's I waited for Mother and Auntie to leave and then I asked him about the doll. He said nothing, taking me up those stairs and handing the doll to me. I began to play with her, when he grabbed her and told me that I could have the doll if I let him kiss me. I was scared, but I wanted that doll. Then as I played with the doll, he ran his hand up my dress. I jumped and told him "no!" This time he was persistent. He wouldn't stop and he just kept fondling and petting me. He removed my clothes and started kissing me all over. I started to cry and gave him a shove.

I didn't want to give up the doll though, and he just ignored my cries. He talked to me ever so quietly and let me put my clothes back on, but he kept up his petting and wanted me to touch him in the no-no places. When I refused, he took away the doll and we went downstairs. I was crying, but he told me to shut up, did I want everybody to know what a bad, bad girl I was?

For almost a year, on and off, this same ritual went on, him promising the doll to me and then him taking advantage of me. Then—it was my eighth birthday. Mother and I went to Auntie and Uncle's so she could buy me a great birthday present. That day was different, for on the bed in Auntie's room was the "Shirley Temple" doll. I pretended not to see it and no one said a thing about it. I was holding my breath as they left to go shopping and ran to it as soon as the car pulled out of the driveway. I grabbed for the doll and he grabbed for me. Down on the floor, his body on my small body. I couldn't breathe from his weight. He smelled and was panting as he pulled off my clothes and forced himself on me. The pain was terrible and I remember screaming and crying, kicking and begging. Then I lay silently crying. It was over almost as quickly as it had begun. Slowly I got up and he shoved me toward the bathroom. I flinched and he laughed at me. I cleaned my aching body and he washed and combed my hair. I was sick, ashamed and betrayed. As I walked to the front door I could not think of anything but to run and run and run. He grabbed me and swung me around, looked at me and told me what a terrible child I was and what a terrible thing I had made him do. In spite of it all, I was so stupid, I asked for the doll. I knew it was not mine and never would be. I also knew that what happened would not happen again. From that day on, rain or shine, heat or snow, I would spend my time in the park across the street and it was never spoken of again. It would be years later that I would tell my Mother—and she called me a liar.

The physical pain would be remembered, but the betrayal and the rejection would hurt me even more. This is the story of my life, getting caught up in circumstances I couldn't control and no one to believe me. But it was one of the first steps in forming my own personality.

I have always been too trusting, too hungry for love, too flirty. At one time I didn't know anything and I found that it took all the events of my young life to prepare me for what lay ahead of me. It would prepare me for the trials of life that I had yet to face. It taught me courage and responsibility for my actions, to understand that even though some people ask "why me," I can ask myself "why not me?" For I think I was created to bear things that others might not be able to bear. Because I can bear it without breaking. I am a survivor. I can bounce back and go on with my life. That is good!

I never knew much about my family as I was growing up, just that I had one. I remember a couple of sailors visiting me, which I know now were my brothers, Carl and Jesse. I remember my real Dad bringing me cherry-chocolates. He always had a smile and called me "Sis."

I remember the first time I saw my real Mom. She had come to the theater and had me paged. She was crying and I was embarrassed, as the other kids were watching. Later I met Rhita and Chester. He teased me about my curls (he said he was going to cut one off) and

I went running to the bedroom and cried. When I met Virginia and Clarence, they had a tiny baby and I thought they were all midgets. They were so small and I was such a big girl. The first time I saw Phyllis, I was about eleven years old. I thought she was beautiful and I wanted to look just like her. She was with my real mom and step-dad, Marvin, at the fair. Vera was also with them and I wasn't too scared, 'cause I knew Vera. Marvin took me on the ferris wheel and when it stopped on top, he rocked it. I was so scared, that I wet myself. He felt bad. He really was sorry, but I never rode a ferris wheel again! I generally spent every day at the fair. I thought I would join up someday and travel around the world. Once, when I was about twelve, my real Mom took me to meet my sister Deloris and her husband, Don. They lived on a farm just north of where I lived. I had a great time and I had my first crush. Don was so good looking. I wanted to marry someone as handsome as he was, someday.

I graduated from the 8th grade feeling like somehow my life was just beginning and found that was an understatement. That summer I was to grow up. I'd lost my father, and with his passing, so did a lot of hopes I had. Who would be my friend? I was scared, so scared. He had left me alone and I didn't know who would help me now. I felt so guilty about the money I had stolen from him. I almost felt it was my fault that he had died and Jesus knew—I did love him so! And now Mother was on the prowl. There were times she didn't come home for weeks. I was on my own. I spent a lot of time with a girlfriend of mother's—at her apartment and became very close to her three kids. I loved staying at their home. It was fun and I needed the feeling of having a family. We did everything together. One night as we were sleeping, their mother woke us up. There was a big fire on the square, and as they lived on the third floor, she wanted to take us somewhere that would be safe. We had a pet opossum called "Delilah," so we grabbed her and were taken to a motel for the night. We placed "Delilah" in a dresser drawer and proceeded to all go to sleep in the same bed. About an hour later, John (the youngest brother) woke us up screaming that there was a big bug in the bed. He was so scared and it scared all of us. I jerked back the covers and it was just Delilah. She had managed to get out of the drawer and had climbed into bed with us, but we laughed for hours. I guess that some of the best times of my younger years was with these kids. After I left home I was lucky enough to see John, again, at my real mother's house, but it took forty years.

Another friend I made as a young teenager was Alice. She was a preacher's daughter who lived around the corner.. She was nineteen and believe me, what people used to say about preachers daughters being wild applied to her. She had a brother that went to school with me and he really was a nice kid. She had four or five sisters and brothers and although they were poor, their home was rich in love. Only Alice seemed to have trouble recognizing it. Her mom and dad were super. Alice showed me a new and grown-up way of life.

I would go on to have a story to tell, but nothing like hers. She finally ended up in jail for stealing from the place where she worked. I felt sorry for her parents.

That summer of 1952 was real exciting. I made a trip to Missouri (as I had for the past eight years) to visit my Daddy's family. I always looked forward to those trips. There were so many kids my age and we did so many fun things. My Aunt Lucille had a great house and two sons just older than me. That summer I had grown up and wanted to do more grown-up things. The boys had a car of their own this summer and we spent a good deal of time just driving around. That summer I made my first pass at a boy. He turned me down cold, because he was a lot smarter than I was. Every year while I was there, we climbed the "mountains" of sand and limestone that was distributed by the mines. We would shoot fireworks on the 4th of July and have picnics on the top. It was great fun! That same summer Alice would bring about a great change in my life. She and I together would venture far beyond our homes and it would mean the start of a new life for me that would last for twenty-five years.

She introduced me to a few guys that she knew from another town—Casey. She was dating one of them and they all thought I was sixteen, not fourteen. They were real cool, had their own cars and I soon took up with one of them. His name was Jack. He really was a nice guy, never fresh, I liked him a lot. But he had a buddy that was dating another girl, and he was so cute. I really wanted to go with him. Bonnie (we'll say) was the cutest little gal in Charleston. Her mother owned one of the saloons. She didn't have a father. Everybody wanted to go with Bonnie, including Jack. Well one Saturday night, Alice and Bob, Willie and Bonnie, and Jack and me all went to Greenup to the burger hangout. I don't recall exactly what happened, but Alice and Bob left and Bonnie and Willie got into a fight. She asked Jack to take her home and that left me with Willie. Jack was supposed to come back but he didn't and the rest became part of my history.

Being that I already had a crush on Willie things couldn't have worked out better for me. He and I became a twosome, me sneaking out of the house, if Mother was home, to meet him. And then October came. I was in school. It was Halloween. I invited Willie to come up to my school's Halloween dance. Well he came. And afterward we took a trip to lover's lane which was simply the end of a cornfield. It only took a few words of persuasion like "If you don't, I'll not be back to see you" to convince me to do anything he wanted. When it was over, I was confused as I had bled. I hadn't done that on the cold, hard bedroom floor so many years ago. He couldn't believe I was still a virgin. "A What?" I didn't know what he was talking about. But I knew it wasn't the same. I just told him I wasn't supposed to kiss him. It was a disaster! I knew in my heart that the same old thing happened again. But I didn't know how to stop it. I was vying for his attention, just as I had back then for the doll.

I didn't see him anymore until Christmas. I had called him

and asked him to take me to the Christmas dance at school. I persuaded Mother that I needed a super dress. She took me to Decatur and I found it. The dress that would bring Willie back to me. It was lush red velvet, strapless and revealing, with teardrop pearls and yards and yards of material in the skirt. I looked great that night. My blonde hair having turned black as midnight, and now my height and full breast made me look eighteen and voluptuous. How excited I was when Willie showed up but how disappointed I was to be for he never took me to the dance. He just told me he wouldn't be back to see me anymore. He didn't even take the time to notice me or the super dress that was supposed to have turned his head. That would be my last chance to go to the school dance. It came and went without me. And never again would I go to a school dance—not ever!

Soon it was March and I hadn't been feeling well. I had been refusing for months to take PE at school, making one lame excuse after another until one day I was called to the Principal's office. "Audrey, we can't find your medical papers which you needed to start High School. I'm afraid you will have to have a physical today." So I was taken to the doctor's office. I had the strangest and most embarrassing exam I ever had. He asked me some strange questions like—when did I have my last period, and did I know what intercourse was? I told him what I could and then he told me "You are going to have a baby." No, no, that's all I could think. No, my mother, she'll kill me. How could I? How did this happen? I don't understand, I can't be pregnant. I didn't know what pregnant meant. I can't be having a baby.

What a surprise to me—my mother stayed calm when she was told. In fact, almost relieved. At that moment she knew she could be rid of me. She took me home and asked who the father was. She explained what had happened to me and calmly dialed the phone. I went to the bathroom and swallowed a dozen or more aspirins. I wanted to just end my life. I knew that Willie didn't want me and I knew that Mother didn't either. She rushed me to the hospital and they pumped my stomach. After a night's rest we headed for Casey.

Willie never denied that this was his baby. And we were married the very next day. After finding that I was fourteen instead of sixteen and he was seventeen instead of nineteen we were faced with the problem of the law in Illinois, so his father and my mother lied about our ages. We were married on Friday, March 13th. Our marriage was doomed from the start. The only great things to come from it were two great kids, and the relationship with his parents that has lasted most of my lifetime. His mother taught me to cook, as I had eaten most of my meals in restaurants, and to clean house, and that I was worth something, if nothing else, to myself.

I believe that Fate does elect a time in your life and events that happen. For that early marriage brought me back to my real mom and a big family that I had never known. But it would be many years until I would feel close to any of them. For a long time I would feel as if I was on the outside—again looking in.

In fourteen years I had experienced many things—enough to make a young girl old. I had been hit by a truck at five and suffered two years of physical therapy for a broken shoulder. At thirteen I was burned badly when I visited a cave in Kentucky. I had been beaten repeatedly, sexually abused, made the brunt of "giant" jokes at school, had few friends, and not very much love and attention, except for a few outsiders.

I had two sets of parents, which I couldn't comprehend, sisters which I couldn't call sisters and now I was married to a young boy who didn't care for me and had a baby that I didn't know how to take care of. Over the next few years I would move back and forth to Chicago to my real moms, to Mattoon to my real dads' and then to Casey to my husband's family. Willie would go to jail for seven months and I would wait for him only to be disappointed again. We only stayed together long enough for me to get pregnant again. In

Audrey Faye Lee

June I would go to Michigan to stay with my sister Margy, meet the boy of my dreams, date him, make the mistake of naming my baby girl after him, and it would haunt me for forty years. Willie and I would be together when my second baby came, but it would be short lived and I headed for a lawyer, divorce and Chicago.

Chicago! That toddling town! How exciting to live in a big city. This would be a new start for me. A real mom and family. How good it was going to be! I didn't know I was the odd apple on the tree. My sisters thought me snobbish. I thought they were loud. There never was any privacy. Mom tried too hard to make me feel at home, then couldn't let go of the past. It made me want to run away. The next few years were like a merry-go-round. Things were happening too fast. I moved back and forth from Chicago to Mattoon. I would have an experience with a brother-in-law that would leave me shaken and an outsider again. I was gullible and thirsty for attention and one of them was so kind to me and my kids, but his intentions went deeper than being a thoughtful brother-in-law. It was one of the first occurrences that left me feeling ashamed and alone again after finding my family. I was just a kid, really, and I reacted in a hateful, smart-alec way in order to hide my feelings. It would stay with me for the rest of my life and I would always be defensive when taking part in family events.

I eventually got my first real job with Sears and Roebuck, downtown Chicago. I got my first apartment, a cold-water flat at $25.00 a month. I also had to work two jobs for awhile and finally settled with the second job, which was for Sunbeam and for better pay. But at Christmas, I was laid off and took a job at Cory Corporation where I soon met the man who was to become my second husband. I was nineteen years old and he was forty-five. He was handsome, Italian, and a great dresser. He gave me encouragement and attention and we dated for nearly two years. He taught me to dress, save money, be gracious. and aggressive. He encouraged me to get a better job, better pay, and made me change my appearance so that I would look older and more worldly. And he was really good to my kids.

Then I got pregnant and it changed everything. No more attention—no more anything. We married only to give the baby a name. We never spent one night of our married life together and divorced as soon as the baby—a girl—was born. I would never see him again. It broke my heart and left me, at twenty-one, feeling as if I wanted to die. And just before the baby was born, I tried. I threw myself down a flight of stairs and ended up with a skull fracture and a healthy baby. And I certainly thank God for her. She has been the light of my life. In fact, my children were the main reason to go on living when things got too rough. They only had me and I had to protect them—always.

I went back to work, but had trouble with babysitters. I had three kids. I got sick at work one night and came home to find my new baby alone in the flat. The baby sitter had the other two children next door at her home. I was furious. She didn't want to watch the new baby and I had to work. Mom lived in the flat in front of me, but she didn't want to baby sit. So I agreed for some friends to keep my children. And through them, I met my next husband.

He was so tall and handsome, so quiet you hardly ever knew he was around. He liked to play with the kids, had two jobs, had money, and I was looking for security for my children. He had been married to my friend's sister but she was now married to someone else. So I set my sights on him and I found that at long last my height, looks, and sex could really get me what I really needed for life. Love really wasn't important—not any more. Life was a rat race and I set out to be the rat. We were married, and we had two added to my three. Two little boys, a nice flat, a little money, and he was Sir Galahad to my friends and family. I had learned now that I had some power of my own and I thought I was controlling my own life. My family loved him, looked up to him, and he helped me to become a part of my family again. They accepted me, now, and I was glad that I finally had settled down, and then Hell broke loose.

Mom had spent a lot of time at my house and noticed something wrong with my husband and eldest daughter who was only seven. She said she saw him put his hands where they shouldn't have been, that it might have been an accident but that it warranted watching. This brought back memories of my own childhood and unwanted hands touching me in unexplored areas. I started sleeping with my girls. One evening as he was at work, I had company and was busy making candy for Christmas and I noticed how quiet my children were. So opening the bedroom door I was confronted with a shocking scene. I guess I went berserk. How had this happened? What did they think they were doing? She simply stated—"Daddy does this all the time." Gone was my confidence, my power, and my security, but worse was the feelings of letting my little girl down. My God, what had I done? How could I have let this happen to her? There were no laws for this kind of situation. So I simply filed for divorce and kept my mouth shut.

Mom wanted me to send my girls away, and to stay with him, but no way. Out he went and with him most of my confidence. I love my kids. I always have, and always will. I have always tried to protect them. I may not have been the best mom, but they soon became my life, totally and without condition. Everything I did, now, would only be for them.

And so after a while I met the man who I felt would be safe for my children. God only knows what I could have been thinking! For I put all my children through a nightmare that was to follow them for the rest of their lives. The next nine years with him brought insanity, and physical abuse that I had not known since childhood. I knew by now that this was to be my destiny. I knew that I had just been hand-picked by God to carry a heavy load because I was bad.

I was a bad person, bad child, bad daughter, sister, mother. Our life together was one beating after another. I finally turned to drinking and my problems only doubled. The drinking kept me from doing right for my own children—protecting them. I should have lost my children at that time. I wasn't fit to have them and he wasn't fit for anything. Three more children and now there were eight. As time went by and the abuse got worse, we bought a tavern.

Strange as it may seem, it was my shelter from the storm. I worked the tavern most all the time, seven days a week, sixteen hours a day. I quit drinking, shaped up, and learned all about life and the people in it. I made some good friends, lasting friends, and my life was slowly turning around. The more I learned, the more I was beaten, the stronger I became. In a short couple of years, I was strong enough to pick up my kids and leave him. I went to work and I learned to survive. Survival is what it is all about. Love, survival and courage. Knowing that you have courage can help through all the bad times. And I had learned to take control and have courage when everything else had failed me. My life with him would leave scars on my children's emotions that would last their lifetime. The scars left on me would end the day he died.

I wonder why I let myself into situations of turmoil and hurt, and most of all why I could not have foreseen the hurt that he was going to cause my children. I divorced him and for the next five years I remained a single parent.

My life, nor my children's, has been charmed. It's been a roller coaster ride all the way. My oldest son was kidnapped when he was only twenty-two months old from my sister's home. It was on Easter Sunday, and it was almost eight hours before the police found him wandering about eighty blocks from where we were. He was okay and I was crazy. Another son was held hostage on the south side of Chicago for seven hours so a fugitive could get transportation out of the city. My son was only thirteen. He was working on Saturdays

Audrey Faye Lee

helping to deliver orange juice to the homes. He was taken hostage and held. The driver of the juice truck took the wanted criminal out of the city. The State's Attorney wanted to let the three people who held my son go, because he had not been harmed, but I went to the newspapers and they went to trial and received five years each for aiding and abetting a criminal. My daughter, when she was only ten, got hit by a car and she was just driven to the hospital and left there unattended. I used a detective friend of mine and we found the car and the driver. It was a doctor at Mt. Sinai's Hospital.

My granddaughter was kidnapped by her father who escaped jail on her first birthday. With the help of some policeman friends of mine, we located her in two weeks and they broke in the house and I brought her home. My youngest daughter was born with a lung disorder. (This was the same disorder that killed John F. Kennedy's baby), but after three years of treatment she was declared well and happy.

I lived in the same house for fifteen years and that corner of the big city was mine. I had a restaurant across the street from where I lived and I had made lots of friends and a few enemies.

The twenty-three years I lived in Chicago, especially the last five or six, I took in a lot of stray teen-age children and with the help of my own kids, we got them on their feet and on their own. I once helped an old man that was being mugged and robbed. I think he might have been killed, but I didn't think about my own safety— at least not until it was all over, and then I was scared to death.

I spent five years building a relationship with my children, but I drank too much, had too many bad experiences with boyfriends. Then I met the man that I *would* spend the rest of my life with.

Our relationship started off pretty rocky. We married only to find out he was already married. I had a wife-in-law. I got an annulment. It was another year before we met again. By this time he was divorced so we resumed our relationship and eventually remarried.

Ten Sisters

I've always been independent. When I was younger, I used to say things that weren't always true to shock my sisters. I always felt that they thought that I was some kind of tramp. And in a way I guess I was close to it. I sure did some running around at that time. But deep inside, buried I guess, was some grass-roots religion, for it seemed to have kept me from going that one step that had no return. I never took drugs, except Bennies. I took them for about two years to stay awake. I simply did not have time to sleep. But it caught up with me and—whammy—it was all over. I did try marijuana, but it certainly wasn't for me.

I spent most of my life making mistakes, some of the same ones over and over. It seems sometimes I was born for trouble and I really have to fight "this sorry for me" syndrome. Do I blame anyone? Well I put my mom to rest and with her went a lot of feelings. She, too, was not perfect. But she, like me, was human. Mom was the best example of that, and I hope my children find that, looking back. I have always had trouble with my self esteem and I wish that I would have changed a lot of things in my life, but I blame no one. Life deals each of us just what we can handle and nothing more.

Not all of the times in Chicago were bad. Years ago in Chicago, we always had the New Year's Eve Party at my house. One Christmas, thirty-six years ago, I worked with my nieces and nephews and Vera and we put on a Nativity Play at Christmas for all the family. Vera made a very good, short Santa Claus.

And music was a big part of my life. I once said I could write my life story around the songs that I knew. Different songs definitely remind me of different people, places and events. I still love music, but today I don't listen to it very much as I always get a little sad, well maybe a little more than that—almost depressed. I have to fight hard with myself—everyday—to keep a smiling face. Most of my own past overtakes and overwhelms me.

And in the past year I have had something to be especially

sad about, the death of my brother, Carl. I was always closest to him and his wife, Bea. We somehow formed a real bond early on in my life. I loved him very much and he was really a big brother to me. He was there so many times when I needed him. I thank God for him.

By 1976, my oldest son married, divorced and remarried. He had given me a grandson that I wouldn't see for nineteen years and a granddaughter that was so sweet. One son was off to the army and one daughter had just graduated from high school. Another son was hospitalized for trying to kill himself. The same son, years earlier, had been kidnapped by his father and lost to me for over a year.

Then my life was to change drastically. My husband and I and the four children that remained moved to Tennessee—Bob's home. We wanted to get our children out of the city and to start a new life. I was also running away from the trouble that always seemed to be around every corner, in the form of my ex-husband, who would not leave us alone. I made the right choice.

The hardest part of leaving Chicago was leaving behind some of my children, my mom, my stepdad, and my granddaughter. I'll never forget the day we left. My stepdad, Marvin, (who was really the only Dad I ever knew) drove our car with the four kids and Bob and I handled the big U-haul. My granddaughter slipped into the cab of the truck an cried so hard I could hardly leave her. The kids all cried, all the way to Tennessee. We put my stepdad on a train for Chicago two days later and two short months after that he died of cancer. I loved and respected him.

The first three years in Tennessee were rough—financially and emotionally. Bob was an alcoholic, and it would be three more years and a separation before we could make things work for us, but when it did, it was worth the wait. He quit drinking and life started to really get good for us.

I guess I know that ten little girls being separated has only made us stronger and closer today. I have finally become closer to my sisters. Maybe it was my own shame that kept us apart. To me they were always so good—no mistakes. And now I know it doesn't make any difference. They love me for me and I love them for letting me be just me.

At this time, I have fourteen grandchildren and two great grandchildren. I have a great husband and lots of hope for a long and happy life with him. We both have lots of interests. I love to cook, quilt, and paint, and I love to work with wood and make small projects and design big projects for my husband to build. He is a great furniture builder and we like to make each piece of furniture just one of a kind. I love new things to do and I love doing the family paper. I love to write—poetry or short stories. I once wrote a song. I like to laugh at myself and I try always to be considerate of others. I love to have company and most of my life my home has been the home of all important dinners, parties, and events for my children and friends.

My grandchildren are my delight. I am very close to two of my grandsons and one of my granddaughters. I give them all the love, time, and attention that I can. And because of them I see so many mistakes that I made with my own children. And that is something I wish I *could* change.

My life with Bob is wonderful and secure. I am proud of him and look forward to that long awaited vacation honeymoon we never took. After twenty years, Dyersburg is my home. I've had to fight a feeling of loneliness with my family up north, but I've made a lot of friends and five of my children have married and are raising their families here. I can't speak for all my children, but I can say how much I love them, how proud of them I am, and although some have their own crosses to bear, I'll always be here for them. My home is always their home. I have finally learned enough to know I must leave them alone, love them, and listen when they want me to hear. After all, each of us has to choose our own life and I had to follow mine.

Doris Evon Jean
(Dorie)

Dedicated to the memory of my parents,
Amanda and Dale Replogle,
who shared their lives with me

Ten Sisters

I was born February 11, 1940, at Paradise Township, Coles County, Illinois in a converted hen house. I lived there for just over two years with my parents, two brothers, and nine sisters. In the third week of March 1942 my sisters and I were taken from our parents and placed in the custody of the State.

On March 30, 1942 I was adopted by a childless couple, Dale and Amanda Replogle. They had responded to a newspaper article and had been told that my sisters and I had been abandoned in the neighboring town of Mattoon on a February evening.

Mother said when she and Dad arrived for the hearing a reporter was taking a photo of us on the courthouse steps. My sisters were crying. My older sister Jenny didn't want to let go of me and resisted when someone pulled me from her arms. Mother and Dad then lined up in the hallway with the other couples seeking children, and we were brought, one by one, for them to view. Mother said she and Dad asked about Vera but were told she had already been placed. When they inquired about me, they were told only that my name was Doris. They would add Jean. They didn't remember seeing our father Glen that day but did see our mother Ruth, a tiny woman who, they said, remained stoic throughout the proceedings. Years later, Mother recalled Ruth sitting alone in the empty courtroom waiting for us to be brought back in to say good-by. She didn't know we had already been taken out a side door to waiting cars. That memory was one Mother, was bothered by her entire life.

The adoption would not be official until July, but Mother and Dad Replogle took me home to North Division Street that very day. Mother said I didn't cry much, but that I dragged a small rug to the living room each morning and sat on it, not wanting to be touched or spoken to. Then one day my father's hunting buddy, Bob Cobble, stopped by to visit. He was a wiry little man. He saw me on the rug and dropped to his knees beside me. Mother said he spoke softly and after a few moments she saw me reach for him. After that, grief gave way to curiosity and I learned, as many adopted children do, to adapt.

The only memory I actually have of that very early time is of sitting on a tricycle, peering out from behind a curtain to see two young men in uniform standing by the front door. They called me "Sis" and wanted me to come to them, but by then I had grown fearful of my brothers who I no longer seemed to recognize.

For awhile Mother said I was afraid of many things. I slept with her, my arms wrapped around her and my fingers locked together. As I grew she explained a scar on my inner left leg just below the knee where I had been tethered, in the house at Paradise, to keep me away from the cookstove. Faded, the scar is still a reminder of another life. She also opened up the cedar chest and showed me the dress I wore the day of the court hearing and the one they purchased on the way home.

Mother and Dad and I lived in a three-bedroom, white frame house with a picket fence. They owned a skating rink and restaurant. Mother was a housewife, but helped out in the business when her "nerves" allowed. When she did, I went along to skate or to hide in the cloakroom playing paper dolls.

Dad's family didn't visit often, but Mother had ten siblings, assorted in-laws, and half a dozen nieces and nephews, all of whom visited often. The Replogles and the Thompsons became my family.

When Dad wasn't running his business, he spent a lot of time running the dogs. I sometimes went with him. During the season he and his friends hunted. Whatever they brought home the women "dressed" and cooked, using the skins or feathers for crafts. Every summer Dad visited the state fair at *DuQuoin*. Mother and I never went along, but he always came home with gifts. Once he brought home a fox terrier. The next year he brought home a pony!

Mother read children's books to me, but other reading material in our house consisted of *The Charleston Daily Courier*, a Bible, and a few religious tracts. I became a regular visitor to the

Carnegie Public Library. *The Boxcar Children*, and *Dandelion Cottage* were favorite books. So were the *Nancy Drew* mysteries, *The Secret Garden,* and the works of Louisa May Alcott. I read comics, too. Trading comics was a nightly pastime.

I don't know when I became aware of Audrey. She was two years older than me and lived across town. She had been adopted by another couple. Her father was considered a nice guy, but her mother had a reputation for being difficult, if not a little "loose." My mother took me to visit one day. Audrey and I went down to the playhouse Jess Cole had built for her in the basement of their home. Shortly after mother left, something frightened me and I ran up the stairs and all the way home. Although I don't recall other times with Audrey when we were small, I apparently saw her on occasion. A photograph of my seventh birthday party includes her among the guests.

At some point, the court returned custody of my six older sisters to our natural mother. It caused Mother and Dad great anxiety. They told me that I might encounter some of my sisters or brothers from time to time, and that if they came by the school, I was to see them only in the presence of a teacher, and that I was *never* to get in a car with any of them—anyplace. I was also asked to call my natural parents by their names—Ruth and Glen.

Ruth and some of my sisters came to visit when I was in the fourth grade. I cried when they left and on and off for several weeks. Mother and Dad decided those visits should be few and far between, and they were. Sometimes I came home from school to find a box of cherry chocolates wedged inside the front storm door—left by Glen. Once he left a soft, white, rabbit-fur muff. But I rarely saw him. Mother seemed to have a higher regard for him than Ruth. I don't know how Dad felt. I received only one letter from Glen. I was a grown woman and the letter has been lost, but I remember the greeting: "Hi Sis." He wrote that he liked history and books.

Mother and Dad had several good friends, most of them

Doris Evon Jean

members of the Friday Night Pinochle Club. Aunt Pearl and Uncle Chalk, Margaret and Vernie McDade, and Bob and Helen Cobble were part of the group. Margaret worked at Dad's skating rink and often baby-sat with me. She taught me to dance, how to make doll clothes, and how to play cards. Unlike most of our other friends, Margaret and Vernie were Catholic. During the holidays they took me to the church bizarre for lunch. I thought the Catholics were a colorful change from our fundamentalist church.

There were other revelations. When World War II was over, cousins Charles and Glen came back, Uncle Walt and Leo came back. But some friends, like Warren Dale Stitt, didn't, or if they did, weren't ever the same. I heard my brothers came back.

Grandpa Replogle lived with us when I was a child. He was a widower. Although he was very thin, he rarely left the table until all the dishes were empty, "You going to eat that?" he'd say, pointing to the fried potatoes or the green beans. When we indicated we were not, he would dig right in.

Grandma and Grandpa Thompson both lived with us, too, but not at the same time. Grandpa, a former trapper and farmer by trade, had a hot temper and because of that had almost always lived down the road from Grandma and their many children, his participation limited to week-end visits. Grandma was a sweet little thing who sat close to the door with her sweater or coat handy so she could go along anytime the car left the drive.

Mother was reared close to Mode, Illinois, a town of about 100 people, most of them friends or relatives. I visited there often, especially in the summer. I would stay for weeks at a time with my cousins, Janet, Roberta, and Carolyn. They lived in a tiny, brown-shingled house they rented for a song from Uncle Chalk. It had two bedrooms, a living room, a kitchen, and a pantry. There was no electricity and the outhouse was at the back of the lot behind the smokehouse and across from the barn. When we weren't climbing apple trees or running from the banty roosters, washing our hair in rainwater or plucking feathers off newly-killed chickens, we were playing "Dr" in the pantry or "Dress Up" in the smokehouse. This was all great fun because I got to go home to indoor plumbing and grocery stores.

By the time we were adolescents, my cousins and I sat under the apple trees or piled into Uncle Clyde's parked car and talked about clothes and boys. On Saturdays, the wash tub was filled with water and we drew straws to see who got to take the first bath. Then we all drove into Shelbyville. Uncle Clyde and Aunt June went off shopping and Carolyn, who was the oldest (relatively speaking), was left to mind us. We were given just enough money for the matinee and a treat. If we didn't spend everything on candy, we pooled our money for paper dolls, movie magazines, little blue bottles of *Evening in Paris* cologne, or tubes of waxy, orange lipstick.

Arriving back at the four-room bungalow at the edge of Mode, Aunt June would light the oil lamps and I would get to squeeze the little pellet of orange coloring into and through the big white block of cellophane-wrapped oleo until it looked just like butter, a similarity the dairy farmers of America objected to.

Thompson family get-togethers were almost a weekly event. Fishing trips were my favorite. Late one summer night we gathered alongside a river bank eating ham-salad sandwiches made with bologna and listening to Joe Louis and Jersey Joe Wolcott slug it out—over a console radio my uncles had connected to a car battery.

Across the street and a few blocks south of our house, a carnival was set up for two weeks of every summer. When the first truck arrived, I packed a lunch of raw potatoes and peanut butter and lettuce sandwiches, grabbed a bottle of *Pepsi,* and made my way to the action. The women were exotic, with glittery earrings and bracelets shimmering in the midwestern sun, their long, braided hair falling heavily down their backs and silk scarves wrapped around their heads or flowing from their waists. The men were interesting, too. Some wore cowboy boots and wide-brimmed hats. Others had silk vests with scarves at their necks. Most wore necklaces or rings and carried pocket watches. I helped set up the booths and fed their pets, including snakes, goats, and mangy dogs. In the evening I'd go home to Mothers' shirtwaist dresses and Dad's *Osh B'Gosh* overalls, a supper of meat and potatoes, and my fat little dog, Tiny.

Mother's nerves continued to be a problem. By the time I was in the fourth grade, Dad hired a nurse to care for her and to help around the house. Her name was Angie Savoia. She was dark and round and was married to a man with large, liquid eyes. Angie's father, Mr. Perry, lived with them at their home in Villa Grove. He was slender, with white hair and dimples, and he walked with a limp. They seemed as solid as stone, those three. Angie taught me to sing *The Old Rugged Cross* and taught me to spell words like Miss-iss-ippi and Ch-em-is-try in a memorable sing-song fashion.

Although we lived a modest life, many neighbors had very little. Dad sometimes ordered a cord of wood for a neighbor and Mother often made candy and gathered canned goods for them at Christmas.

Our house sat in almost the last residential block on North Division Street. The hard road ended there and turned into a dead-end lane, dotted with a few dilapidated houses and sheds, that ran another half mile or so, eventually disappearing into woods and farmland, except for the last house north, a white farmhouse with a few out buildings, and across the road from the farmhouse a fenced-in pasture, overgrown with native plants, hid a coarse, one-room dwelling. Lilly McCandless lived there, with her stray dogs, cats, and geese. The animals wandered in and out her door at all times of the year. You had to be careful where you stepped and I carried a stick to ward off the honkers. Inside was worse. An enamel pot sat in the corner and everything else was heaped with boxes, sewing materials, and paper. The cookstove was the only source of heat and it was piled high, too, with pots and pans and bits of this and that. A bed sat in the corner, but you couldn't see anything except the bedstead. Years of collected bric-a-brac completely covered the mattress. It was clear Miss McCandless didn't use the bed to sleep in. She slept where she worked—in a heavy rocker between the cookstove and the window—next to her treadle sewing machine. She was a wonderful seamstress and Mother hired her to make and alter clothes for me. The only pretty things in the room were the scraps of material she'd place on the window sill. They were swatches of color, and texture, and pattern enhanced by natural light. I looked for them each time I visited. They were like a cool oasis in the hot, dense atmosphere of the crowded room.

One night Mother, and Dad, and I were awakened by sirens and flashing lights. We threw on our robes and ran outside. All the neighbors were gathered in the middle of the street watching a red glow at the North end of the lane. Animals were howling in a frenzy of fear. Miss McCandless' house was burning. We soon learned that everything had been destroyed, everything except Miss McCandless. Come morning, her familiar bent figure emerged from the smoky distance. She stopped to thank those who had tried to help and walked on toward town, a part of her daily routine.

By the following spring, her little home had been rebuilt, she had collected dozens of abandoned animals, and she was altering my clothes again. Years later I visited her in a retirement home. She sat on the edge of her bed beside her a stack of linens. I gave her some swatches of material. She smiled and nodded to the linens and said she was happy to earn her way mending.

Not all the memories are inspirational. Art Bloomstrom, a tall, heavy-set cousin of my Dad's was a deputy sheriff in Coles County. He also worked on his off hours at the skating rink. He used to tease me and my friends and we were intimidated by his size, but he was a trusted friend. One afternoon, we were having one of our frequent family gatherings at Aunt Pearl and Uncle Chalk's when we received news that Art had been shot. They said a woman had come into the Sheriff's office saying her husband was out of control. Art knew the irate man and said he would go out to the farm and settle him down. Several officers went with him. We were told that Art eased himself out of the car and walked across the yard, calling out the man's name and telling him to put down any weapons so they could talk. When Art stepped onto the porch, the man aimed and shot. It threw Art back into the tall grass and he lay moaning. Because of his size, it was some time before they could drag him back to the police car. He lingered a few days and died. His oversized casket sat in the parlour of the Victorian cottage next to the County Jail.

Other people made lasting impressions, too. My first-grade teacher was not much taller than me and had a hump on her back. Uncle Chalk had one arm. Uncle John had half a foot. Aunt Eva had a shrunken leg and walked with the help of a crutch. The girl down the block had a large head and was confined to a wheelchair. Aunt Ruth, because of medical treatment, was addicted to morphine, and a midget lived next door to her. The world was an imperfect place. But, Mrs. Ferguson controlled the classroom like a general. Uncle Chalk and Uncle John worked on the railroad until they retired. Aunt Eva took in ironings. The girl with the large head conned the neighborhood kids into pushing her the full length of her porch for hours. On good days, Aunt Ruth crocheted doll clothes for me and took me to see the elusive Amish. And the midget kept trying to French kiss me. I grew up knowing everybody was good at something.

School was always an influence—of one sort or another. Twice, I got my hands smacked. One night I sat on the floor in our living room and drew my version of a picture that hung high on the wall. I took it to school the next day and the teacher showed it to the class saying, "Doris Jean traced this." I tried to explain that I hadn't, but after a few minutes of my insistence she smacked my fingers with a ruler for "lying." I didn't tell my parents. The edict was: "If you get a spanking at school, you'll get another when you get home!"

I didn't tell Mother and Dad about the other time I got smacked, either. It was the winter of third grade and I was bundled up with a new scarf around my neck. Leslie Hickenbottom ran past me, grabbed the scarf, and kept running. I took off after him, tackling him just west of the slides and was giving him "what for" when the teacher grabbed me by the collar. She took me inside and had me hold out my hands. "The smacking," she explained, "was for unlady-like behavior."

By the fourth grade Miss Kincaid called me her "little artist," but her interest probably had more to do with the fact that she was the sweetheart of the accomplished Illinois painter, Paul Sargent. Forty years later Miss Kincaid sat in her home and told me about the last time she saw Mr. Sargent and talked of the picture I had drawn of her when I was in her class. She was almost blind by then, but remembering she said, "See, you even drew my sloping shoulders."

Teacher and friend, Helen Harrington, introduced me to poetry and theater and it was on a school trip with her that I met the first black person of my life. He was a tall, good-looking boy. I danced with him once and thought he wasn't any different than the other boys I knew. He stepped on my feet and talked about sports.

Another influence was Glendon Gabbard. He taught theater at Eastern Illinois University when I was in high school and for many years after. For two wonderful seasons he cast me in his summer productions, *Our Town* and *The Night of January 16th*. Eventually, I would make part of my living on the stage and in front of a camera.

By the time I was reaching puberty, the physical similarities between Audrey and me were evident. We even saw one another socially on a few occasions. I remember going with her to the Coles County Fair when I was eleven or so. We got on all the rides free because Audrey attracted the boys and they were eager to impress her with favors, even if it meant tolerating a younger sister. I don't think Mother and Dad knew much of these outings.

A couple of years later I attended Jefferson Jr. High. Audrey had attended two years before. She had been a favorite student of Mr. Whitman's and he often mistakenly called me by her name. One day he took me aside and asked if I knew Audrey was getting married because she was going to have a baby. She was only fourteen. I was surprised and a little embarrassed. I told him I didn't really know much about her life.

Vera visited once and told me about Pizza Pie she'd eaten in Chicago (a delicacy then unknown in Charleston). Sometime later Mother, Dad, and I stopped to visit her at the house on Moultrie Avenue. Vera wasn't there, but Ruth's brother, Uncle Nolan was. We sat on the porch and talked with him for a few moments.

About that same time, I went to the horse races at the Coles County Fair. A girl in a red dress was standing by the fence. She was a few years older than me, but the resemblance was striking. I approached her and asked if her name was Waggoner. She said it was and that her first name was Phyllis. We were sisters. We stood, for a few minutes, looking toward the horses parading around the track, and then I went back to my friends.

There were a few other early encounters with family members. Carl visited when I was in Jr. High, and Jesse sent a photo of himself and his family at their home in Hawaii. I saw them, too, at the only reunion we all had together thirty-six years after our family had been disbanded. Jesse died of a heart attack in his prime. I looked on him more with curiosity than understanding. It was romantic, then, to interact with all these people on some distant, infrequent level, like unrequited love, all mystery and full of promise—and it didn't require my becoming too attached.

Over the years I was invited to an occasional wedding or

party, but my parents worried about contact with my former family and it was easier to stay away. Photos, though, document some rare visits to my home. One even included Grandma Coen.

In 1957, at the age of seventeen, I dropped out of high school and married. My husband was teaching and coaching at the Jr. High and we bought a house a couple of blocks from the university and two blocks from his parents. Ten days short of our first anniversary, Brian Harvey was born. We brought him home on a beautiful June day, the yard filled with the scent of roses. Fourteen months later, I gave birth to Todd Mitchell. Teresa Francine arrived the following year and Cullen Jerome was born a year to the month after Teresa. There was little time to think about the past.

By the time I was twenty-one we had added to our house and were providing room, and often board, for fourteen college boys. That fall Mother watched the children while I took the test for the High School Equivalency Diploma, and a few months later I enrolled at Eastern Illinois University. I had taken the first step on a long academic road.

Contact with my sisters was minimal. They tried to keep the lines of communication open. Jenny and some of the others visited in the early 1960's. At some point my sisters started hosting an annual reunion and published a family newspaper. I attended a couple of the reunions for a few minutes and read an occasional newspaper, but I was never very comfortable with it. Besides, though they denied it publicly, contact with my sisters and brothers, or my natural parents, still upset Mother and Dad.

In 1963 we moved to DeKalb, Illinois. Son Brian started kindergarten. My husband spent a lot of time at work and with so many little ones to tend to, I found it difficult to cultivate new friends. On November 22, Brian and I sat stunned as his brothers and sisters nibbled at their lunch. The world would never look quite the same. We didn't know about the backstairs life of Jack Kennedy, then. We only knew his family and friends were mourning. Years later I stood on the grassy knoll in Dallas, amazed at the smallness and familiarity of the area. That night we returned to son Todd's apartment to learn that Jackie Kennedy Onassis had just died. It seemed life had gone full circle.

Aaron Matthew was born in May of 1964, three weeks before we moved from DeKalb to Wheaton, Illinois. The following year we moved to Glen Ellyn. The Walshes next door had a dozen children and there were forty more in our block. We lived on Hillside Avenue, across from the Chatholic church, for the next twenty years. During that time, Quintin Mathias and Michelle René were born, but their father had developed a roving eye and within a few weeks after Michelle's birth, our marriage began to disintegrate.

It was during this time that Ruth and my sisters re-entered my life. It was Christmas. Mother and Dad were visiting. During all those years, they had continue to worry about the influence of my natural parents and my sisters. To appease them, and because I found the situation difficult to handle, I had kept my distance. But that Christmas I received a call. It was Ruth. She and her husband, Marvin, were in the area and wanted to stop by. I asked Mother and Dad if it would be alright. In a holiday spirit, they acquiesced.

A few minutes later Ruth and Marvin appeared at the door. I worried there could be a scene, as Mother was possessive and Ruth was rumored to have a temper, but both women were polite. I learned that my brother Carl and his wife Bea lived in the neighboring town of Lombard, but it would be years before I saw them.

Dad died shortly after that encounter and I went back to rearing children and working at various part-time jobs, including several years as an interviewer with Leo Burnett Advertising Agency and a brief stint selling real estate.

In 1974 we were invited to an anniversary party for Ruth and her husband Marvin. By that time I felt my children should know about my origins. Brother Jesse didn't attend this event and not much communication took place in the crowded hall, but following the party there was more contact with some of the sisters. Sister Dodo and her husband Don even became camping buddies. For three years we traveled together, with Jim and Sharon Hayes and several other friends, to beautiful Ft. Pickens in Florida. And once in awhile Jenny, Bede, Margy, or whoever else was in the area, would stop to visit us in Glen Ellyn. But life was becoming a whole lot more complex. Over the next few years most of my attention would be focused on other people and other events.

The children were growing. Brian graduated early from High school and went in to the Marine Corps. When he came home, he, Todd, Teresa, Cullen, and I enrolled at the College of Dupage. After a year or so, Todd went off to Central College in Pella, Iowa; Teresa left for Eastern Illinois University in Charleston; and I moved on to North Central College in Naperville. But by that time it was clear that the problems in my marriage weren't going away.

By 1981 I'd earned a B.A. and had written and produced, with the help of an undergraduate fellowship,*Without Discretion*, a play about Mary Todd Lincoln. One of my grandsons and one of my grand-nephews had small roles, and several family members attended opening night. The research for the play had renewed a childhood interest in history, but things at home were deteriorating rapidly. I was not contributing much to the income, and believing money was the problem, I borrowed from friends and family. But my husband's interest was no longer on Hillside Avenue and mine, I'm afraid, wasn't always, either. On June 9, 1982, after a surprise 25th Anniversary party organized by daughter Teresa and attended by Carl and several of my sisters, my husband left home. For the next month he would come and go at will.

Mother was bewildered. I hadn't told her until I had to, and she thought I could somehow salvage the marriage. The children were confused. Some were hostile. All were very sad. One awful morning daughter, Teresa, suggested a trip to my sisters might lesson the tension in our house. I sped to Phyllis and Dick's in Charleston. Dodo and Bede were there. I was a mess. My sisters fed me and fixed my hair. They took me to a doctor. And that night they sat with me for hours, listening to my heartache. When I finally tried to rest, Dodo slipped in beside me and held my hand until I drifted into an uneasy sleep. There would be other times that summer when my sisters and my brother came to my rescue. And Ruth took a long ride to southern Illinois one warm summer night, and talked about her life and mine. My family, like my children, and friends, and a few amazing strangers, came to my aide when I could barely cope with the loneliness and change.

On the July 4th weekend of 1982, my husband left for good, but late that month I received a call from Lilla Heston at Northwestern University. She said they were prepared to offer me an assistantship if I could arrange to enroll for the fall term. I applied for a school loan and plunged ahead. Northwestern was like a dream, studying under noted instructors, playing a major role in the fall play, making new friends. It all made the daily ride back and forth from Glen Ellyn to Evanston worthwhile, and I thought I had prepared myself for the inevitable. But when the divorce papers came in mid-November, the children and I were devastated. I walked away from Northwestern and went home to hold things together. I wrote Ms. Heston that I was at peace with my decision, but it was short-lived. I couldn't eat, or sleep, or concentrate long enough to read. Michelle slept with me some of the time and we kept a hammer under the pillow, from a general fear of the unknown. We also left the bedroom door open so we could hear the comforting voices of the older children and their friends floating up from the first floor.

Depression seized me. Because I woke *very* early each morning, I walked to *Glen Oak* restaurant and drank coffee and watched the people go by. Some of them became friends. I often carried a book, but it was almost two years until I read for pleasure, not until a friend from Maine sent *The Log of the Skipper's Wife*. I read it, line by line, from beginning to end, repeatedly.

Over time, family, and some remarkable friends, dragged me out of the awful depression. One helped me secure a teaching position at the College of DuPage and I worked as an actress, mostly in industrial films. During this time a friend surprised me with a visit to see my brother Carl and his wife Bea in Tennessee. It was the only time I was to spend a night in my brother's home.

By 1985, I again tried my hand at Graduate school. Michelle and Quint in tow, I took refuge at Illinois State University. In moving some cartons Quint dropped a picture and the frame was broken. Out from behind the photo fell a small negative. I took it to my friend Tom Dyba and he enlarged it. It was the picture taken on the courthouse steps in 1942. That Christmas, Tom made a copy for each of my sisters.

Going through it, 1985 seemed one of the worst years of my life. I taught undergraduate classes, worked as a house painter, attended graduate classes, and tried to deal with my sizable family. Times were awful, but friends provided continued help and very good company. And, as in Glen Ellyn, I met several good and lasting friends at a local restaurant. I completed my course work within the year, including the research of, then, Secretary of State, Jim Edgar, but the thesis remained unfinished.

In 1986 I received a Visiting Teaching Assistantship at the University of Illinois and Michelle and I moved to Mahomet. As in Glen Ellyn and Normal, I made a lot of good friends over coffee, especially at the *J & K*.

I loved teaching at the University of Illinois, but the pay was terrible, so I also taught part-time at the Bloomington campus of Lincoln College and at both the Rantoul and Champaign campuses of Parkland College. We could still barely make ends meet.

1987 wasn't so good either. I had no teaching assignments during the summer and I was broke—flat broke. I didn't have a job, and I hadn't completed my thesis. The future looked bleak. I contacted every friend I had and asked them to help. They didn't let me down. Before long I had several interviews. One day I got a call from *The Welcome In*, the little restaurant in Normal. They said someone had been asking for me. They gave me the number. A few weeks later I had a good position at Champion Federal with a salary we could live on, but I was concerned about the unfinished thesis.

In December of 1987 I began spending time with Harry Wenzel. A Civil Engineer, educator, and administrator, he urged me to get back to work on the thesis and I did. He also bought me *two* new winter coats, included me in his social life, and took care of me when I was sick. In a word, he changed my life. One night, over Chinese food, he leaned back and laughed, and I knew I was hooked. In May of that year, Michelle graduated from high school and a week later Harry and I were married, a scant five months after our first meeting. We honeymooned in Italy. There were adjustments, some simple—some very complex, but life had definitely taken a turn.

In 1990 I resigned from Champion and taught one last year at the U of I. In the spring, I started a small publishing company. Contact with my sisters and Ruth had dwindled to a few calls or an occasional greeting card, but in the fall of 1992, Mother and I were driving around Charleston when she asked if I knew where Ruth lived. I drove to C Street. It had been twenty years since the two women had seen one another. Ruth was sitting on the porch and when we pulled up she called to us to come have a glass of tea. Both women were in their eighties. Ruth brought out a chair and placed it beside me, for Mother, and she sat down across from us. They talked about their health, about their husbands, and about their common grandchildren. I was happily incidental to the visit.

After an hour or so, when both women looked a bit tired, I suggested it might be time to leave. As we walked to the car, Mother put her arm around me. "I've always wanted to do that," she said.

A few months later, Ruth died. Mother, Harry, and son Cullen went with me to the Visitation. Ruth, with little encouragement, had been especially kind during the early 80's when I most needed kindness. Now my sisters, our brother, my mother, and I gathered to say good-bye to a woman who had earned our respect.

The next day, son Quintin accompanied me to the funeral. Because of the nature of our gathering, someone said it would be nice if we could have our photo taken on the courthouse steps as we had that day in March 1942. I called a local reporter and suggested there might be a story within this photo. He agreed and we gathered in an upstairs room at the Coles County courthouse. Bill Lair interviewed all ten of us at once, with children, husbands, grandchildren, and great-grandchildren milling about. His article won a prize and added to the information we had about our family. And he took another photo on the courthouse steps. The 1942 photo had heralded a remarkable change in all our lives. This one would, too.

In the summer of 1995 nine of us met to say good-by to brother Carl. Like Jesse, he had died of a heart attack in his prime. Vera couldn't be with us because of her treatment for Non-hodgkins Lymphoma. But we left the little church that day, sisters closer than we had ever been, and determined to leave a record for our children and our friends.

In the sum of life some influences are obvious and some are subtle, but everything counts. Nothing has counted more than the circumstances of my birth and the brothers and sisters who have indirectly influenced who and what I am. Over the course of my life, if I told a friend or stranger just one thing about me it was usually that I was one of many.

Epilogue

For most of our lives, the *why's* of what happened to our family were answered in rumors and myths. We all felt the decision to separate us from our parents and from one another was made in haste during a single month in 1942. Most of us thought it had been a surprise to both Mom and Dad. But in 1993 we found among Mom's things a sort of journal of her daily activities, kept sporadically over the year preceding the 1942 court decision. Sprinkled, almost casually, among the comments about routine activities, social events, and crude accounting notes, were comments that shed a good deal of light on the events of 1941 and 1942. The following are excerpts, with editing comments, from that journal:

> Wed. Feb. 26, 1941: "We went to see Kidwell. Glen talked to Mrs. Allen."
> [Kidwell was an attorney. Mrs. Allen was assigned by the state to work with Mom and Dad—perhaps at their request.]

> Fri., Feb. 21: "Charleston trial."
> [We know nothing of this "trial." A search of court documents do not include anything about it, but Mom's subsequent notes suggest at least a hearing in this case.]

> Sat. March 1: "I got things from Mrs. Caton."
> [Mrs. Caton was a County Probation Officer. A book on sterilization was found among Mom's things, and at some point she told the older girls the state wanted her to do something so she would not have any more children.]

> Tues. March 4: "Mrs. Allen was here."
> [This was at least the second visit by Mrs. Allen.]

Thurs. March 6: "Glen went to Ellen's."
[Dad was seeing another woman during this time. He later lived with her family in Mattoon and in Chicago.]

Mon. March 10: "Glen went to Huffman's."
[The Huffman's were related to Dad's woman friend.]

Wed. March 12: "Glen went to Huffman's."

Sat. April 5: "Carl was home. We had a racket. Glen knocked me out."
[There is no further explanation of this event, except that Mom did see a Dr. a few days later. The older sisters say Mom would sometimes 'pick a fight,' but the situation may have initiated this incident.]

Wed. May 11: "I came after Glen."
[There is no explanation of where she "came after" him.]

Tues. Oct. 28: "Had supper with Mrs. Allen at the hotel."

These notes made by Mom in 1941 indicate that the decision of the court was based on observations and events of over a year. Although we sisters regret that we were separated, we have all come to understand that the situation in our home had probably become untenable and the prospect of dealing with ten minor sisters presented exceptional problems for the court. We will always wish help had come in other ways, and we know we may never understand the entire events of that time, but discovering the truth, even if it is painful, is preferable to living with rumors and myths.
